Property Law
in Hong Kong
An Introductory Guide

Second Edition

Property Law
in Hong Kong
An Introductory Guide

Second Edition

Stephen D. Mau

The research funding for this book was sponsored by
the Hong Kong Institute of Surveyors

THE HONG KONG INSTITUTE OF
SURVEYORS
香港測量師學會

香港大學出版社
HONG KONG UNIVERSITY PRESS

Hong Kong University Press
The University of Hong Kong
Pokfulam Road
Hong Kong
www.hkupress.org

© Stephen D. Mau 2010, 2014
First edition 2010
Second edition 2014

ISBN 978-988-8208-61-6

British Library Cataloguing-in-Publication Data
A catalogue record for this book is available from the British Library.

10 9 8 7 6 5 4 3 2 1

Printed and bound by Cheer Shine Enterprise Co., Ltd. in Hong Kong, China

Contents

Foreword

Over the past 30 years, the Hong Kong Institute of Surveyors has been committed to serving the needs of its members in the surveying profession. One of the Institute's recent initiatives is to support the production of reference books relevant to local surveying practice. In 2013, the Institute proudly sponsored the publication of *Hong Kong Legal Principles: Important Topics for Students and Professionals, Second Edition*, by Stephen D. Mau, which has been well regarded as a useful and popular tool for non-legal professionals and students in Hong Kong. Following the success of the title, the Institute has decided to fund the second edition of a series of three books authored by Stephen D. Mau, namely *Contract Law in Hong Kong: An Introductory Guide*; *Property Law in Hong Kong: An Introductory Guide*; and *Tort Law in Hong Kong: An Introductory Guide*.

As reference books intended for a general readership, these three titles seek to provide a general but comprehensive introduction to the three important fields of the law in simple, accessible language. The books are specifically designed for guiding readers through key legal principles. In order to reflect the changes in the law in the past few years, the revised edition of the books have included a number of new case authorities and legislation.

Dynamic changes have been taking place in the landscape of the construction industry over the past decade, and the development of the law has played a vital role in these transformations. With this updated series of introductory law books, members of the surveying profession and other lay readers will certainly find it easier to explore the principles and implications of the law.

On behalf of the Hong Kong Institute of Surveyors, I would like to thank Dr Stephen D. Mau for his invaluable contribution in penning this up-to-date series of books on contract, property and tort laws.

Sr Simon Kwok
President
The Hong Kong Institute of Surveyors

Preface to the Second Edition

For many non-law students and professionals, the study of law has often been regarded as a complex and difficult subject. Nevertheless, acquiring legal knowledge is an essential part of the professional development of practitioners in many industries. The law also plays an important role in business operations and the daily lives of every citizen. In response to the need for an introductory guide to legal principles for the general public, in 2010 I decided to develop a series of books that cover three fundamental areas of law, namely contract, tort and property. Since then, the common law and the statutory law have continued to evolve dynamically, and it is now time to update these books to ensure that they reflect the current legal position in Hong Kong.

The technical terms are usually the major obstacles to beginners of legal studies. To facilitate understanding, simple language has been used in these three introductory guides. Where the use of technical terms is inevitable, the terms are defined using simple English. Chinese translations of most of the terms are provided either in the main text or in the notes. Additional information can be found in the notes, including detailed explanations and discussions of the corresponding topic, and references to supplementary sources.

In this second edition, a number of chapters and sections have been revised and consolidated to help comprehension. In response to the latest developments in the law, discussions on new case law and statutes have also been included.

The author wishes to acknowledge the invaluable assistance provided by the following individuals in the preparation of the second edition: Chow Man Ho, Rocky (周文浩); Fong Man Hin (方文軒); Ken Lee Kin-wang (李健泓); and Lit Ka Ki, Andy (列家麒).

Preface to the First Edition

The purpose of this book is to provide general coverage of matters in the field of property law. As such, this title is intended for the general public rather than legal professionals or those studying to become legal professionals. Consequently, this title is also suitable for beginners or students who require some legal knowledge but not to the extent of a legal practitioner. Other titles are available offering more extensive and more in-depth coverage of the subject for those who wish to pursue further studies.

The study of law is difficult — due to concepts, application and/or technical terms — with language being an obstacle to many. With this and the readership in mind, we have attempted to strive for "simple English" rather than more academic prose or technical legal language. Where technical terms are used, we have attempted to define those terms in simple English rather than using "legalese." Furthermore, we have provided a Chinese translation (in traditional characters) of most legal terms, either in the main text or in the endnotes.

This book contains endnotes for each of the chapters. In these endnotes, the reader may find additional information. This information may consist of more detailed explanations and/or discussions of the corresponding topic in the main text. This information may also consist of references to other sources where additional information on the particular topic may be found.

The author wishes to acknowledge the invaluable assistance provided by following individuals in the preparation of this publication: Sebastian Yat Fung Ko (高一鋒), BSc LLB(Hons), PCLL; Terence Lam (林蓬源); Krystal Lee Yeuk-ying (李若瑩); Li Tai Chiu, Ryan (李泰釗); Hazel Mah Hau-sung (馬孝笙); Pun Cheuk Lun, Eric (潘卓倫); and Shao Wai Chun, Wilson (邵尉晉).

Table of Cases

Table of Legislation

1

Introduction to Property – Generally

A. Overview

This book is about property and the general legal principles which apply to this area of law. Rather than a specialized textbook for law students, this book seeks to introduce property law to readers from different fields such as construction, accountancy, social work, and, other professions. As such, this publication will not review all aspects of property. This book will cover property topics that are, in general, governed by the common law. Areas of property that are statute-based will be reviewed but not in substantive detail. Conveyancing, because of its importance, will be reviewed in some detail.

Before continuing on this subject of property law, however, we should discuss a related matter. That matter is the common law legal system. Hong Kong and the United Kingdom, along with most Commonwealth countries and the United States, all follow the common law legal system. Continental Europe and China are examples of jurisdictions which follow the civil law legal system. The major difference between the two legal systems is that the common law legal system relies upon precedent.[1] *Common law* historically refers to the law common to all England. *Precedent* refers to prior examples found in preceding court decisions which would be followed in subsequent cases concerning the same facts and issues. Consequently, this is the reason for referring to cases and for discussing cases in this book.

Finally, in preparing this work, we assumed that the reader has some basic knowledge of contract law as most transactions concerning property involve legally-binding agreements.

B. Organization

This book is concerned with property, its definition and the general principles of property law. Both personal and real property will be examined. This publication is divided into three parts. Part 1 focuses on real property. The discussion on real property will include a review of freehold and leasehold estates, and co-ownership. Then, in Part 2, focus turns to land-related issues, such as servitudes and mortgages. Part 3 of this book provides a detailed review of Hong Kong conveyancing and follows the process of creation and transfer of interests in real property.

C. Definition

This section is the introduction to property in general. Here we will review the definition of property; what it means to own property; how property is acquired or disposed; and, some general rules about property. Later, we will discuss in more detail the aspects of what is commonly known as real estate.

The definition of *property* we use is: title to, or, rights of, ownership in goods or other valuables. *Title* means one's right to property, or the evidence of that right to property. *Ownership* means the complete and the exclusive right to control property, subject to law.[2]

In Hong Kong, the *Interpretation and General Clauses Ordinance* (Cap 1) also provides some definitions, which are as follows:

> "immovable property" (不動產) means –
> (a) land, whether covered by water or not;
> (b) any estate, right, interest or easement in or over any land; and
> (c) things attached to land or permanently fastened to anything attached to land;
> "movable property" (動產) means property of every description except immovable property;
> "property" (財產) includes –
> (a) money, goods, choses in action and land; and
> (b) obligations, easements and every description of estate, interest and profit, present or future, vested or contingent, arising out of or incident to property as defined in paragraph (a) of this definition.[3]

Ownership involves certain rights.[4] Someone who owns property has the following rights:

- to use the property
- to enjoy the use of the property
- to enjoy the property aesthetically (e.g., works of art such as paintings or sculptures)
- to destroy the property
- to dispose of the property
    - by gift
    - by succession,[5] through a document known as a *will* made by the testator[6] or through intestacy[7] where the probate court applies of the laws of intestate succession[8]
    - by sale
    - by abandonment[9]

How does a person obtain these rights of ownership? Methods by which ownership of property may be acquired include the following:

- original, i.e., taking possession of property which has never been owned[10]
- taking property which has been abandoned by the original owner
- creation or invention, i.e., creating property such as when a carpenter creates a piece of furniture from raw materials[11]
- derivatively:
    - by sale/purchase of the property
    - by gift of the property
    - succession: either in accordance with a will or the laws of intestacy if the person died without a will

Notice how some methods of disposing of property by one person may also be the manner through which property is obtained by another person. For example, property may be disposed of by gift and can be acquired by gift. The sale of property by the original owner may result in the purchase of the property by a new owner. As a final example, a person may come into ownership of property abandoned by the original owner.

With ownership comes the right of control. However, ownership and possession may be exercised separately. Property may thus be controlled by a person who exercises fewer rights than an owner, but who nonetheless may control access to and use of the property. This person has possession of the property. This concept of possession of personal property is discussed immediately below.

D. Possession and Bailment

Possession is the actual physical control of that property; or, the intent to possess exclusively that property intending to prevent others from using the property. The word *possession* "may mean effective, physical or manual control, or occupation, evidenced by some outward act, sometimes called *de facto* possession or detention as distinct from a legal right to possession. This is a question of fact rather than of law."[12]

What happens when an owner of property lawfully parts with possession of the property? Two situations may arise. In the first situation, if the owner has no intention for any other person to have exclusive control, then the other person has no rights to possess the property. This person is a custodian. *Custodian* is defined as a "person or institution that has charge or custody of property, papers, or other valuables." *Custody* is defined as the "care and control of a thing or person for inspection, preservation, or security."[13]

In the second situation, if the owner, upon parting with possession, gives full control over the property to another person, a bailment is created. A *bailment* is a transaction under which property or goods are delivered by one party (referred to as the *bailor*) to another party (known as the *bailee*) with provisions which normally require the bailee to hold the goods and ultimately to return the property to the bailor or to dispose of the property according to the bailor's instructions.[14]

> Acts as diverse as lending a book to [a] friend, leaving luggage in a storage area at a train station, and renting a car are all bailments. . . . in a bailment one person is entitled to ownership of a chattel but a different person has lawful possession of the good. In general, the good is to be held for a purpose and to be returned or redelivered when the purpose for which it was delivered is accomplished. The quintessential characteristic of a bailment, however, is a change in possession (control) over the good with the result that two sets of property rights exist in the same object – those arising from the bailor's title and those resulting from the bailee's possession.[15]

A bailment is usually based upon a contract. Three essential concepts are linked with the creation of a bailment. First, the bailee is to take care of the goods and return them in accordance with the bailor's instruction. The extent of the duty of care varies, depending upon whether the bailment is for payment or free. Second, the bailee is liable for the loss or damage of the property should the bailee be negligent. Finally, the bailee cannot deny the bailor's ownership of the goods.[16] Thus, the bailee is given both physical and legal possession over the goods but does not become the owner of the goods. The bailor keeps the ownership or title to the property, and, may recover possession upon the end of the bailment.

E. Possession and the Finder Doctrine

Where an owner is unintentionally separated from its property, the common law[17] recognises the Finder Doctrine.[18] Under this doctrine, if the owner loses or misplaces property, the finder has better rights to the found object than anyone except the owner. The case of *Armory v Delamirie* (1722) 93 ER 664 introduced this doctrine that a finder "does not by such finding acquire an absolute property or ownership. Yet he has such a property as will enable him to keep it against all but the rightful owner." Thus a finder has a right in the found property that is good against everyone in the whole world except the owner.[19] Some examples include the following:

- if someone finds an object in a public place (such as a park), that person is entitled to the object unless it is claimed by the owner
- if someone finds an item in a private place where the public is invited (such as a store, mall, restaurant), that person is entitled to the item unless it is claimed by the owner
- if an object is found in a private place where the public is not invited, the object becomes the property of the owner of the land where the object is found
- if the owner was never in actual possession of the land, then the finder will be the individual who obtains lawful possession, except against the lawful owner

Parker v British Airways Board [1982] 1 QB 1004 is a case that applied the Finder Doctrine. Parker, a passenger of the airline, found a bracelet in the airline's lounge. Parker handed the bracelet to the airline, requesting that if the bracelet remained unclaimed, it should be returned to him. British Airways sold the bracelet and kept the money from the sale. Parker sued and the court determined that he acted properly. The airline did not show an intention to exercise control over the lounge such that the bracelet was in its possession before Parker found it.[20]

The Finder Doctrine illustrates the common law's concept of relativity of property: the law determines which claimant of particular property has better title, rather than determining the true owner. Thus, in a court case claiming conversion,[21] the finder only needs to prove better title than the other party who cannot rely on the defence that a third party has a better title than the finder.[22] This common law rule still applies in Hong Kong. Further, at common law, possession is assumed as evidence of title.

> The right to have legal and de facto possession is a normal but not necessary incident of ownership. Such a right may exist with, or apart from, de facto or legal possession, and in different persons at the same time in virtue of different proprietary rights. Thus, when an owner has been wrongfully dispossessed of his goods by theft, or has lost them, he retains the right to possess them; but, where he has bailed them for a term or by way of pledge, this right is temporarily suspended.[23]
>
> . . .
>
> The presumption of law is that the person who has de facto possession also has the property, and accordingly, such possession is protected, whatever its origin, against all who cannot prove a superior title. This rule applies equally in criminal and civil matters. Thus, as against a stranger or a wrongdoer, a person in actual or apparent possession, but without the right to possession, has all the rights and remedies of a person entitled to and able to prove a present right to possession.[24]

F. Classification of Property

Here, we review the different types of property. Property may be categorised in many ways. Some of these categories might overlap so that a particular type of property could be classified under more than one category. We discuss these categories below.

One method of classification is designating property as either *tangible* property or *intangible* property. Tangible property includes goods or other things which can be touched, that is, objects which have a physical shape or a physical being. Intangible property refers to things which do not have a physical shape or being, such as rights arising under a contract.

Another method of classification is to designate property as being *realty* (real property) or *personalty* (personal property). Realty includes all things such as freehold estates and interests in land; trees and other plants which grow in the land; and, things that are permanently attached to the land, such as buildings, structures and plants. Real property can be further sub-divided into corporeal hereditaments and incorporeal hereditaments.

Corporeal refers to something which has a physical being, in other words, tangible property. *Incorporeal* refers to rights over objects rather than the property itself. *Hereditament* means those rights which are capable of being inherited. Corporeal hereditaments thus are physical objects over which rights may be exercised and incorporeal hereditaments are intangible rights over objects. Therefore, an incorporeal hereditament means any rights attached to, arising out of, or exercisable within a corporeal hereditament, e.g., a right of way. *Personalty* is all other types of property, sometimes referred to as *chattels*.

These classifications of property resulted from historical developments. In the past, an individual's status in society depended upon that person's relationship to the land. Thus, someone who lost land should be able to recover that land rather than receiving financial compensation. Courts would protect real property by requiring that the realty be returned to the owner. Thus, a law suit concerning land is known as a *real* action, which is sometimes termed an action *in rem*.[25] A legal right in land is a right *in rem*. This right *in rem* attaches to the land, binding all those who come into ownership or possession of that land. This is in part because land is considered to be unique in character. On the other hand, a lawsuit against a person for loss or damage to property other than land would be an action *in personam*, that is, a court action against the wrongdoer. The claimant in an action *in personam* would generally seek monetary payment for damages resulting from the wrongdoer's acts rather than for the return of the property.

Another historical development involved the common law being more concerned with the form and the strict application of law. As a result of the harsh application of the statutes by the courts of law, equitable notions began to be applied in the courts of equity. Equity sought to lessen the severity of the common law in order to make the law more fair and just.[26]

An equitable right is a right *in personam* which can be enforced against the whole world except a person who acquired the land in good faith,[27] for value and without notice of the equitable interest.

Equitable remedies apply in property law and will be discussed in further detail in the following sections. For now, as an example, equity will be discussed in terms of trusts involving land.[28] Equity permits the creation of a *trust* where the legal title is in one person while another person enjoys the beneficial, or equitable, interests in that property.[29]

With a trust involving land, the common law recognises that one party owns the land. This person has the legal estate in the land. If a trust is created allowing another person to enjoy the land and its benefits, then this other person (referred to as the *beneficiary*) has an equitable interest (also known as an *equitable estate*) in the land. Equity would protect the interests of the beneficiary against those of the legal owner (known as the *trustee*).

PART 1

Real Property

The common law definition of land includes the surface of the earth, together with all things of a physical nature above and below the land surface, such as buildings, trees, and, minerals.[1] In Hong Kong, there are several statutory definitions of real property. One set of definitions is found in the *Interpretation and General Clauses Ordinance* which was provided earlier.[2]

Section 2 of the *Conveyancing and Property Ordinance* (Cap 219) provides the definitions concerning conveyancing and property. As these definitions are used throughout this book, section 2 is quoted in full as follows:

> In this Ordinance, unless the context otherwise requires –
> "assignment" (轉讓、轉讓契) includes –
> > (a) the transfer of the whole of the interest in land held under a Government lease;
> > (b) a legal charge;
> > (c) a lease (other than a Government lease);
> > (d) a surrender;
> > (e) an assent; and
> > (f) every other assurance or conveyance of land by any instrument;
>
> "bankruptcy" (破產) includes winding up;
> "borrower" (借款人), where used in the First, Second and Third Schedules, includes "mortgagor";
> "encumbrance" (產權負擔) includes a legal and equitable mortgage, a trust for securing money, a lien, a charge of a portion, annuity, or other capital or annual sum; and "encumbrancer"

(產權負擔人) . . . includes every person entitled to the benefit of an encumbrance, or to require payment or discharge thereof;

"equitable interest" (衡平法權益) means any estate, interest or charge in or over land which is not a legal estate or a freehold;

"instrument" (文書) means any document having legal effect except a will;

"land" (土地) includes –

(a) land covered by water;

(b) any estate, right, interest or easement in or over any land;

(bb) the whole or part of an undivided share in land and any estate, right, interest or easement in or over the whole or part of an undivided share in land; and

(c) things attached to land or permanently fastened to anything attached to land;

"legal charge" (法定押記) means a mortgage expressed to be a legal charge;

"legal estate" (法定產業權) means –

(a) a term of years absolute in land;

(b) the legal interest in any easement, right or privilege in or over land for an interest equivalent to a term of years absolute; and

(c) a legal charge;

"lender" (貸款人), where used in the First, Second and Third Schedules, includes "mortgagee";

"mortgage" (按揭) means a security over land for securing money or money's worth;

"mortgage money" (按揭金) means the money, or money's worth, secured by a mortgage;

"mortgagee" (承按人) includes any person claiming under a mortgagee;

"mortgagor" (按揭人) includes any person claiming under a mortgagor;

"sale" (售賣), in relation to the sale of land, includes the disposition of all or part of the vendor's estate and interest under a Government lease; . . .

"term of years absolute" (絕對年期), includes a term for less than a year, for a year or years and a fraction of a year and from year to year.

Thus, under the *Conveyancing and Property Ordinance*, land is defined in sections (a) and (c). Intangible rights which might exist over or in the land are given in sections (b) and (bb).

These definitions include some concepts which might be unfamiliar. The following sections of this book will attempt to explain the application of these concepts to land law. The next sections, in particular, review the doctrine of estates, examining the principles involving rights and interests in land. Servitudes and mortgages will be discussed later in Part 2.

2
Estates

An *estate* is an interest in land. This interest in land gives its owner certain rights over that land for a period of time.[1] There are two types of estates: freehold and leasehold. The differing types of freehold estates will be examined before proceeding to a discussion of leasehold estates.

It should be noted that the freehold estates are practically irrelevant to Hong Kong, but their discussion assists in the analysis of leasehold estates. Leasehold estates are the predominant form of estates in Hong Kong.

A. Freehold Estate

Traditionally, there are three types of freehold estates: (i) fee simple, (ii) fee tail and (iii) life estate. These will be discussed below. Before doing so, however, two terms should be introduced: *grantor* and *grantee*. A *grantor* is the person (or company, trustee, etc.) who grants, gives or sells the property or a property right. A *grantee* is the person (or company, trustee, etc.) who receives the property or property right.[2]

i. Fee Simple

The first type of freehold estate is known as a fee simple estate. The term *fee simple* is the shortened version for the proper name of this estate: fee simple absolute in possession. The word *fee* means an estate which can be passed to another person. The word *simple* means that the estate can be passed on to anyone, that there are no restrictions upon who can own the land. The term *absolute* refers to the unlimited or unrestricted time period of ownership. An absolute interest is an interest in an estate which "is not determinable or conditional, i.e., it is not granted on such terms that it is liable to end prematurely on the occurrence of some specified event."[3] The term *possession* is self-explanatory. The owner of the estate is entitled to possess the estate, i.e., to live on the premises or to rent the premises. Consequently, a fee simple estate is the highest and most unrestricted form of ownership.

There are two sub-types of fee simple estates, neither of which has an absolute interest. One sub-type is known as a *conditional fee simple* where the person granting or creating this estate may take possession of the property in the future when a specified event either takes place or does not take place. A conditional fee simple requires the event (as the condition) to occur after the granting of the estate rather than as a pre-condition (a requirement which must be satisfied before granting the estate).

> A conditional interest arises where a fee simple is granted subject to a limitation which provides that the grantor will be able to re-enter the property at some date in the future on the occurrence (or non-occurrence) of specified events. In such a case the grantor appears initially to be giving a fee simple absolute, but then reserves the right to recover the land (right of re-entry).[4]

For instance, a grantor grants to a grantee a fee simple estate on the condition that the grantee will not marry someone with red hair. If the grantee marries an individual with red hair, the grantor has the choice of taking back the estate. Note, however, that this fee only gives the grantor the opportunity to take back the estate. The grantee's interest in the land does not end until the grantor actually takes back the estate.

The other sub-type of fee simple estate is known as a *determinable fee simple*, where the grant of the interest in the land lasts until a specified event occurs (or does not occur). The fee is a determinable estate even where a specified event is unlikely to occur. This is because, from the beginning of the grant, the period of the interest in the estate has been reduced. For example, a grantor grants to a grantee the estate until the grantee buys a flat in Causeway Bay. When and only if the grantee buys such a flat, the grantee's interest in this estate ends. A determinable fee simple automatically determines (or *ends*) when the specified event occurs.

At times, it is difficult to know whether a conditional fee simple or a determinable fee simple is being created because the end result, return of the estate to the grantor (known as *reversion*, see Chapter 4 endnote 10 for further discussion), is quite similar. However, the wording used in the grant might assist in classifying whether the estate is of one sub-type or the other.[5]

Conditional Fee	Determinable Fee
on condition that	until
providing that	as long as
but if	or the duration of
	while

The common law and equity affect these sub-types of fee simple in different ways. A conditional fee is a legal estate, while a determinable fee exists only as an equitable interest.

ii. Fee Tail

The second type of freehold estate is the *fee tail* estate. This estate continues so long as the original grantee or any of the grantee's descendants survives. Once the family line is broken, the fee tail estate ends. Thus, the grantee cannot sell the land and only familial descendants may inherit the estate. Once the fee tail ends, the estate returns back to the grantor.

iii. Life Estate

The third type of traditional freehold estate is the *life estate* which is measured by the life of a person. Thus, this estate exists only for the duration of someone's lifetime. The life estate may be granted for the life of the grantee or the grant may be based on the life of any another individual.

B. Co-ownership – Types

Having reviewed the types of estates which a person may possess, presented below are the ways in which those estates may be held by more than one grantee. There are various types of co-ownership.[6] The two types of co-ownership most commonly found in Hong Kong are joint tenancy and tenancy in common. Here, we use the term *tenant* to refer to the grantee rather than to someone who rents property under a lease and we use the term *tenancy* to refer to ownership.[7]

i. Joint Tenancy

Joint tenancy is the co-ownership of an estate.[8] Each owner is entitled to the whole property, rather than to an undivided share in the estate. A joint tenant does not hold any interest in the property as an individual. The interest is held equally and jointly with the other joint tenant(s).[9]

> A joint tenant is said to hold the whole [estate] with another but nothing of himself. There is thus only one estate in the land which is held jointly and, although the joint tenants as between themselves have distinct rights, to everyone else they are like a sole owner.[10]

A joint tenancy as a form of co-ownership also:

> dictates that no co-owner is entitled to the possession of any particular part of the land to the exclusion of his fellow co-owner. He is entitled to the possession of the whole, with and not to the exclusion of his fellow co-owners. If A and B are co-owners of a flats [sic] they are both entitled to occupy the whole flat. Neither A or B can exclude the other from the kitchen, bathroom, 'their' respective bedrooms, or any other part of the flat.[11]

The right of survivorship (known as *jus accrescendi*) applies in a joint tenancy: the last survivor among all the joint tenants becomes sole owner of the whole property. The heirs of the joint tenants who predecease the surviving joint tenant have no share in the property. For example, assume there are three friends: Au, Chan and Tang. Each is married with a family. These three friends own a flat as joint tenants. When Au passes away, Au's ownership interest in the property will go to Chan and Tang. Au's family will receive nothing from Au's share in the flat. The same result will happen when Chan passes on. In the end, Tang will solely own the whole property.

Formerly, at law, a joint tenancy must always remain a joint tenancy. Dividing the ownership (known as *severance*) was not possible. Equity recognised an injustice and allowed severance under the rules established in the case of *Williams v Hensman* (1861) 1 John & H 546:

> a joint tenancy may be severed in three ways; in the first place, an act of any one of the persons interested operating upon his own share may create a severance as to that share (e.g., selling his "share") . . . Secondly, a joint tenancy may be severed by mutual agreement. And, in the third place, there may be

a severance by any course of dealing sufficient to intimate that the interests of all were mutually treated as constituting a tenancy in common. When the severance depends on an inference of this kind without any express act of severance, it will not suffice to rely on an intention, with respect to the particular share, declared behind the backs of the other persons interested. You must find in this class of cases a course of dealing by which the shares of all the parties to the contest have been affected . . . [12]

The law in Hong Kong regarding severance of a joint tenancy can be found in section 8 of the *Conveyancing and Property Ordinance*,[13] which provides for severance by instrument or by notice.[14]

The main characteristics of a joint tenancy are:

- A joint tenancy has a right of survivorship. *Survivorship* means that the interest of the deceased joint owner is acquired by the surviving joint tenant(s). The deceased owner's interest does not pass to its heirs. Title in a joint tenancy passes upon death and by the process of elimination. The last joint tenant to survive acquires the sole ownership of the property.
- Following the above principle, the interest of a joint tenant is extinguished upon death and is incapable of being passed on to an heir under a will or on intestacy.
- Each joint owner has the legal right to equal participation in the land's actual profits.

Again, the premise underlying the joint tenancy form of co-ownership is that each joint tenant has no individual interest in the realty. The only interest a joint tenant has is held jointly with fellow joint tenant(s). Although the joint tenants as between themselves have separate rights and obligations, they are regarded as a sole owner.

Because of this premise that a joint tenant holds the property with others as a single owner, the requirements for the creation of a joint tenancy reflect this premise. Thus, provided no words of severance are present,[15] there will be a joint tenancy if the four *unities* are present, namely:

1. unity of possession: each owner has possession of the whole, and none of the joint tenants may claim possession of any particular part of the estate
2. unity of interest: the interest of each joint tenant is equal both in quantity and quality in terms of nature, extent and duration, so that no share is larger or smaller than another

3. unity of title: each co-owner derives title from the same document
4. unity of time: the interest of each co-owner comes into being at the same time

ii. Tenancy in Common

A tenancy in common is another form of co-ownership. Under a tenancy in common, each owner has an undivided share in the property.[16] This share in the property will pass to the heirs with the decedent's other assets at the time of death.[17] The right of survivorship does not apply to this form of co-ownership. Hence, a deceased tenant's interest in this type of property can be inherited by the heirs. Unity of possession must exist in a tenancy in common, because all co-owners are entitled to possession of all parts of the land. However, the other unities of interest, title and time are not required for a tenancy in common.

The *Conveyancing and Property Ordinance* provides for a presumption in favour of a tenancy in common rather than a joint tenancy.[18] Section 9 of this statute provides:

*   Where a tenancy in the same estate or interest in land vests in two or more persons under an instrument or a will, it shall be presumed, unless the contrary intention is expressed in that instrument or will, that the tenancy vests in those persons as tenants in common rather than as joint tenants.[19]

*   This section shall not apply to any instrument or will made before the commencement of this section.

*   This section shall not apply to a tenancy vesting in trustees or personal representatives.

The important points to note about the tenancy in common form of co-ownership are:

*   Each tenant owns an individual portion. The portions are not physically divisible but each tenant has an undivided share. Unlike a joint tenancy, the ownership shares or portions need not be equal in a tenancy in common so long as together they make up the whole. In the example above, in a tenancy in common situation, it would be possible for Au to have a 65% share in the flat, Chan to have a 30% share and Tang to have a 5% share.

*   Each tenant may deal with its individual share, e.g., sell its share.

*   There is no right of survivorship in a tenancy in common. If a tenant in common dies, that tenant's share in the land will be distributed

to the beneficiaries according to the tenant's will or under the rules of intestacy. Again using the previous example, should Au pass away under a tenancy in common, Au's heirs (e.g., spouse and children) will become tenants in common with a 65% share in the flat with Chan and Tang.

C. Co-ownership – Creation

The following is a brief discussion on the creation of co-ownership, reviewing the guidelines used to determine whether a co-ownership is a joint tenancy or a tenancy in common. Where the co-ownership does not state whether the property is held either at law or in equity, a court will look to the presumptions that arise both at law and in equity.

If one or more of the four unities is absent, then the co-owners must hold the realty as tenants in common both at law and in equity. Additionally, where all four unities are present, the existence of a joint tenancy or a tenancy in common will depend on whether the relationship came into existence before or after the *Conveyancing and Property Ordinance* of 1 November 1984.

Prior to the Ordinance, the common law favoured a joint tenancy. This was to avoid the fragmentation of the property's title that results from a tenancy in common, where each owner's share was being disposed of separately from the other owners. A tenancy in common is created by words in the grant of title which indicate each grantee will take a distinct share in the property, i.e., the words in the grant amount to words of severance. Words or phrases which have been held to have this effect include: *equally, between, share and share alike*, and, *to be divided amongst*. Additionally, words showing that the grantees were to take unequal interests or shares in the realty create a tenancy in common.[20]

If an intention is to create a tenancy in common (indicated by words of severance) this intention will be recognised by the common law. Thus, the words used in the grant will determine if there is an intention to sever or divide the shares in the estate. If there are words of severance, the grant will be a tenancy in common. If there are no words of severance, the grant will be a joint tenancy.[21]

Section 9 of the *Conveyancing and Property Ordinance* changed this common law presumption. Today, according to the Ordinance, co-owners are presumed to hold an estate as tenants in common even if no words of severance are used. In order to create a joint tenancy, the document by which the co-owners acquire their interest in the property must express a clear intention against a tenancy in common.

Because equity favours fairness rather than conveyancing convenience, equity prefers a tenancy in common. Although a legal estate might be held by joint tenants, equity will presume an intention to create a tenancy in common. Equity will actually impose a tenancy in common in three situations:

1. Unequal contributions: where the money used to purchase the realty is provided in unequal shares, the parties providing the funds are presumed by equity to be tenants in common in the same proportions as their contributions to the purchase price.[22] "If two or more persons together purchase property and provide the money in equal shares they are presumed in equity to be joint tenants."[23] These presumptions may be overturned by evidence that the parties intended a tenancy in common despite equal contributions or that they intended to hold as joint tenants despite unequal contributions.[24]

2. Money advanced on a mortgage: where two or more people lend money for a mortgage they are presumed to have made the loan as tenants in common.

    > So if two people join in lending money upon a mortgage, Equity says, it could not be the intention, that the interest in that should survive. Though they take a joint security, each means to lend his own and take back his own.[25]

    Again, this presumption may be countered by evidence showing the contrary intention.

3. Business assets: the concept of survivorship does not generally apply to the commercial field. Equity will presume a tenancy in common over partnership assets or the assets of a joint business, or where the premises are held jointly for several individual business purposes.[26]

D. Co-ownership – Determination

Co-ownership of an estate may be ended by several methods. The first method of termination of co-ownership is by union into a sole owner, where one person becomes the sole owner of the estate, e.g., by purchasing it from the other co-owner or is gifted the share from the other co-owner.

Co-ownership among joint tenants also can be terminated by death. As the term implies, survivorship occurs where the co-ownership is ended by the death of the other joint tenant(s), leaving one remaining joint tenant.

In a third method, co-ownership may be terminated by severance, when a joint tenant changes the relationship with the other co-owners to that of a tenant in common. The joint tenant maintains an undivided share in the property but is no longer affected by the right of survivorship.[27] *Severance* converts a joint tenancy into a tenancy in common. Any act destroying one or more of the four unities results in a severance, as will the intention by the joint tenants to exclude the operation of survivorship.

Partition is a procedure available to end either type of co-ownership of land.[28] Partition may be done voluntarily by a conveyance of a part of the realty by all of the co-owners jointly to each one individually. Partition can be compulsory through an application to a court. The *Partition Ordinance* (Cap 352) gives a court the power to partition or to sell jointly owned property.

For example, the *Partition Ordinance* allows a court to partition the realty in one of the following ways:

- into parcels to be held by the single owners individually
- into parcels to be held by two or more persons as joint tenants
- into parcels to be held by two or more individuals as tenants in common[29]

In conclusion, this section has reviewed briefly the types, creation and determination of freehold estates. We will now discuss the second category of interest in land, leasehold.

3
Licence and Leasehold Estate

A. Introduction

Having reviewed freehold estates, we now review the other type of estate: leasehold. Leasehold estates are a type of interest in land that do not rise to the level of freehold estates. Leasehold estates are held for a certain duration "and usually involve a continuing relationship between the grantor and the grantee, such as the grantee's [e.g., lessee's/tenant's] obligation to pay rent to the grantor [e.g., lessor/landlord]."[1]

> Generally, the relationship of landlord and tenant arises as a rule when one person ('the landlord') grants to another ('the tenant') a right to the exclusive possession of land for a term less than that which the landlord has in the land . . . and it usually carries with it the right to receive from the tenant payment of rent for the use of the property.[2]

Leases were not considered to be a legal right to real property. Leases were regarded as commercial contracts which created *in personam* rights between the parties. Unlike freehold estates, leases historically did not affect the tenants' social class or position in the society of that time. Thus, leasehold estates were not subject to a real action. A dispossessed tenant could not recover the land from the landlord but would only be awarded damages for breach of contract. Since the interests contained in a lease were protected only by an action *in personam*, the lease was regarded as personal property. Consequently, classification of the lease had become fixed as personalty.

In the case of *Street v Mountford* [1985] AC 809, the court stated that "[t]o constitute a tenancy the occupier must be granted exclusive possession for a fixed or periodic term certain in consideration of a premium or periodical payments."[3] Yet, not all occupiers of land are tenants. A tenant holds a legal estate.[4] Some occupants of land only have a licence or permission to use the premises which creates no interest in the land. Thus, there are differences between a lessee and licensee. For example, the tenant of a shop in an arcade is different from a licensed hawker set up in a marketplace. In this example, the tenant has a lease and the hawker has a licence. Both pay for the space, but the hawker receives no interest in the premises. A lease is not revocable; a licence is revocable. A licensee whose licence is illegally revoked will have to sue in court for breach of contract rather than for possession of the land. Furthermore, leases can be assigned to third persons whereas licences are generally personal and not assignable.

Thus, a "licence is a permission to use land, without which an occupier would be a trespasser."[5] The distinction between a licence and a lease is important because the *Landlord and Tenant (Consolidation) Ordinance* (Cap 7) applies only to leases. This classification assists in determining whether a provision against subletting has been broken and determining the way in which an occupation can be ended. A tenant may also be entitled to statutory benefits.

> There is, therefore, an incentive for owners to grant licences rather than leases, and in many cases the court has to determine whether a document before it, which is expressed to be a licence, is in fact a tenancy either mislabelled or disguised as a licence.[6]

As both licenses and leases are routinely encountered, the topic of licenses will be set out briefly below, followed by an introduction to leases.

B. Licence – Types[7]

The case of *Thomas v Sorrell* (1673) Vaugh 330 provides the classic definition of a licence: "A . . . licence properly passeth no interest, nor alters or transfers property in any thing, but only makes an action lawful, which without it had been unlawful."[8] Another source states that:

> a licence creates no interest or estate in the land. It is merely a personal right providing a remedy only against the licensor and not against the land. Nor is the licensee considered to be in possession of the land, and he is unable to sue in either trespass or nuisance.[9]

In addition to the criteria set out in *Street v Mountford*, the courts may consider the following factors in determining whether there is a license or a lease:

- The power to grant a lease
- The *nemo dat quod non habet* rule that a seller cannot give better title than that which the seller possesses.

  A similar situation applies to the granting of leases. If the grantor has no interest or estate in land, the grantor cannot grant a lease to others. In *Torbett v Faulkner* [1952] 2 TLR 659, the court decided that an agreement between an occupant and a company was an invalid lease because the company's director, rather than the company, was the true owner of the house in question.[10]

- The substance of the agreement

  The parties cannot create a licence simply by calling it a licence. The courts will look at the substance, rather than the form, of the agreement.

  For example, terms like *the landlord reserves the right to enter and inspect the state of repair of the premises* or *the tenant is forbidden to transfer his interest* suggest that exclusive possession has been granted. Accordingly, a lease is created.

- Family arrangements, acts of friendship or generosity

  Where the parties have no intention to create any legal relationships, no lease is created.

A full discussion of licences is beyond the scope of this work. Below is an introduction to different types of licences most commonly encountered. A court classified licences thus: "The threefold classification of licences is well known. There are licences coupled with an interest, contractual licences and bare licences."[11] Presented first is the lowest form of licence which affords licensees the least protection under the law.

i. Bare Licence

A bare licence is permission to enter land without any payment by the entrant. For instance, a visitor's entry onto land is allowed with the owner's permission. The visitor, with this permission, is a licensee and not a trespasser. Should the owner request the visitor to leave and, failing to do so, the visitor will become a trespasser.

A bare licence can be created expressly or impliedly. For example, a dinner guest will have the owner's express permission to be on the land to attend the dinner; a postman has an implied permission to come to a home's front door to deliver the mail; the public has an implied licence to come up to the entrance of privately owned land for any lawful business.

A bare licence can be cancelled or revoked by either party. Revocation may be made by express notice or by any act inconsistent with the continuance of the licence. For instance, the express licence of dinner guests ends when they leave. Another example involves the implied license of members of the public: this licence ends when they are asked, by words or conduct, to leave. The death of one of the parties to the licence will end a bare licence. The assignment by the licensor of its interest in the land to another person will also terminate a bare licence.

ii. Licence Coupled with an Interest

A licence coupled with an interest is comprised of two components: a licence and an interest.[12] A licence coupled with an interest occurs where a right to enter land (the licence) is granted in order to support an interest in that land. Thus, the grantee of a *profit à prendre* has an interest in land of another person in the form of a right to take the land's natural products such as wild animals, soil, or minerals. Coupled with this interest is the license to enter that person's land in order to remove the products. Another example: an interest in land in the form of the right to fish is of little value unless permission is also given to reach the fish. Licences coupled with an interest are uncommon in Hong Kong because some of the natural products entitled to one who holds a *profit à prendre* are in low abundance.

iii. Contractual Licence

A contractual licence arises where the permission to use or to occupy land is made pursuant to a contract. Contractual licences serve many functions. Contractual licences are found in the right to enter a cinema, concert hall, sports venue, or in the right to park a vehicle in a commercial car park. Contractual licences may govern the right of a building contractor to enter a building site to carry out the building works. Contractual licenses may also govern the right to use and to enjoy the facilities of a club.

The creation and the terms of contractual licences may be express or implicit. Termination of a contractual licence will depend on the terms of the licence. "For instance, the length of the licence may be expressly stated, but in many cases the courts will have to ascertain the parties' intention from the terms of the licence and the surrounding circumstances."[13]

C. Leases – Definition

Distinguishing between leases and licences can be difficult. Conceptually, the distinction is clear, but its application is difficult. Each situation is judged on a case-by-case basis. Since the mid-1980s, the decision in the case of *Street v Mountford* [1985] AC 809 has been the authority: to be a lease, every tenant must have exclusive possession for a fixed duration.[14]

i. Exclusive Possession

Exclusive possession means that a tenant must have the right to take possession and to exercise all the rights that come with possession.[15] "Exclusive possession enables the tenant to exclude strangers and to exclude also the landlord unless the landlord is exercising rights to enter the land granted to him under the tenancy agreement."[16] A tenant's exclusive possession is thus the basis for the tenant's estate. If a tenant does not have exclusive possession of the realty, there is no estate.

In determining whether the occupants have exclusive possession, the courts will look to the substance, rather than to the form, of the agreement. Thus, the parties cannot create a licence simply by labelling the agreement as a licence. Some terms in the agreement may indicate that exclusive possession has been granted, for example, where the landlord reserves the right to enter and inspect the condition of the premises, or to restrict the occupant's right to transfer any interest in the property.

Formerly, exclusive occupation meant exclusive possession. In *Street v Mountford*, the court made a clear distinction between a tenant and a lodger. An occupant with exclusive occupation is not considered to be in overall control of the premises. The provision of services to an occupant or the restriction of access to the premises may indicate that the occupant does not have exclusive possession.

The court in *Lam Man-yuen v Lucky Apartment* [1964] HKLR 689 held that the degree of control is a factor in deciding whether there is exclusive possession. In this case, Lucky Apartment owned three floors of a building. Each floor was divided into rooms which were hired out to various occupants including Lam. The rooms were furnished and bed linen provided. The rooms were cleaned and the linen was changed by staff. Electricity was supplied at no extra charge. Keys to the rooms were kept at the building's entrance. The gate to the building's entrance was locked after midnight. The occupants had no key to the gate; if they returned late, they had to call for the security guard. In the lobby and in each room was a notice, *Regulations for Guests*, concerning such matters as noise after midnight and the keeping of pets. New occupants had to complete a registration card. Rooms could be hired at a daily rate. A manager, who was a partner of Lucky Apartment, lived on the premises.

Lam refused to leave his room, contending he was protected by the law concerning tenants and could do what he liked in his room (e.g., have as many visitors or occupants as he wished). Further, Lam claimed Lucky Apartment was concerned only with the payment of rent. All these factors indicated a landlord-tenant relationship according to Lam. Nonetheless, Lucky Apartment claimed that Lam was not a tenant but a licensee. Lucky Apartment won the case by showing that it maintained some control over the property and that the occupants' interests were too temporary to be a lease.

In *May King Development Co v Young Ching Huo Ltd* [1981] HKLR 280, the developer of a building assigned the flats in the building to Young Ching Huo. The assignment stated that the premises were for residential purposes. There was a similar stipulation in the Crown lease to the developer. An agreement between the developer and the assignees, including Young Ching Huo, required that the building not be used for boarding or lodging. Young Ching Huo hired out individual rooms in the flats generally to short-term occupants. The issue was whether Young Ching Huo had retained enough control over the flats to make the occupants only licensees. The following facts in this case made it different from the *Lam Man-yuen* case:

- no shared facilities with the occupants of other rooms
- no cooking was allowed in the rooms
- rooms were furnished as bedrooms with their own telephones
- each occupant had a key to its room and to the flat in which the room was situated
- cleaning and linen services were provided and were charged to the occupant
- rooms were hired on a weekly or a monthly basis and a deposit was required
- the management staff registered occupants and visitors, and collected payments
- the management staff were not present on the premises between 7:00 pm and 10:00 am
- there were no regulations or rules except that occupants should not create any disturbance

Despite the foregoing, the court found that Young Ching Huo did not retain sufficient control of the premises because:

- occupants kept their own keys and thus had ready access to their rooms at all times (in the *Lam Man-yuen* case, the room keys were kept at the entrance and the front gate, to which the occupants had no key, was locked at night)
- there were no regulations (there were regulations in the *Lam Man-yuen* case)
- management did not live on the premises (unlike in the *Lam Man-yuen* case)

Thus the occupants did not have a licence but a lease. As the court stated in the case of *Marchant v Charters* [1977] 1 WLR 1181:

> What is the test to see whether the occupier of one room in a house is a tenant or a licensee? . . . the answer depends on the nature and quality of the occupancy. Was it intended that the occupier should have a stake in the room or did he have only permission for himself personally to occupy the room . . . [17]

ii. Fixed Duration

The length (or *duration*) of the lease period must be ascertainable at the commencement of the lease.[18] The duration may be a fixed term (e.g., 1 April 2009 to 31 March 2015) or a periodic term (e.g., weekly, monthly or yearly). There must be certainty of the duration of the lease; there must be a definite length of term.

A lease "for the duration of the war" failed to meet this requirement in the case of *Lace v Chantler* [1944] KB 368 where the court stated:

> a term created by a leasehold tenancy agreement must be expressed either with certainty and specifically or by reference to something which can, at the time when the lease takes effect, be looked to as a certain ascertainment of what the term is meant to be. In the present case, when this tenancy agreement took effect, the term was completely uncertain. It was impossible to say how long the [war] . . . would last.[19]

D. Leases – Types

In this section, the different categories of leases will be presented. Included in this discussion will be an analysis of the components which distinguishes the different categories of leases.

i. Fixed-term Lease

A fixed-term lease is for a specified duration. The length or duration of the lease is fixed to end at a specified time. The key points to note about a fixed-term lease are the following:

- a lease for a fixed term is created by an express agreement
- the start and end dates of the fixed-term lease must be stated or ascertainable
- under the common law, no notice to quit is required for the fixed-term lease as it will expire at the end of the fixed term

ii. Periodic Lease

Another type of lease is a periodic lease, which consists of an initial period of time and automatically renews for successive periods until notice is given by one of the parties.[20] Examples of periodic leases include quarterly, monthly or weekly tenancies. A yearly lease continues from year to year and is known as a tenancy from year to year.[21] Periodic leases are created by express agreement or by implication of law, or where no intention to create a particular form of lease has been expressed.[22] Unless otherwise agreed, periodic leases can only be terminated at the end of one of the periods of tenancy. Periodic leases require notice of one full period in order to terminate the lease. In other words, a weekly periodic tenancy will, unless otherwise agreed, require one week's notice. Likewise, a monthly tenancy will require one month's notice to quit in order to end the lease. One exception is that the required period for the notice to quit in order to terminate a yearly lease, unless agreed otherwise, is six months' notice which expires at the end of one of the years of tenancy.[23]

iii. Tenancy at Will

Another type of lease is a tenancy at will.[24] This type of tenancy is not a proper lease because of its unknown or uncertain duration. Nonetheless, this tenancy is more than a contractual relationship because the parties' relationship is one of landlord and tenant. A tenancy at will may be likened to a tenure with no estate.

> Like a licensee, the tenant at will has no estate in land. However, a tenancy at will is different from a license in that the tenant at will is in 'possession' of the land, and may bring an action in trespass against a stranger.[25]

A tenancy at will arises when a tenant takes possession of the landlord's realty with consent and with the understanding that the tenancy might be ended at any time.[26] In the case of *Errington v Errington and Woods* [1952] 1 KB 290, the court said: "it is of the essence of a tenancy at will that it should be determinable [i.e., ended] by either party on demand."[27] This type of tenancy comes into being when a person occupies land as tenant, with the owner's consent, and, with the understanding that either party may terminate the tenancy at any time.[28] This occupation might be the result of an expressed or an implied tenancy.[29] If expressed, the rent should be stipulated, although the tenancy at will can be rent-free. The offer and acceptance of rent generally changes a tenancy at will into a periodic tenancy unless otherwise stated.

Most frequently, a tenancy at will is created when a tenant remains in possession of the estate after the end of lease, with the landlord's permission. This will not be the case if the tenant is relying on the *Landlord and Tenant (Consolidation) Ordinance*.[30] There is no tenancy at will where the original tenancy is for a one-year period, which, upon expiry, will result in another tenancy from year to year.

A tenancy at will may be ended at any time when either party gives notice. No formal notice to quit is required. Alternatively, either party may commit an act inconsistent with the continuation of the tenancy.[31] For example, a purported transfer of either party's interest will end a tenancy at will. Finally, as the relationship between the parties to a tenancy at will is a personal one, the tenancy at will ends if either party dies.

iv. Tenancy at Sufferance

Another type of lease is a tenancy at sufferance. Tenancy at sufferance is not a true lease as there is no tenure of the land and no estate in the land. "A tenancy at sufferance arises where a tenant wrongfully holds over on termination of a previous tenancy without the landlord's consent or dissent. The absence of the landlord's consent distinguishes a tenancy at sufferance from a tenancy at will."[32] The term *tenancy* is used because the occupier was originally a tenant who entered the land with the owner's permission, and in this respect the tenant differs from a trespasser. A tenancy at sufferance may be terminated at any time by the landlord suing for possession of the property or otherwise evicting the tenant.[33]

In sum, tenancies at sufferance arise by law, without any agreement between the landlord and the tenant. A tenant originally had a tenancy but then continues to occupy the property after the termination of that tenancy.

This occupation must be without the landlord's consent; otherwise, the occupant becomes a tenant at will rather than a tenant at sufferance. If the landlord objects, the tenant is considered to be a trespasser.[34]

E. Leases – Formal Requirements

Under the *Conveyancing and Property Ordinance*, a lease is defined as a type of legal estate.[35] Section 4 of the Ordinance requires that a legal estate be created, extinguished or disposed of by deed.[36] There are some exceptions. One of these exceptions to the general rule is

> the grant, disposal or surrender of a lease taking effect in possession for a term not exceeding three years (whether or not the lessee is given power to extend the term) at the best rent which can reasonably be obtained without a premium.

In calculating the three-year term of a lease, any option to renew is disregarded. Thus, a monthly periodic lease is for a term of less than three years. Where an oral lease does not satisfy the exemption requirements, a tenancy at will is created.[37]

Leases and agreements for lease are subject to an *ad valorem* stamp duty calculated on the average annual rent.[38] The amount of the stamp duty will depend upon the length of the lease term. The duty should be paid within 30 days after the lease is signed. Both landlord and tenant are responsible for the duty under the *Stamp Duty Ordinance* (Cap 117), but frequently a lease will specify which party is to pay. A premium paid for the grant of a lease requires payment of an *ad valorem* stamp duty. An unstamped agreement cannot be used in court proceedings and cannot be registered in the Land Registry.

Only leases that are both stamped and written can be registered in the Land Registry. Written leases lasting longer than three years must be registered to protect their priority. As with title documents and mortgages, in order to be prioritised by the day of signing, i.e. execution date rather than the date of registration, leases must be registered within one month of signing.[39] A registrable lease which is not registered is void against a *bona fide* purchaser or mortgagee for value, regardless of notice.[40] A written lease for a term of three years or less at market rent does not need to be registered.

A lease option is considered to be a disposal of an interest in land. An option to renew a lease is an interest in land that is independent of the lease itself.[41] In order to be enforceable, the option to renew must be in writing and signed by the party against whom enforcement is sought.[42] The instrument creating the option must be registered to bind a subsequent purchaser or mortgagee for value.

Domestic tenancies must be notified to the Commissioner of Rating and Valuation.[43] For each new letting or renewal, Form CR109 needs to be completed, signed and lodged, in triplicate, by the landlord. The Commissioner endorses two copies, returns one to the landlord and sends the other to the tenant. There is no time limit for filing but a charge is made if not done within one month. More importantly, if the filing is not made, the landlord or principal tenant shall not be entitled to maintain a court action for unpaid rent unless Section B of Form CR109 is endorsed by the Commissioner. The Commissioner cannot endorse the form until it has been filed.[44]

F. Obligations of Landlords and Tenants

Having discussed the types of tenancies under a leasehold estate, the manner by which the landlord and the tenant's obligations and rights are allocated will now be presented. A leasehold estate is governed by the agreement made between the parties. This agreement provides the responsibilities and the rights between the parties. The following section presents some of those burdens and benefits.

A *covenant* is a promise made by one party (the *covenantor*) for the benefit of another party (the *covenantee*).[45] The covenant(s) is contained in a deed which is signed, witnessed and delivered by the covenantor to the covenantee. As all leases for more than three years should be made by deed, the promises made in the lease will be covenants.[46]

Covenants should be differentiated from *conditions*, which may also impose obligations on a tenant.[47] If a tenant breaches a lease condition, the landlord will have an automatic right to end the tenancy. If a tenant breaches a covenant, the landlord does not automatically have such a right. The landlord must make an express provision in the lease for automatic termination. In a lease, this provision is usually known as a *forfeiture clause*. The parties' intentions determine whether a provision in a lease should be construed as a covenant or a condition. A provision is a condition if the continuance of the lease is premised upon the tenant fulfilling the provision. Generally, courts presume lease provisions are covenants unless the obligations are clearly expressed to be conditions. Most obligations[48] will thus be considered as covenants rather than conditions.[49]

Usually, the parties will negotiate the provisions governing their relationship as landlord and tenant. In leases, these provisions are usually referred to as covenants. Leasehold covenants consist of three categories:

- *implied covenants* are those provisions that are so essential to the landlord-tenant relationship that those provisions are implied by law into the lease
- *express* covenants are the expressed or stated provisions agreed between the parties
- *usual covenants* are those covenants that will be imposed where a lease agreement provides that the usual covenants are to be given

In Hong Kong, implied covenants are particularly important because of the small number of express covenants usually made by a landlord. The Government makes no express covenants in a Government lease. In short-term tenancy agreements, the landlord usually provides only an express covenant for quiet enjoyment and an express covenant for the payment of the Government rent due under the Government lease. The established test for the implication of terms is the *business efficacy* test. The rules to be applied under this test are the same as the rules which govern the implication of terms into contracts generally. A court cannot imply into an agreement any term:

> unless, on considering the terms of the contract in a responsible and business manner, an implication necessarily arises that the parties must have intended that the suggested stipulation should exist. It is not enough to say that it would be a reasonable thing to make such an implication.[50]

i. Landlord's Implied Covenants

A landlord's implied covenants or obligations include the following:

(1) Quiet enjoyment: a lessee (i.e., a tenant) shall have quiet enjoyment and use of the premises, free from any interference with the tenant's use of the premises by the landlord or the landlord's agent or any person claiming any interest in the realty through the landlord.[51] The case of *Kenny v Preen* [1963] 1 QB 499, CA considered the covenant of quiet enjoyment. The landlord supposedly gave the female tenant a valid notice to quit. Thereafter the landlord threatened, both by letters and by shouting at the tenant and banging on her door, to physically evict the tenant and remove her belongings from the premises. The tenant succeeded in court against the landlord for breach of the covenant for

quiet enjoyment and for a court order preventing the landlord from further interference with her enjoyment of the premises.[52]

In *Yeung Wah James v Alfa Sea Ltd* [1993] 1 HKC 440, the court found the landlord liable to the tenant for breach of the covenant for quiet enjoyment. The tenant was away from Hong Kong for three months during which time renovation was carried out. The tenant later found the flat full of debris and waste materials; and, the bedroom was no longer fit for that purpose. The court awarded the tenant $50,000 general damages for the discomfort, inconvenience and distress caused and an additional $50,000 exemplary damages for the landlord's harassment of the tenant with the intention of eviction.

Other examples of breach of the quiet enjoyment covenant include:

- scaffolding: *Owen v Gadd* [1956] 2 QB 99
- foul air: *World Realty v Kwan Ngar Yin* [1987] 3 HKC 148
- frequently changing the name of the building: *Union Assurance Society of Canton v Hong Kong Land Co Ltd* [1977] HKLR 597

(2) Derogation from grant: a landlord must not do anything which might cause the premises to become unfit.[53] This obligation may overlap with the covenant for quiet enjoyment, but applies even when there is no physical interference by the landlord. The court will consider the purpose(s) for which the premises are let. If that purpose is frustrated or made impossible by the landlord's action, there will be derogation. There might not be any derogation, however, when that purpose is made more difficult, more expensive or less profitable.

In the case of *Aldin v Latimer Clark, Muirhead & Co* [1894] 2 Ch 437, an assignee of the landlord built on adjacent land in such a way as to obstruct the flow of air to the drying sheds in the tenant's timber yard (the reason which the tenant had leased the premises). The court held that the covenant had been breached and awarded damages to the tenant.

In the case of *Secretary for Justice v Wisename Ltd* [1998] 1 HKC 128, the court held that the Government derogated from its grant where it granted an easement, which included vehicular use, and subsequently carried out works that made vehicular use no longer possible. However, in the earlier case of *Lam Kwok-leung v Attorney General* [1979] HKLR 145, the court found no derogation where the erection of a latrine adjacent to the granted realty adversely affected the classification of the subject realty.

(3) Condition of premises: generally, there are no implied obligations upon the landlord that the premises are fit for habitation,[54] or will remain fit for habitation. The exception is if the house or flat let is furnished, in which case there is an implied covenant of habitability.[55] A landlord is not under any implied obligation to carry out repairs on the leased premises unless it is expressly agreed otherwise between the parties.[56]

ii. Tenant's Implied Covenants

A tenant's implied covenants or obligations include the following:
(1) To repair:[57] the tenant is to use the premises in a tenant-like manner.
(a) At common law, a tenant is liable for *waste*, an act or omission that changes the condition of the land.[58] The obligation to use the premises in a tenant-like manner might vary with the type of tenant and the length of tenancy.

There are various categories of waste:
(i) Equitable waste: equity will not excuse acts of wilful or unjustifiable destruction even if an agreement purports to exclude a tenant's liability for waste.
(ii) Voluntary waste: voluntary waste is an act, which does not amount to wanton destruction, but which nevertheless harms the property. Voluntary waste "consists of doing something which should not be done (e.g. knocking down a wall)".[59] Voluntary waste occurs when a tenant deliberately or negligently commits an act which destroys or lowers the property's value.[60] All tenants are liable for voluntary waste unless their liability is expressly excluded.
(iii) Ameliorating waste: ameliorating waste consists of an act that changes the premises but in such a way as to improve the property.[61]
(iv) Permissive waste: permissive waste is the failure to repair the premises or to do what ought to be done in order to maintain the property. "Permissive waste implies an omission through which damage results to the premises, as, for example, where houses are allowed to fall into decay."[62] The duties of a particular tenant vary according to the type of leasehold interest held, particularly the length of tenancy. The longer the tenancy, the higher the duty imposed upon the tenant.[63]
(b) The tenant's liability for waste depends upon the lease involved.

A weekly tenant must take proper care of the property.[64] Yearly tenants must carry out minor repairs but they are not responsible for any substantial repairs, e.g., mending the roof or fixing the foundation. A fixed-term tenant must carry out all the repairs that are necessary to enable the return of the premises at the end of the term in the same condition as when occupation commenced, normal wear and tear excepted.[65]

(c) Trespassers, tenants at will, tenants at sufferance and short-term periodic tenants are not liable for permissive waste. Tenants at will and tenants at sufferance are not liable for voluntary waste, but such acts would end the tenancy and make the tenants liable for the damages as trespassers.

(2) To pay rent: the rent must be paid promptly.[66] A sub-tenant must also pay rent even though there still is an obligation to pay the rent on the part of the original tenant. Privity of contract exists between the original tenant and the landlord.[67] Privity of estate exists between the under-lessee and the original tenant.[68] A tenant is also under an implied covenant to permit the landlord to re-enter and take possession when in arrears of rent.

(3) Not to repudiate the landlord's title: a tenant may not do anything to affect the landlord's title.[69]

(4) To pay government rates, management fees and other taxes: in the absence of any agreement to the contrary, a tenant is liable to pay government rates, management fees and other taxes.[70]

(5) To allow the landlord entry and inspection: where the landlord is liable for internal repairs, the right to enter the premises to inspect and/or make repairs will be specifically stated in the lease. If not, it will be an implied term.

(6) To deliver up the premises at the termination of the lease: it is implied that the tenant should return possession of the premises in good condition at the lease's end.[71]

(7) Not to assign or to under-let/sublet or to change the tenant's possession of the leased premises without the landlord's consent.[72]

(8) To insure.

iii. Usual Covenants

Usual covenants will be read into a lease if the lease is stated to be subject to the usual covenants or if the lease is an open contract where only the basic terms are recorded (i.e., parties, rent, premises, length of term and commencement date).[73] Usual covenants may be divided into two classes. The first category consists of covenants regarded as usual in every lease. These include the following covenants:

- by the landlord
  - for quiet enjoyment
- by the tenant
  - to pay rent and rates
  - to keep the premises in repair
  - to permit the landlord to enter and inspect where the landlord is liable for repairs
  - a condition for re-entry for non-payment of rent

The second class of usual covenants consists of promises considered to be usual in a particular letting. This class of usual covenants could vary with the area, nature of the premises, the length of the lease, and, purpose of the lease. However, a covenant which commonly appears in leases of a particular nature might not be classified as a usual covenant. Courts do not like to find a covenant to be a usual covenant because it limits the estate granted to the tenant. For this reason, agreements against assignment or subletting, and covenants against carrying on a specified trade, or usage for certain purposes, have not been regarded as usual covenants.

iv. Remedies for Breach of Covenants

A tenant may seek damages, injunction and declaration for any breach of covenant by the landlord.[74] A landlord may seek the same remedies for a tenant's breach of covenant. In certain circumstances, a tenant may make repairs for which the landlord is responsible and deduct the repair costs from the rent. A landlord has additional remedies for non-payment of rent and breach of covenant, including forfeiture and distress, which are discussed in the next chapter.

4
Alienation and Determination of Lease

A. Alienation of Leases

A tenant may assign or sublet the premises unless expressly prohibited.[1] Most written Hong Kong leases restrict assignments, sublets or licences. A tenant's breach of the prohibition could result in forfeiture of the premises to the landlord for breach of a covenant. A landlord can assign its reversionary interest subject to the lease. Assignments and sublets are considered to be dispositions of an interest in land. Therefore, the requirements of the *Conveyancing and Property Ordinance* should be followed.[2] The normal practice is for the lease to prohibit assignment and subletting without the landlord's consent, such consent not to be unreasonably withheld.

B. Determination of a Lease

A lease may end either by its own terms or prematurely through a breach of a particular covenant. The methods of determination discussed below are the most commonly recognised ways, albeit not necessarily all the ways by which a lease may be terminated.[3]

i. Lapse of Time

With the exception of periodic tenancies, one way in which a lease will end is by passage of the specified time. A tenancy for a fixed term ends automatically upon expiry of the last day of the term. If a fixed term tenancy ends and the landlord continues to accept rent, a new periodic tenancy will be created by conduct.[4]

ii. Notice

A lease may also be terminated by notice. The lease itself may specify the notice period required for determination. If there is no provision in the lease, the notice period for periodic tenancies is generally one full period for short-term periodic tenancies and six months for tenancies from year to year.[5] Where a periodic tenancy is determinable by notice of a specified length, the notice must be given to expire at end of the year[6] unless otherwise agreed in the lease, namely in a break clause.[7]

The notice must comply with any requirements set out in the lease. Where no requirements are specified, the notice must be in writing.[8] A notice to terminate a tenancy pursuant to the *Landlord and Tenant (Consolidation) Ordinance* must be in the prescribed form, but otherwise the only requirement is that the notice must be reasonably clear and certain. The notice must describe the premises so that the property can be ascertained with certainty. A notice to quit only part of the premises is ineffective because a landlord cannot be forced to take back only a portion of the leased property. The notice must also give a clear date when the tenancy will end.

iii. Surrender

A third manner of terminating a lease is by surrender.[9] Upon the tenant's surrender of the lease, the lease will merge with the landlord's reversion,[10] and come to an end. A surrender does not affect any rights to sue which arose prior to the surrender. A surrender has no impact upon any sub-lease; the surrender will only affect the lease being surrendered.

A surrender must be made by agreement of both parties, either by a term in the lease itself or by a special agreement.[11] The *Conveyancing and Property Ordinance* requires that a surrender must be by deed and that the surrender must be registered at the Land Registry unless the lease falls within section 4(2)(d) of the Ordinance (i.e., one which takes effect in possession at best rent for a term not exceeding three years). If the lease is an equitable lease, the surrender may be made in writing under section 5 of the *Conveyancing and Property Ordinance*.[12] A surrender requires the payment of stamp duties.

Surrender can be implied or inferred by the conduct of the parties. Any action which is contrary to a continuing landlord-tenant relationship results in an implied surrender of the lease. For example:

- a new grant to the tenant, with the tenant's consent, of a new lease, results in the old lease being surrendered;[13]

- the tenant delivering actual possession to the landlord during the term of the lease with the landlord's consent and acceptance;[14]
- change of capacity of the tenant which is inconsistent with the tenancy;[15] and
- the landlord granting a new lease to a third person with the consent of the tenant.[16]

iv. Merger

Merger is another method to determine a lease. A merger occurs when the different interests merge into one interest. A merger occurs when both the landlord's reversion and the lease are acquired by either the tenant or a third person.[17]

> Merger is similar [in effect] to surrender. In both cases the reversion and the lease become vested in one person so as to extinguish the lease. In a surrender, that person is the landlord – in a merger, it is the tenant or a third party. . . .
>
> A merger at law is automatic, but in equity it is dependent on intention and will not occur unless intended by the person acquiring the lease and reversion.[18]

v. Forfeiture

Another method of determining a lease is by forfeiture.[19] A lease can be forfeited for breach of covenant where the lease contains an express provision for such action. A lease can also be forfeited for breach of condition. In a lease subject to section 126 of the *Landlord and Tenant (Consolidation) Ordinance* (Cap 7), failure by a tenant to pay rent may result in forfeiture of the lease.[20] As such, a breach of a covenant does not automatically give a landlord the right to re-enter and to take possession unless this right is stated in the lease. If the breach is a breach of a contractual condition, then the common law grants a right to repossess. A breach makes the lease voidable; there is no automatic termination of the lease. In the event of non-payment of rent, a formal demand must be made by the landlord before re-entry, unless either the right of re-entry expressly excludes a need to do so, or the rent is at least six months in arrears and the value of the goods on the premises that may be subject to distress (discussed in section vii) would not cover the cost of the arrears.[21] Forfeiture does not exclude any rights to sue which arose prior to the forfeiture.

Where the forfeiture is for breach of either a covenant or a condition (other than for non-payment of rent), section 58 of the *Conveyancing and Property Ordinance* obligates the landlord to serve notice on the tenant. Section 58(1) provides:

> A right of re-entry or forfeiture under any proviso or stipulation in a lease for a breach of any covenant or condition in the lease shall not be enforceable, by action or otherwise, unless and until the lessor serves on the lessee a notice –
>
> (a) specifying the particular breach complained of; and
>
> (b) if the breach is capable of remedy, requiring the lessee to remedy the breach; and
>
> (c) specifying the compensation, if any, which the lessor requires in respect of the breach,
>
> and the lessee fails, within a reasonable time thereafter, to remedy the breach, if it is capable of remedy, and to make reasonable compensation in money, to the satisfaction of the lessor, for the breach.

If the tenant fails to make good the breach, the landlord may re-enter by self-help or through court proceedings. The landlord will usually start court proceedings for possession of the premises as forcible entry has risks. If the tenant does not comply with the notice, forfeiture of the lease may proceed. Positive covenants, e.g., the tenant's covenants to make certain repairs or to pay management fees, usually can be corrected. Negative covenants, e.g., a covenant not to assign, appear to require a court to determine whether late compliance and/or compensation could make good the injury to the landlord arising from the breach. Some covenants are incapable of remedy, such as covenants against assignments, sublets and immoral use.

a. Relief against Forfeiture

A tenant may contest forfeiture proceedings if either waiver or estoppel exists, and may also seek court relief. Hong Kong courts have equitable powers to order relief against forfeiture where the action is based upon the tenant's failure to pay rent. These equitable powers have largely been replaced by statutory powers.[22] Section 58(2) of the *Conveyancing and Property Ordinance* also provides a tenant with the right to apply for relief from forfeiture for breach of covenant. The right, however, cannot be exercised until the landlord starts proceedings, and this right may still be exercised after the landlord has taken possession without an order. If relief is granted, conditions may be imposed. Note that the grant of relief from forfeiture revives the lease. However, once the landlord has re-entered, the court's statutory power to grant relief ends.

Forfeiture of a head lease also ends a sub-lease. A sub-tenant can apply for relief against the head landlord under the *Conveyancing and Property Ordinance*. If the relief is granted to a sub-tenant, a new lease is granted to the sub-tenant but not for a term longer than the sub-tenant's original sub-lease.[23]

The lease is considered ended from the date the court proceedings are started or when the landlord writes to the tenant forfeiting the lease. The tenant is to pay *mesne* profits, i.e., market rent, to the date on which the tenant actually leaves the premises.[24]

b. Waiver

For a breach of covenant other than non-payment of rent, the landlord may waive the breach and continue with the lease.

> A landlord will be unable to enforce a right of re-entry if he has waived the breach that gave rise to the right. . . .
>
> A waiver will not prevent a landlord from forfeiting the lease where the tenant again breaches the same covenant. Thus, where the breach is continuing the landlord may rely on a future breach despite an earlier waiver of the same breach, unless this waiver condoned the future as well as the past breaches, or was so soon after waiver that the landlord must have known that the breach would still be continuing.[25]

To establish the defence of waiver, a tenant has to prove that the landlord knew of the breach but continues with the lease.[26] A waiver usually arises where the landlord accepts or demands rent from the tenant with the knowledge of a breach of covenant. Some breaches, such as a breach of the covenant against assignment, are once-and-for-all breaches. Other breaches are continuing breaches so there can be no waiver of a continuing breach. In the case of *Chinachem Investment Co Ltd v Chung Wah Weaving and Dyeing Factory Ltd* [1978] HKLR 83, the tenant covenanted not to use the car park for purposes other than parking, and, loading and unloading vehicles. Later, with advice from the landlord, the tenant installed machinery in the car park. The landlord sued for possession claiming forfeiture for breach of covenant. The court held that the landlord had waived the tenant's breach for the duration of the lease.

vi. Estoppel

Estoppel is an equitable remedy which courts use to do justice and prevent unfairness. Estoppel has undergone changes in recent times, with the traditional categories of estoppel having merged to some degree. Nonetheless, the essential purpose of estoppel has remained unchanged: to prevent unfairness. As applied in this section of the chapter, estoppel would prevent, for example, a landlord from supposedly waiving a breach of the tenancy agreement by the tenant only to claim later that the tenant had breached the agreement. Such a course of action by the landlord would be unfair to a tenant who had relied upon the landlord's waiver.[27]

vii. Distress

Due to non-payment of rent, the landlord may forfeit the lease, if legally possible, or may recover the overdue rent by a lawsuit for non-payment and distraint. Also known as *distress for rent*, *distraint* is defined as taking the tenant's personal property in order to pay the arrears of rent under a current lease. Distress is the seizing, holding and selling of the tenant's goods.[28] Distress for rent is a common law remedy, which is now only available to landlords and only while they remain as landlords.[29] Further, distress is only available for unpaid rent. Distress is not available for other outstanding obligations such as property management fees. A landlord cannot distrain for more than 12 months' rent. A landlord loses the right to distrain upon the sale of the landlord's reversion. At the time of any sale of reversion, the purchaser cannot distrain for rent in arrears as the purchaser is not entitled to the arrears as landlord.

Distress for arrears of rent can only be made under Part III of the *Landlord and Tenant (Consolidation) Ordinance*.[30] The landlord makes an *ex parte* application to the District Court for a distress warrant.[31] An affidavit is attached to this application setting out details of the landlord, premises, rent due, and the period for which rent is owed. There is no duty of full disclosure as in other *ex parte* applications, e.g., the landlord need not disclose any dispute with the tenant.

The court issues a warrant directing the bailiff to execute distress within six days. Prior to performing the distraint, the landlord is obligated to pay the fees for the warrant. In carrying out the distraint, subject to some exceptions, the bailiff may seize goods in the tenant's apparent possession, such as:
- movable goods
- property in or on the premises

- property in of the debtor tenant, except for:
  - things in actual use
  - tools and implements not in use, if there are other moveable property
  - property of another
  - clothing
  - goods delivered to the tenant as part of his trade

The bailiff seizes the property and prepares an inventory for the purpose of selling the property by public auction. During this process, there is no opportunity for the tenant to be heard in court prior to seizure.

As the seized items will be subject to sale, the defaulting tenant, when confronted with this situation, usually will pay the outstanding rent. The tenant may apply to the court for an extension of time to pay the rent which is in arrears. Alternatively, the tenant may challenge either the distraint action itself or the right to seize an article under the distraint warrant.[32] If these acts are not taken or the tenant is unsuccessful, the failure to pay will result in a sale of the seized items. The proceeds of the sale will generally be distributed in the following order:

- the costs of the distress for rent action in the court
- payment of the debt owed to the landlord
- the remaining funds, if any, to the debtor

Further, a distraint seizure of third-party goods in the tenant's apparent possession may be challenged by the goods' rightful owners under sections 93 and 95 of the *Landlord and Tenant (Consolidation) Ordinance*. Challenges under section 93 must be brought within five days of the seizure. Such proceedings are known as *interpleader* proceedings.[33]

C. Domestic Leases

Part IV of the *Landlord and Tenant (Consolidation) Ordinance* pertains to domestic tenancies.[34] A *domestic tenancy* is defined as "a tenancy of premises let as a dwelling."[35] *Tenancy* is defined to include an oral or written tenancy and includes a sub-tenancy and agreement for tenancy,[36] but is not defined to include a licence or tenancy at sufferance.[37]

The *Landlord and Tenant (Consolidation) (Amendment) Ordinance 2004* revised the *Landlord and Tenant (Consolidation) Ordinance* with effect on 9 July 2004. The amendments removed the security of tenure provisions for domestic tenancies. As of that commencement date, there was no longer any statutory control for domestic tenancies in regards to security of tenure or rent. For domestic tenancies in existence before 9 July 2004, and where the Part IV tenancy renewal procedure had commenced before this date, the Part IV procedure, which allowed a tenant the right to renew the tenancy, continues to apply.

For the sake of completeness, this section will provide a brief survey of the pre- and post-amendment domestic tenancies.

As a result of the amendments imposed by the *Landlord and Tenant (Consolidation) (Amendment) Ordinance 2004*, there can be three scenarios:

1. Post-amendment domestic tenancies, i.e., those tenancies created on or after the commencement date of 9 July 2004.
2. Transitional domestic tenancies, i.e., those tenancies in existence prior to the commencement date and where the Part IV tenancy renewal procedures have not commenced.[38]
3. Pre-amendment tenancies, i.e., those tenancies in existence prior to the commencement date and where the Part IV tenancy renewal procedures have commenced.[39]

Each of these will be presented in turn, with the last scenario being presented as if the *Landlord and Tenant (Consolidation) (Amendment) Ordinance 2004* had not come into being.

Under the first scenario, pursuant to the amended Ordinance, a domestic tenancy created on or after 9 July 2004 will end upon expiry of the tenancy agreement. Domestic tenancies will terminate according to the terms of the lease agreement or as the parties may mutually agree. Without a contractual notice period or mutual agreement, a fixed term tenancy will end upon expiry while a periodic tenancy will be terminated by a notice to quit in accordance with the common law.

Under the second scenario, where a domestic tenancy existed prior to the amendments and where no Part IV tenancy renewal procedure had commenced before 9 July 2004, there will be transitional provisions. The former Part IV tenancy renewal procedures will no longer be available. In place of those procedures, a *Transitional Termination Notice* [hereinafter referred to as "TTN"] should be served on the other party after expiry of the tenancy's term.[40] For landlords, the TTN should be served on a tenant not less than 12 months before the intended termination date.[41] For tenants, the TTN should be served on a landlord not less than one month before the intended termination date.[42] A tenancy will continue in effect, despite expiration of the original term or duration, on its existing terms until terminated by a TTN.[43] The TTN requirement applies equally to sub-tenancies. A head or principal tenant who wishes to terminate a sub-tenancy will need to serve a TTN.

A TTN will not be required where, on or after 9 July 2004, a tenancy is assigned to a new tenant; the terms of the tenancy have changed; or, the landlord and tenant mutually agree to the notice period for termination of the lease agreement.[44]

Note that the *Landlord and Tenant (Consolidation) (Amendment) Ordinance 2004* repealed a substantial portion of the provisions of Part IV of the *Landlord and Tenant (Consolidation) Ordinance*. However, certain Part IV provisions will remain in force: the requirement of filing Form CR109 with the Commissioner of Rating and Valuation,[45] the implied covenants and forfeiture clauses,[46] and, the prohibition of harassment of a tenant. Note that consequential amendments to the *Landlord and Tenant (Consolidation) Ordinance* and other ordinances affecting the landlord-tenant relationship have been made.[47]

In relation to the third scenario, the termination of a lease on a domestic tenancy was complicated.[48] Thus, only a summary of the procedures will be provided. Until the amendment came into effect, the *Landlord and Tenant (Consolidation) Ordinance* afforded security of tenure to tenants but not rent control. Here, the Ordinance is briefly reviewed, particularly Part IV, as it is this part which applied to domestic lettings or domestic tenancies.[49] A domestic tenancy falling under Part IV of the *Landlord and Tenant (Consolidation) Ordinance* will not end by the passage of time or by the landlord's notice to quit. Such a tenancy is continued until ended in accordance with this law. A landlord must follow these provisions in order to end a tenancy by means of notice.[50] Under section 116(1)(a) the parties may not contract out of Part IV of the Ordinance.

The benefits and protection of Part IV of the *Landlord and Tenant (Consolidation) Ordinance* are available to the spouse, mother, father, or children aged over 18 of the tenant (if residing with the tenant at the time of the tenant's demise).[51] Only one person is entitled to the benefits and protections under the Ordinance and that person will, in the absence of agreement, be nominated by the Lands Tribunal. The benefits and protection of Part IV do not pass by will or under the intestacy rules.

i. Landlord's Procedures under the Former Provisions

A tenancy regulated by Part IV shall not end unless terminated in accordance with Part IV, i.e., through forfeiture, surrender or the tenant giving notice to quit.[52] Another method of terminating a tenancy is by notice in anticipation of a new tenancy. In this situation the existing tenancy may be ended by the landlord giving notice on Form CR101 not more than four nor less than three months from the date of stated termination, which cannot be before expiry of the lease term. If the landlord desires possession of the premises, the landlord is required to give the reasons for which possession is demanded and the tenant is required to reply in Form CR102 within one month whether the tenant will hand over possession.[53]

A notice received on the first of a month will expire, at the earliest, on the first of the month that is six months later. In *Lo Ping-kwong v Siu Lai Yung* [1995] 2 HKC 612 the landlord gave notice through registered post, by mailing the notice on 14 November. The notice contained a termination date six months after the posting date, i.e., 14 May. The court found the document to be invalid for failing to provide six months' notice, as the earliest date that the tenant could have received the notice via post was 15 November. "The effect of a valid notice will be to terminate the current tenancy on the date of termination unless the tenant takes the proper steps to apply to the Lands Tribunal for new tenancy . . . "[54]

ii. Tenant's Procedures under the Former Provisions

A tenant must reply on Form CR102 within two months of the landlord's Form CR101 notice.[55] In Form CR102, the tenant states whether possession of the premises will be surrendered to the landlord. If the tenant is willing to give up possession and makes no application to the Lands Tribunal for a new tenancy, the current tenancy will end on expiry of the landlord's notice of termination.[56] If the tenant will not be giving up possession of the premises, the landlord must be so notified in order for the Lands Tribunal to consider the tenant's application for a new tenancy.[57]

If the tenant fails to reply in a Form CR102, the Lands Tribunal will not consider an application for a new tenancy unless the tenant receives an extension of time to serve a Form CR102 from the Lands Tribunal "for good cause."[58] After expiry of the landlord's notice in the Form CR101, no extension will be granted.[59]

A tenant is not required to assume a new tenancy of the premises by stating in Form CR102 that there will be no surrender of possession.[60] Consequently, should a tenant be in doubt of the desire to remain in the realty, the tenant should state in the Form CR102 that possession will not be given up and that the tenant will apply for a new tenancy.

Alternatively, a tenant need not wait for the landlord to start the action. A tenant may start the procedure for a new tenancy by filing a Form CR103 requesting a new tenancy beginning with a date not more than seven nor less than six months after the making of the request and nominating the date of commencement of the new tenancy. A tenant dissatisfied with the high level of rent could use this procedure in an attempt to lower that rent. A request for a new tenancy may not be made if the landlord has already served a notice to terminate or if the tenant has already served a notice to quit.[61]

If the landlord opposes a new tenancy, the landlord must reply in Form CR104 within two months of receiving the tenant's Form CR103, giving the reasons of opposition.[62] The landlord need not reply on Form CR104 if there is no opposition to the grant of a new tenancy.

iii. Landlord's Grounds for Opposition under the Former Provisions

A landlord can oppose the granting of a new tenancy on one of the following six grounds, which are similar to the Part II grounds for possession.

One reason for opposition is the non-payment of rent or a breach of a covenant which, if provided in the agreement, will be a ground for forfeiture.[63] Concerning a breach of a covenant:

> To establish this ground . . . the landlord must show that a covenant or condition of the tenancy has been broken or not performed and that breach or non-performance is, under the tenancy, a cause of forfeiture. . . . Unless the term which has been broken or not performed is a condition, a forfeiture clause is required, for the law does not imply a term that the tenancy will be forfeited in the event of breach . . . To enforce a forfeiture for reasons other than non-payment of rent, the landlord is required to serve notice upon the tenant stipulating the breach and calling for its remedy . . . and for compensation . . . It has however been held that while such notice would be required in order to enforce a forfeiture, it need not be given where the landlord is proceeding under one of the statutory grounds of possession . . . [64]

A second ground of opposition by a landlord to a new tenancy is a reasonable requirement of the premises by the landlord for its own occupation or its co-landlord, the father, mother, son or daughter (aged eighteen or above) of the landlord, including a parent or child (aged eighteen or above) of one of the joint landlords.[65] *Reasonable requirement* of the landlord requires a:

genuine present need for the premises. A genuine present need is more than a desire, but less than a necessity. The reasonableness of the landlord's requirement is a question of fact and is different from whether it is reasonable to refuse to make an order for a new tenancy.[66]

There are limitations on a landlord who wishes to use this ground of opposition. One limitation is that the landlord must not have recently purchased the premises (i.e., the date of termination in the Form CR101 must be at least 12 months after the purchase date of the property). The landlord's application will also be rejected if:

- in the case of a tenancy, the tenant satisfies the Lands Tribunal that refusal to grant a new tenancy would be manifestly unjust and inequitable;[67] or
- in the case of a sub-tenancy, refusing to grant a new tenancy would result in greater hardship than granting one.[68]

There are also restrictions and penalties upon a landlord who successfully opposes a request for the grant of a new tenancy based upon the landlord's statement that the premises are needed for self-use. The principal restriction is that no person other than the landlord may occupy the premises for a period of 24 months following the Lands Tribunal's decision not to grant a new tenancy to the tenant. Thus, a landlord cannot lease, sell or otherwise part with possession or use of the premises for a period of 24 months.[69]

Should circumstances change, a landlord may apply to the Lands Tribunal for authorisation to lease or sell the premises. Alternatively, a landlord may apply to the Commissioner for Rating and Valuation for permission to lease the premises for a particular purpose for a period of not more than 12 months.[70] Should the landlord fail to comply with the order or where the landlord obtains the order through false statements or concealment of facts, the landlord may be required to pay compensation to the tenant.[71]

A third ground for objection to the grant of a new tenancy is the landlord's intention to rebuild the premises.[72] The landlord is required to establish at the time of the Lands Tribunal hearing that the rebuilding will result in increased accommodation, that the site is suitable for any change of use, or rebuilding is in the public interest, or that it is not economically viable to restore or repair the premises. A landlord must satisfy the Lands Tribunal of a genuine intention to rebuild and that the landlord has the ability to rebuild.[73]

The Lands Tribunal may impose any reasonable condition[74] upon the landlord and shall order:

- that the plans be lodged with the Lands Tribunal and that the building shall comply with those plans;
- that the rebuilding work commence and that the new building be ready for occupation by specified dates; and/or
- that compensation be paid to the tenant(s). The amount of compensation is set out in the Ordinance.[75]

The Land Tribunal's order is filed in the Land Registry and the conditions imposed apply to the landlord's successors in title.

The fourth ground for objection to the grant of a new tenancy is based upon the tenant causing unnecessary annoyance, inconvenience or disturbance to the landlord or to any other person.[76] In order to succeed on this ground, a landlord should prove that a written warning has been given to the tenant. "The annoyance, inconvenience or disturbance must continue after the warning. It seems that one repetition of the annoyance, inconvenience or disturbance is sufficient even in the case of a persistent failure to pay rent."[77]

The fifth ground for opposition to the grant of a new tenancy is based upon the tenant's immoral or illegal use of the premises.[78] The landlord is required to prove that the tenant has used, has tolerated or has consented to the use of the leased premises for an immoral or illegal purpose. The use need not be continuous or repeated but an isolated offence by a lawful user is insufficient.[79]

The sixth and final ground for objecting to the grant of a new tenancy is the tenant's subletting without occupation. As explained by one authority:

> the landlord must show that the tenant has sublet the whole or any part of the premises of which he is tenant and does not occupy any part of the premises as his dwelling. This ground is not confined to cases where the subletting is in breach of covenant. A subletting of the whole premises, even with the landlord's consent, would give rise to this ground. Even if the tenant has not sublet the whole premises, he will be in breach of this ground if he does not live upon the part which he has not sublet . . .[80]

iv. Lands Tribunal's Procedures under the Former Provisions

After the issuing Form CR101 and receiving a reply in Form CR102, or issuing a Form CR103 and receiving reply in a Form CR104, the parties may negotiate a new tenancy. Should the parties fail to negotiate a new tenancy agreement, the tenant must make an application in Form 22 to the Lands Tribunal for a new tenancy. This must be accomplished within two months after the landlord gives notice in Form CR105, but no later than the expiry of the landlord's Form CR101 notice or the new tenancy's commencement date specified in the tenant's Form CR103 request.

Form CR105 moves forward the time for the tenant's application for a new tenancy by requiring the tenant to file a Form 22 applying to the Lands Tribunal for a new tenancy. Form CR105 cannot be served until two months have passed since the landlord's service of Form CR101 or the tenant's service of Form CR103. There is no practical advantage in the landlord serving a Form CR105 less than two months before the expiry of the landlord's notice in the Form CR101 or the date of commencement of the new tenancy specified in Form CR103.

Thus, a tenant's application to the Lands Tribunal in Form 22 should not be made before two months after the landlord has sent Form CR101 or the tenant has made a request on Form CR103. The tenant's application to the Tribunal must be served on the landlord. Should the tenant fail to file a Form 22 within two months of the landlord's Form CR105, the tenant's application for a new tenancy cannot be considered by the Lands Tribunal.[81]

The Lands Tribunal cannot extend the time limits for a tenant's application for a new tenancy.[82] The Lands Tribunal has the authority to grant an order for possession in situations where a tenant fails to apply for a tenancy in time.[83]

If the landlord opposes the tenant's application in Form 22, the landlord has 14 days to file a notice of opposition on Form 7.[84] At this stage, the landlord can only refer to the grounds set out in that particular case in the Form CR101, which cannot be amended. Thereafter, either party can apply to list the case for hearing.

Upon failure of the parties to reach an agreement, the Lands Tribunal will decide the terms other than duration and rent.[85] The Lands Tribunal should have regard to the terms of the current tenancy and all relevant circumstances.

The agreement's length of term must be "reasonable in all the circumstances," but must not exceed three years.[86] Normally, the Lands Tribunal will grant a term of the same duration as under the old agreement.

The party asking for a different duration must provide a good reason for a different duration to be ordered, e.g., because the landlord wants to live in the premises but recently purchased them and therefore cannot claim possession immediately. In such an instance, a landlord may be able to persuade the Lands Tribunal to grant a shorter lease.

The term will start on the day following the expiry of the landlord's notice in Form CR101, or on the commencement date specified in the tenant's request in Form CR103, or on a date fixed by the Lands Tribunal. In the case of a sub-tenancy, the term must end no less than three days before the end of the term of the main tenancy.[87]

Where the parties have agreed the terms of a new tenancy but have not agreed the rent, either party may refer the rent for determination by the Lands Tribunal[88] under former section 119K of the *Landlord and Tenant (Consolidation) Ordinance*.[89] Thus, in the absence of agreement between the parties, the rent will be the prevailing market rent determined by the Lands Tribunal or a valuation surveyor appointed by the Lands Tribunal. The Lands Tribunal must determine the prevailing market rent at the date the current tenancy is ended by notice pursuant to a Form CR101 or at the commencement date of a new tenancy requested by the tenant under a Form CR103.

Where the terms of the new tenancy are agreed between the parties or set by the Lands Tribunal, a new agreement is signed and a Form CR109 is lodged with the Commissioner of Rating and Valuation in triplicate. The Commissioner will endorse receipt of the Form CR109 and return an endorsed copy to each party.

A tenant, within one month of the Lands Tribunal's decision on the new tenancy's provisions, may provide notice in Form CR106 to the landlord and the Lands Tribunal informing these parties that the tenant will not take up a new tenancy. The tenant will specify a date within two months of the Form CR106 when the tenant will leave. Rent at the new rate must be paid to that date from the expiry of notice in the Form CR101 or from the starting date of the new tenancy as specified in Form CR103.[90]

A sub-tenant has the same rights as a tenant provided there is no breach of the principal tenancy. If the sub-tenant's interest in the premises has been given in Form CR107 to the head landlord, future copies of notice(s), request(s) or application(s) must be provided to the sub-tenant.

A subtenant may apply in Form 22 or request in Form CR103 a new tenancy direct from the head landlord. If the head landlord successfully opposes a new tenancy based on self-use or rebuilding of the premises, the sub-tenancy also terminates. If the tenant has sublet in breach of the tenant's agreement with the landlord, the sub-tenancy terminates when the tenancy terminates. If a new tenancy is refused on other grounds and the sub-tenant is not in default of any of the grounds of opposition, the subtenant becomes the tenant of the head landlord but the head landlord can apply for an order that the new tenancy be of the whole premises.

D. Commercial Leases

Part V of the *Landlord and Tenant (Consolidation) Ordinance* applies to non-domestic tenancies,[91] with certain exceptions.[92] Non-domestic leases concern premises used primarily for commercial activity, e.g., offices, shops, restaurants, etc. The previous sections of this chapter concentrated on domestic tenancies. This section will review briefly commercial leases and tenancies, although in many respects both tenancies are governed by the same law. Therefore, this section addresses the matters particular to commercial leases: rent increases and determination.[93]

Commercial premises' rents tend to be higher than that of similar residential premises and be of longer duration. To protect a landlord's interests, there frequently are provisions for rent adjustments at regular intervals throughout the term of the commercial lease. The revised rent, nonetheless, must be capable of being calculated with certainty.[94]

One method employed by landlords to implement a rent increase is the *rent escalation* clause which may permit rent increases linked, for example, to increases in the Consumer Price Index. Another method available to landlords is the *turnover rent* clause which permits rent increases to be directly proportional to the success of a tenant's business. Rent review clauses may also be accompanied by *break clauses* which allow commercial tenants to end or determine the lease without any breach of the agreement if the tenants are dissatisfied with the rent increase. Finally, absent a provision in the tenancy agreement to the contrary, the tenancy may be subject to forfeiture if the rent is not paid within 15 days after its due date.[95]

From 9 July 2004, the *Landlord and Tenant (Consolidation) (Amendment) Ordinance 2004* removed from Part V the six-month written notice requirement for the termination of non-domestic tenancies.

If the commercial lease has not expired and thus no Part V notice has been served by 9 July 2004, the tenancy may be ended in accordance with the terms of the lease agreement or as agreed between the parties.[96] Absent any agreement to the contrary, a fixed-term tenancy will end upon the expiry of the term and a periodic tenancy may be ended by a notice to quit at the length of a full notice period in accordance with the common law.[97]

If the commercial lease has already expired but no Part V notice has been served by 9 July 2004, the lease continues as a month-to-month tenancy. The parties may end the tenancy by agreement or by serving a notice to quit on the other party one month before the intended termination date.[98] Alternatively, the parties may mutually agree to other arrangements.

A tenant of commercial premises may also give notice of termination. If the lease is for a periodic tenancy, the tenant must give notice of at least one month before determination can lawfully occur.[99] If the lease term is for a fixed period, then the notice should be given at least one month before the tenancy's expiry. If the tenancy agreement so provides, the notice by the tenant may be more than one month in advance of the termination date.[100]

E. Transfer of Deposits

Usually, a tenant pays a deposit to the landlord as security. The landlord agrees to return the money at the end of the lease when the tenant has surrendered the premises. A common provision allows the landlord to deduct any loss or damage resulting from the tenant's breach of any lease covenants. Any remaining funds from the deposit will then be returned to the tenant.[101]

If there is a sale of the premises and thus a change of landlord, the practice of transferring the deposit money to the new landlord should be avoided. Repayment of the deposit is a personal obligation of the original landlord who remains liable to the tenant. The tenant cannot recover the deposit from the new landlord. An agreement between the three parties, that the deposit money will be repaid by the purchaser to the tenant following termination of the tenancy, would solve the matter.

5
Fixtures

At common law, the ownership of a piece of land includes everything above the land and everything beneath the land. The maxim *quicquid plantatur solo, solo cedit* means whatever is attached to the soil becomes part of it. Thus, land includes any buildings that are erected on the land. This maxim also applies to the law relating to fixtures.

The concept of fixtures affects both freehold estates and leasehold estates. *Fixture* is a term given to anything that becomes so attached to the land or a building as to become part of the land, and is therefore treated as realty. The distinction between fixtures and *fittings*, i.e., chattels that are not attached to land, is crucial whenever there is a transfer of a freehold or leasehold estate. For example, purchasers ought to know the chattels being sold to them and sellers ought to know which chattels are removable.[1]

Whether an object is a fixture is not always easily determined. Frequently, the determination is for a court to decide on a case-by-case basis. Whether a chattel has become a fixture depends on the degree of annexation and the purpose of annexation.[2] If these guidelines are applied correctly, the purpose of annexation should be shown by the degree of annexation.

A chattel is not considered a fixture unless it is actually fastened to, or connected with the land or a building.[3] A chattel attached to land, however slightly, is *prima facie* considered to be a fixture. For example, in *Buckland v Butterfield* (1820) 2 Brod & Bing 54, a veranda connected to a house was considered a fixture because it was attached to land. The burden of proof that a chattel is not a fixture rests upon the party claiming the contrary.

The *purpose of annexation* test helps determine whether a chattel has been attached for its more convenient use as chattel or for the more convenient use of the land or building. In *Australian Provincial Assurance Co Ltd v Coroneo* (1938) 38 SR (NSW) 700, the court determined that the test would be whether an object is fixed with the intention that the object remains in position permanently (or for some substantial period) or whether the object has been fixed with the intention that it shall remain in position only for some temporary purposes.

For example, in the case of *Holland v Hodgson* (1872) LR 7 CP 328 the court held that blocks of stone placed one on top of another without any mortar or cement for the purpose of forming a dry stone wall would become part of the land. Those same stones, if located in a builder's yard and for convenience were similarly stacked on top of each other in the form of a wall, would remain as chattels.

A greenhouse attached to the external wall of a house is a fixture because it cannot be moved.[4] A movable greenhouse might be considered a chattel.[5] An air conditioner which fits into a window is presumed to be a fixture as it could not be enjoyed separately from a room and its purpose is to improve the premises.[6] A court determined that air conditioning machines resting by their own weight on the floor of a garage adjoining a restaurant were not to be considered fixtures.[7] Likewise, another court found an air conditioning system to be a fixture because the air conditioning system was either affixed to the building or affixed to an item which is already a fixture.[8]

If a chattel becomes a fixture, its ownership will belong to the landowner. Therefore, ownership of the fixture will pass to the new owner upon sale of the land. A seller is not entitled to remove fixtures upon any sale of land without having agreed with the purchaser to do so. The right to remove fixtures also arises in the following situations:

- Mortgagor and mortgagee: fixtures, whether annexed to the land before or during the life of the mortgage, will become subject to the mortgage and can only be removed with the agreement of the mortgagee. Thus, the fixtures will pass with the land to the mortgagee even though they are not mentioned in the mortgage document. This rule applies to both legal and equitable mortgages. If the fixtures are attached by a third party, and the mortgagor and the third party agree that the mortgagor will allow removal, the third party's rights are superior to the mortgagee's.

- Seller and purchaser: fixtures pass to the purchaser. Subject to any stated exceptions, a conveyance would pass the title of the fixtures to the purchaser. Fixtures are considered to be part of the purchase price.

If a seller wishes to remove fixtures, the seller must make specific arrangements with the purchaser.

- Landlord and tenant: all fixtures attached by a tenant *prima facie* form part of the property to be returned to the landlord. Because of the unfairness this rule might cause, the law has developed so that a tenant has a right to remove trade fixtures or ornamental and domestic fixtures during its tenancy, provided that these items can be removed without substantial or irreparable damage to the land.

  - Trade fixtures are considered to be fixtures used for the purpose of conducting a trade or a business and thus can be removed by the tenant. For example, pipes and vats for a brewery, or petrol pumps and car lifts at a garage/repair shop are considered to be trade fixtures.[9]

  - Ornamental and domestic fixtures are chattels attached for decoration of the land or the building, or, for convenience.

    Objects which have been fixed to the land by way of ornament or for domestic convenience and utility have from the earliest times been removable by the tenant provided that the lease does not provide to the contrary and that they are capable of being severed without irreparable injury to the land.

    Articles which form an essential part of a house at the time of its construction may not be removed; and it is doubtful whether such articles may properly be called fixtures of any description. Skylights are not fixtures but form part of the roof.[10]

These fixtures may be removed, provided that the removal does no substantial damage to the land or the building.

So long as a chattel can be removed without doing irreparable damage to the demised premises, neither the method nor the degree of annexation, nor the quantum of damage that would be done either to the chattel itself or to the demised premises by the removal, have any bearing upon the tenant's right to remove it, except in so far as they indicate the intention with which the tenant affixed the chattel to the premises. Where trade fixtures have to be taken to pieces in the removal, in general it is essential that they are capable of being put together in the same form in some other place. Buildings of a permanent nature are not removable, but a temporary corrugated iron shed used for trade is removable. Glasshouses are removable when

> erected for the purpose of his business by a market gardener but, when erected for ornament or convenience, are not removable. Slight buildings, erected for the purpose of trade, and buildings which are accessory to removable machinery are removable.[11]

If a tenant removes fixtures, the tenant must repair any damage to the property caused by the fixtures' removal.

In summary, although the concept of fixtures is relatively easy to understand, the application of this concept may be difficult. An example of this difficulty is provided by several court cases concerning whether window-type air conditioners are fixtures or personalty. The concept of fixtures is further demonstrated in the endnotes.

Items considered to be fixtures become part of the land and ownership in the items or fixtures will be transferred with the title to the land. Whether an item is to be considered as a fixture will depend upon the reason for attaching that item to the land and the extent of that attachment.

6
Adverse Possession

Adverse possession refers to the occupation of land by a person against the rights and interests of the owner. A landowner has the right to keep unwanted or uninvited people off the land. A landowner has the right to go to court for an order for possession against any trespasser.[1] However, if the person has adversely possessed the land for the period of time specified by law, the actual owner may not enforce its rights against the occupier.[2]

P J Dalton explains the policy behind this principle as follows:

> . . . statute has placed a limit on the time after which a claimant to an interest in land may bring an action to establish it in the face of the possession of another person holding under a later title . . . [Title] is only extinguished or "barred" because the claim it gives to land has been allowed to remain unpressed for a long time in face of a rival title . . . [3]

The following points should be considered in cases involving claims of adverse possession.

- The length of the period: section 7 of the *Limitation Ordinance* (Cap 347) provides that the limitation period for actions brought for the recovery of land by the Government is sixty years, and by any other person the period is twelve years.[4]
- The running of time: section 8 of the *Limitation Ordinance* provides that time will begin to run against an actual owner of land only where:
  - the owner had been dispossessed or discontinued possession. Possession with a licence, that is permissive use, does not constitute
  - adverse possession unless the licence is revoked and the licensee continues in possession.

- Adverse possession of the land has been taken by some other person. An owner is presumed to be in possession of the land, even without any physical possession, unless the contrary is proved.

In *Boosey v Davis* (1987) 55 P & CR 83, CA, the judge referred to the case of *Wallis's Cayton Bay Holiday Camp Ltd v Shell-Mex and BP Ltd* in his decision concerning adverse possession. The judge determined that possession by itself is not enough to give a title. It must be *adverse* possession. The true owner must have discontinued possession or have been dispossessed and another must have taken it adversely from the true owner.[5]

The Court of Final Appeal in *Incorporated Owners of San Po Kong Mansion v Shine Empire* (2007) 10 HKCFAR 588 set out the requirements for someone to claim adverse possession:

> . . .
>
> (2) . . . he must be shown to have both factual possession and the requisite intention to possess (*animus possidendi*).
>
> (3) Factual possession signifies an appropriate degree of physical control. It must be a single and conclusive possession . . . The question what acts constitute a sufficient degree of exclusive physical control must depend on the circumstances . . . acts of possession done on parts of land to which a possessory title is sought may be evidence of possession of the whole. Whether or not acts of possession done on parts of an area establish title to the whole area must, however, be a matter of degree . . . is that the alleged possessor has been dealing with the land in question as an occupying owner might have been expected to deal with it and that no-one else has done so.
>
> (4) . . . the *animus possidendi* involves the intention . . . to exclude the world at large, including the owner with the paper title . . . so far as is reasonably practicable and so far as the processes of the law will allow.
>
> . . .
>
> An owner or other person with the right to possession of land will be readily assumed to have the requisite intention to possess, unless the contrary is clearly proved. This is why the slightest acts done by or on behalf of an owner in possession will be found to negative discontinuance of possession. The position, however, is quite different from a case where the question is whether a trespasser has acquired possession. In such a situation the courts will require clear and affirmative

evidence that the trespasser, claiming that he has acquired possession, not only had the requisite intention to possess, but made such intention clear to the world. If his acts are open to more than one interpretation and he has not made it perfectly plain to the world at large by his actions or words that he has intended to exclude the owner as best he can, the courts will treat him as not having had the requisite *animus possidendi* and consequently as not having dispossessed the owner.[6]

. . .

There is a recent adverse possession case in Causeway Bay. A family occupied the land near the Lee Theatre claiming to have been in possession of the property for approximately 50 years. The developer attempted to remove the occupiers in order to develop the property, estimated to be worth HK$60 million. The Court of First Instance determined that the family squatting on the land did not have exclusive possession of the land and that the family did not occupy the land for the requisite period. On appeal, the Court of Appeal decided that the family did exercise exclusive possession of a portion of the property for the requisite period.[7]

Another case of adverse possession involved a residential flat in To Kwa Wan. Here, the tenant lived in the flat since 1973. After 1984, the owner seemed to have disappeared. For more than 25 years, the tenant paid the rates and other related expenses. By 2010, despite the wide publicity of this case given by the media, the owner could not be located. The court decided that the tenant had met the requirements: prescribed time period, exclusive possession and the intent to exclude the owner. The court decided that the title of the flat now belonged to the tenant.[8]

In the cases of *Chu Kwok Wai v Tang Wing Tung Anthony* [2013] HKEC 545, *To Hin Cheung v All Occupiers(s) of a portion of Lot No 240 in Demarcation District No 128, Yuen Long* [2013] HKEC 546, *Hero Smart Corp Ltd v Tse Mei Kuen* [2012] HKEC 579, *Lam Kin Chun v Lin Xiumei* [2011] HKEC 932 and *Tsui Kwong On v Koo Ling Sung* [2011] HKEC 1473 the court in each case followed the principles for determining whether there had been adverse possession: whether there had been exclusive and continuous possession of the land for the required time period, and, whether the occupants had the intention to possess the land to the exclusion of the everyone, including the true owner. In the cases of *Chiu Si Hon v Estate of Chan Shui Kiu* [2012] HKEC 607 and *C & C Joint Printing Co (HK) Ltd v Chen Bei Tsen* [2013] HKEC 57, adverse possession was used to clarify and settle title in favour of the plaintiffs rather than to dispossess the defendants of ownership. In the case of *Cheung Pak Cheong v Tong Keng* [2013] HKEC 42, the court allowed husband and wife to take adverse possession of a factory unit against the defendant. The wife and the defendant were the legal co-owners of the property and the husband was the tenant.

In summation, adverse possession allows another person to claim title of the property from the true owner. Therefore, if an owner ignores or allows another person to use or claim ownership of land without any challenge or assertion of ownership for the statutory time period, the owner has a risk of losing the property to the adverse possessor. Note, however, the exception. The court in *Wealth Hill International Investment Ltd v Wong Kwan Siu* [2013] HKEC 838 stated that in regards to land belonging to a *Tong*, the arrival of a newborn member can defeat a claim of adverse possession as a new limitation period starts to run and will not expire until six years after the new member ceases to be an infant, i.e., 24 years after the birth of the newest member of the *Tong*.

PART 2
Encumbrances

.

7
Servitudes

Earlier, the introduction to Part 1 defined *encumbrance*. An encumbrance may also be defined as a: "claim or liability that is attached to property or some other right and that may lessen its value, such as a lien or mortgage; any property right that is not an ownership interest."[1] Thus, an encumbrance may be considered as a legal obligation or duty imposed upon the land. In other words, this obligation or duty remains with land regardless of changes in ownership.

Servitude is a term from Roman law meaning an encumbrance consisting of a right to the restricted use of land without the possession or ownership of that parcel of land.[2] Because of the physical closeness of land possessed by different parties and the potential flexibility of land use, the law has recognized rights allowing use of a neighbour's land for occasional purposes. Thus, it is possible to create either rights over or interests in a neighbour's land, known as the *servient tenement*, without the right to occupy or to possess that neighbour's land. These servitudes restrict a landowner's rights to use the land in some manner. The three main types of servitudes are:

- easements
- *profits à prendre*
- restrictive covenants

As easements and *profits à prendre* are similar, they will be presented first. Restrictive covenants will then be reviewed. This will be followed by a survey of a different type of encumbrance, known as *mortgages* in the following chapter.

A. Easements

An *easement* is the right attached to land to use, or to restrict the use of, the land of another person in some way. An easement is a right enjoyed by an owner of one parcel of land over another owner's parcel of land. Examples of easements include: right of way, right of light and right of support.

Easements are generally positive, examples include: a right of way, a right of support for a building, a right to draw water, or a right to discharge water. Easements may also be negative, examples include: a right to prevent another from using the land in a particular way, or a right to light and air, which a neighbour may not obstruct by erecting a building.

"Incidents of a novel kind cannot be devised and attached to property at the fancy or caprice of any owner."[3] Consequently, what does it take to create an easement? The creation of an easement requires the same conditions as the creation of a profit.[4] In *Re Ellenborough Park* [1956] 1 Ch 131, the owners of nearby houses claimed compensation for the loss of their right to walk in and enjoy the neighbouring park. The court held that damages would only be awarded if the right amounted to an easement. The judge stated the requirements for finding the existence of an easement:

> . . . (1) there must be a dominant and a servient tenement; (2) an easement must accommodate the dominant tenement, that is, be connected with its enjoyment and for its benefit; (3) the dominant and servient owners must be different persons; and (4) the right claimed must be capable of forming the subject-matter of a grant.[5]

Easements thus have four characteristics. First, there must be two pieces of land: a dominant tenement and a servient tenement.[6] An easement is a right over one piece of land (the *servient tenement*) enjoyed by another piece of land (the *dominant tenement*). An easement must be attached to, and benefit, a dominant tenement. Without a dominant tenement, the right to use the servient tenement would be a licence only.

The second characteristic is that the easement must accommodate the dominant tenement. An easement "must . . . have some natural connection with the estate, as being for its benefit."[7] This right must also be connected with the usual and normal enjoyment of the dominant tenement so that this right benefits the dominant land and is not simply a personal benefit to the current owner of the dominant tenement.[8]

The third characteristic is that the right must lie in grant.[9] In other words, the right must be capable of being transferred by deed. A right over land cannot amount to an easement unless it is capable of being granted to another individual.[10] A right will not be considered an easement if the right requires the servient land's owner to incur any expenditure or take any action. The servient landowner's role in an easement is passive: to allow the dominant landowner to use the easement and not to interfere with the easement or its use. A servient landowner cannot generally be required to repair the easement. A right will not be considered as an easement if the right excludes the servient landowner's occupation of the servient land or if it constitutes joint occupation of the servient land.

The fourth characteristic is that the dominant and servient owners must be different persons. A person cannot have an easement over his or her own land because identical ownership of the dominant tenement and the servient tenement would eliminate the need for an easement. Two tenements may, however, be owned by the same person in different capacities. For instance, a person may own the dominant tenement as a beneficiary and own the servient tenement as a trustee.

B. *Profit à Prendre*

The court in *Duke of Sutherland v Heathcote* [1892] 1 Ch 475 defined *profit à prendre* (also known as a *profit*) as "a right to take something off another person's land."[11] A profit differs from an easement in that a profit is the right to take some part of the servient tenement, e.g., its natural produce, including any wild animals, soil or minerals. (An easement, by comparison, merely confers a right to use the servient tenement in some way.) The right to remove something from another person's land generally means that this product must be something of value taken off the soil, e.g., sand, gravel or topsoil, or the produce of the land, e.g., firewood, fish or fodder for livestock.

A profit may also be a right to "hawk, hunt, fish and fowl," that is the right to take creatures living on the land. The creature(s) taken must be capable of ownership. The right to take water from a river, spring, and the like is an easement rather than a profit because water is not considered to be part of the land nor is it owned by anyone.

A profit can be enjoyed by one person to the exclusion of all others, in which case it would be considered as a *several profit*. Alternatively, a profit can be enjoyed by one person in common with others, in which case it would be considered as a *profit in common*.

A *profit appurtenant* is a type of *profit à prendre* where the benefit is attached to a dominant tenement by act of the parties.[12] As a profit appurtenant is linked to the ownership of another parcel of land, four conditions, the same as those for the existence of an easement, are required for a profit appurtenant:[13]

- there must be a dominant and a servient tenement
- the benefit must add to the amenities of the dominant tenement and not just confer a personal benefit
- the right or the benefit must be capable of being granted by deed
- there must be separate ownership of the dominant and the servient tenements

A *profit in gross* gives the benefit of the land to the grantee personally regardless of occupation or ownership of land. A profit in gross thus requires no dominant tenement. For example, a right to take fish from a canal without stint[14] can exist as a profit in gross.[15]

A *profit pur cause de vicinage* only exists in the form of a common of pasture. It is a right enjoyed by commoners of adjoining commons, for example where the cattle on one common are allowed to stray on the other common.[16]

A *profit appendant* is one which is attached to land by operation of law.[17]

C. Creation of Servitudes

Servitudes may be created by several methods. These methods will be discussed below in brief detail.

i. By Statute

Through legislation, the Government may acquire certain rights over private property for public works. The right to carry electric power, gas and telephone lines over or under land will often be negotiated if this right affects private property. This right of way is sometimes referred to as a *wayleave* or as a *statutory easement*.[18]

ii. By Express Grant

In law, the grant of an easement or a *profit à prendre* must be for an interest equivalent to an estate for a term of years absolute. Additionally, the profit or easement must be granted by deed and registered. A legal easement in Hong Kong must be created for a term of years.

The term of the easement must not exceed the period of the lease of either the dominant or servient land . . . An easement for another period than a term of years, for instance for life, cannot exist at law but only in equity.[19]

iii. By Express Reservation

Sometimes, a legal easement may be created when a vendor sells only part of the land and reserves easements or profits over a portion of the land sold. This is known as a *reservation* because the owner has reserved a right for the benefit of the retained land (the dominant tenement) from the land sold (destined to become the servient tenement) rather than granting a servitude.

iv. By Implied Grant

A grantor has to make the reservation expressly in order to create a servitude. The law will only imply a grant of a servitude if it was obviously intended or is of necessity. An implied grant of a servitude is "based upon the presumed common intention of the parties. In order to give effect to the transaction contemplated by the parties, it may be necessary to imply an easement where the parties have failed to mention the right expressly."[20]

For instance,

where an owner has been accustomed to using one part of his land in a particular way, which is of benefit to the rest of his land, his use is commonly termed a quasi-easement. All the elements of an easement are present except the diversity of occupation of the dominant and servient tenements. On the sale of part of the land, there is diversity of occupation and the right may develop into an easement displaying all the characteristics we have examined.[21]

Following are some instances where a grant of a servitude may be implied upon the sale of the quasi-dominant tenement:

a. Under the rule in the case of **Wheeldon v Burrows**[22]

The court in this case identified the rule as being one of intention, based upon the principle that a person cannot derogate from his or her grant, that is:

> on the grant by the owner of a tenement of part of that
> tenement . . . there will pass to the grantee all those continuous
> and apparent easements (by which . . . I mean quasi-
> easements), or, in other words, all those easements which are
> *necessary to the reasonable enjoyment of the property granted,*
> and which have been and are at the time of the grant used by
> the owners . . . for the benefit of the part granted.[23]

Three requirements must be satisfied before a quasi-easement can develop by implication into an easement:

* the quasi-easement must be continuous and apparent
* the quasi-easement must be reasonably necessary for the enjoyment of the property sold
* the quasi-easement must be in use at the time of the sale

b. Arising by Necessity

"An easement of necessity is a right that is so essential to the enjoyment of the land that the land would be useless without it."[24] For instance in *Wong v Beaumont Property Trust Ltd* [1965] 1 QB 173 the court determined that "to use this place as a restaurant, there must be implied an easement, by the necessity of the case, to carry a duct up the wall."[25] In this case:

> [the] basement premises had been let upon the express
> understanding that the property was to be used as a restaurant.
> Later, after assignment by the original tenant, the assignee was
> required to improve ventilation if the restaurant business were
> to continue.[26]

In *Nickerson v Barraclough* [1981] 2 WLR 773, the court held that a way of necessity could exist only with a grant of land and depended on the intention of the parties; an implication from the circumstances that unless some way was implied, the land in question would be inaccessible.

An easement of necessity can only be implied if the needs of the dominant tenement are the same as they were at the date of the grant.

c. Servitudes of Common Intention

The *Wong* case discussed above might have been decided by implying that "the parties *intended* all rights which permitted the use of the premises as a restaurant."[27] The law will imply either the grant or the reservation of easements as necessary to give effect to the intention of the parties, with reference to the purposes for which the land is to be used.[28] "That intention may arise because the right is necessary for the use of the land . . . or because surrounding circumstances are such that the parties must have contemplated such a right."[29] In the case of *Stafford v Lee* (1993) 65 P & CR 172, Stafford was the owner of a woodland lot fronting on to a drive which ran to a public road. Stafford sought to build a house on the land. Lee, the owner of the drive, objected. Lee contended that Stafford's right of way over the drive was for the purposes of using this land as woodland. No express right of way had been reserved on conveyance of the land in 1955. Stafford obtained a declaration that he was entitled to use the drive for the purposes of building and using a house on the woodland lot.

This category of implied easements may include a claim of a profit or an easement, even though *not* necessary to the enjoyment of the property, provided it can be shown that both parties intended to make such a grant.[30] An example is found in the case of *Cory v Davies* [1923] 2 Ch 95, where a row of terraced houses had been built with a drive in front and an exit to the road at each end:

> One of the owners barred the exit at his end of the terrace, requiring all traffic to go the other way. There was no express grant of an easement in favour of all the house owners over all parts of the drive, but the court found that the original parties had a common intention that the drive should be used in this way, and thus an intended easement was implied.[31]

d. Implied Reservation

Courts hesitate to find the implication of a reservation in favour of the grantor when the quasi-servient tenement is sold. This reluctance is because a grantor should not be allowed to derogate from its grant unless it is clearly known to the grantee.[32]

> An easement may be implied, reserved in favour of the grantor on the basis of necessity, or due to the common intention of the parties; but the courts will adopt a stricter test than in the case of the implication of a grant in favour of the quasi-dominant tenement.[33]

e. Presumed Grant (Prescription)

The word *prescription* refers to the method by which those who retain land for an uninterrupted period (usually ten or twenty years) acquired ownership of that property. Common law prescription is based upon the presumption that where a person is in undisturbed enjoyment of a right, that person is deemed to be in possession as of right. The following Latin maxim applies: *omnia praesumuntur rite er solemniter esse acta* – all acts are presumed to have been done rightly and regularly. Where a right is enjoyed for a sufficiently long time, it will be presumed that the right is by virtue of an original grant of an easement or of a *profit à prendre* by prescription. In other words, a prescriptive easement is an acquisition of an easement by adverse possession. The user must have been as of right: that the right was acquired without force, without secrecy, and without permission. The term *as of right* means that "the use must have been exercised as if the right had properly granted" to the user.[34]

There are three ways in which an easement or a *profit à prendre* may be acquired by prescription:

(1) Prescription at Common Law – User since Time Immemorial

The common law presumes an easement or a *profit à prendre* if it is proven that the right has been used since time immemorial.[35] Hence, a claimant had to show that the right had been enjoyed after 1189. The presumption may be rebutted by proof that it did not or could not have existed at some time after 1189. Prescription has little, if any, application in Hong Kong.

> It is an established feature of prescription at common law that the right must be acquired by a fee simple owner of the dominant land against the fee simple owner of the servient land. The leasehold nature of land in Hong Kong thus excludes prescription at common law.[36]

(2) Doctrine of Lost Modern Grant

The difficulties of proving use since time immemorial resulted in the courts creating the fiction of a lost grant. This legal fiction provides that if use could be established for at least twenty years, a formal grant to the user is presumed. This legal fiction "is so well established that it cannot be rebutted by evidence that no such grant was made."[37] Thus, the fiction further provides the assumption that the grant has since been lost, so that it cannot be produced.

Courts will accept proof of a continuous use for at least 20 years as evidence that the right has been used or enjoyed since 1189. Thus, it is necessary to prove the continuous use as of right for a minimum period of 20 years.[38] Once this is done, the courts will presume that there was a grant.

(3) Prescription Act 1832

This statute was known for its poor drafting. The statute did not simplify the requirements for demonstrating use by prescription under the common law or under the fiction of the lost modern grant. Instead, the statute further complicates the situation. Nonetheless, Parliament made no attempts to rectify this Act. The *Application of English Law Ordinance* (Cap 88) applied the *Prescription Act* 1832 to Hong Kong. Note that this Ordinance has not been adopted as a part of the Laws of the Hong Kong SAR. As the *Prescription Act* no longer applies to Hong Kong, no further mention of this Act will be made.

D. Extinguishment of Servitudes

Rights under both easements and *profit à prendre* may be terminated. The several ways in which they may be ended are discussed below.

i. Legislation

As statutes might create an easement or a *profit à prendre*, an easement or a *profit à prendre* may also be terminated by legislative action.

ii. Express Release

An express release, either by deed or court order, may end a servitude. To be effective, the express release must be by deed. Equity, however, may recognise a release made by less formal means.[39] With the release, the easement or profit reverts back to the servient owner, at which time the servitude merges with the servient owner's estate and ceases to be a servitude.

iii. Implied Release

An implied release may occur when the dominant owner has abandoned its right to the easement or profit. Failing to use an easement or profit does not prove abandonment. "Non-use will only constitute abandonment if it is explicable only on the assumption that the dominant owner intended to give up the right."[40] There needs to be evidence of an intention to abandon the right because a person need not exercise his/her rights. For example, in the case of *Cook v Mayor & Corp of Bath* (1868) LR 6 Eq 177, a door had been bricked over for more than thirty years. The court decided this did not constitute an abandonment of a right of way. A prolonged non-use may demonstrate that the dominant owner has impliedly abandoned the right. In *Moore v Rawson* (1824) 3 B & C 332, Moore had demolished a wall containing windows and built a window-less wall in its place. The court held this act to have shown an intention to abandon a right to light.

> If, however, the dominant tenement has been altered in such a way that the right claimed becomes unnecessary or impossible to exercise, then the alteration may be regarded as evidence of an intention to abandon the right. This presumption may be rebutted by evidence that the original character of the land may be restored in the future and that the need for the easement or profit would revive.[41]

The case of *Re Yateley Common* [1977] 1 All ER 505 suggested that to establish abandonment of a right, it must be established that the owner of the right has ceased to use it and never intends to use it again. If the dominant owner explains the non-use, the owner is likely to be regarded as not surrendering that right.

iv. Unity of Possession and Ownership

When the same person becomes owner and possessor of both the dominant and the servient tenements, the requirement of diversity of ownership is destroyed. Thus, an easement or a profit appurtenant to land will be extinguished when the tenements come into common ownership. The exception is where that individual owns the dominant and servient tenements in different capacities.

v. Effluction of Time

Easements in Hong Kong must be granted for a term of years. This grant generally will be for the shorter of the terms created by the Government leases of the dominant and servient lands. At the end of the term for which the easement is granted, the easement will simply expire. Where there is a statutory renewal or extension of the Government lease term of the servient land, the grant may also be deemed to continue.[42]

vi. Alteration in the Dominant Tenement

Where the dominant tenement is altered so that use or enjoyment of a profit appurtenant is no longer possible, the servitude is extinguished. For example, in *National Guaranteed Manure Co v Donald* (1859) 4 H & N 8, a canal, the dominant tenement, was converted to a railway. The conversion ended the easement of water for the canal.

E. Restrictive Covenants[43]

The development of covenants may be attributed to the need for land use control.

> The major function of the rules about restrictive covenants, is the control of land use. When the rules were initially developed in the nineteenth century, there was no public planning law . . . A person selling land for building might extract a promise that only homes would be built (no shops or factories), and initially this was only enforceable in contract law, that is only against the person who made the promise (the covenantor) and not against his successors on the land.[44]

Restrictive covenants were first recognised in the case of *Tulk v Moxhay* (1848) 41 ER 1143, which is discussed below.

Recall that easements may be positive or negative. A negative easement is one which "is enjoyed without any action by the dominant owner."[45] In other words, a negative easement restricts what the servient tenement's owner may do with its property.

A *covenant* is a formal deed between at least two parties and which creates obligations. One party (the *covenantor*) agrees with the other party (the *covenantee*) to perform or refrain from performing some act. The covenantor is bound by the obligation and the covenantee may enforce the benefit of the obligation.[46] A positive covenant requires the performance of some act. A negative covenant forbids the commission of some act. "In *Phipps v Pears* [1965] 1 QB 76 . . . courts would not readily accept the creation of new *negative* easements, because they have a tendency to restrict the servient tenement owner and hamper development of his property."[47] There is great similarity between easements and restrictive covenants, including requirements for a dominant and a servient tenement, proximity, and accommodation or benefit.

If the agreement is a personal covenant with a landlord and lessee or with another landlord, the covenant only affects the concerned parties. Their successors cannot enforce the covenants, as there is no privity of contract.[48] The exception to this general rule is an equitable easement, where an agreement is not to perform some act but to restrict the use of the land for the benefit of another. These equitable easements are known also as *restrictive covenants*. Thus, some covenants may run with the land, i.e., they can be enforced by and against assignees of a lease and the purchasers of a leasehold estate when there is privity of contract between the parties. A restrictive covenant must be negative in nature. Equity will allow covenants that "touch and concern" the land to run with the land (i.e., to go with or become part of the land). This is because of the unfairness to allow a person, who might have paid a lower price for the land due to restriction placed on its use, to disregard these restrictions with impunity. For example, in the case of *Tulk v Moxhay* (1848) 41 ER 1143, Tulk sold part of Leicester Square to Elms who covenanted on behalf of himself, his heirs and assigns not to build on the land. Elms sold to Moxhay who, knowing of the covenant, started to build on the land. The court held that it would be inequitable that Elms, who paid a lower price for the land on account of restrictions, be able to sell it for a much higher price free from restrictions. The court found that Moxhay was bound by the restrictive covenant.

A restrictive covenant may be enforced by an injunction brought by the original covenantee or its assignee against the original covenantor or its assignee who has notice of the covenant.

The following are the major points to note about restrictive covenants:

- The common law requires the covenant to be negative in form, i.e., a covenant to build only a one-storeyed house will not be enforceable, whereas a covenant to build house of not more than one storey will be enforceable. This common law principle has been modified by the *Conveyancing and Property Ordinance*, sections 41 and 42, allowing the enforcement of both positive and negative covenants.

- The covenant must touch and concern the land, i.e., the covenant must confer a benefit on the land by protecting its value or amenities, and, not confer a personal benefit. Section 39 of the *Conveyancing and Property Ordinance* assumes that all land-related covenants intend that the covenant's benefits should run with the land unless otherwise stated.[49]

- The person seeking to enforce the covenant must be the landowner – a lesser interest in the property is insufficient to support a claim. As the law only acknowledges legal estates, the covenantee and assignee must hold the same legal estate. Section 39 of the *Conveyancing and Property Ordinance* permits an assignee who takes a legal estate to claim the benefit of a covenant by an assignment at law. A legal lessee or a legal mortgagee can thus claim the benefit upon satisfying the stipulations.[50]

- If the claimant of a covenant's benefit is not the original covenantee, the claimant must demonstrate that the equitable benefit of the covenant has been expressly assigned to the claimant, that this benefit was originally annexed to the land, or, that this benefit relates to land subject to a building scheme or development.
- When a claim is made against the assignee of the original covenantor, it must be proved that the assignee has knowledge (also known as *notice*) of the covenant which burdens the land. Notice can be actual or constructive. Constructive notice is when there has been no exercise of proper diligence in searching documents of title and records in the Land Registry. Sub-lessees are deemed to have notice of covenants contained in the head lease and are therefore bound in equity.
- The right or benefit conferred is enforceable only by injunction rather than by damages.

8
Mortgages

A. Mortgages

The definition of *mortgage* is: the transfer, or the creation, of an interest in land for securing the repayment of a debt or for the performance of an obligation. A mortgage is thus a security interest in real property. The manner in which such an interest can arise in Hong Kong is discussed in this section.

The *mortgagor* is the borrower/debtor in this transaction, and the *mortgagee* is the lender/creditor (usually a bank). The amount of money borrowed is referred to as the *principal*. The mortgage is a personal promise to re-pay the principal and the interest by a certain date, together with a formal conveyancing of the land to the mortgagee as collateral. The mortgagor's possession of the land, however, remains undisturbed. The mortgagor has the right to redemption of the mortgage. In other words, on payment of the debt or fulfilment of the obligation, the mortgagor can exercise this right to re-convey the land back to itself.

Tacking, also known as the right to tack, is a feature of mortgages. Tacking is the right to add a further advance, i.e., a later loan, to the earlier debt which is secured by the mortgage. In effect, this gives the later loan the same priority as the earlier debt. The purpose of tacking is to give priority to the later loan over any intervening mortgages or loans. For example, the mortgagor gives a mortgage for $1 million to Bank A in January. In February, the mortgagor gives another mortgage on the same property for $750,000 to Bank B. In March, the mortgagor gives another mortgage on the same property for $500,000 to Bank C. In April, the mortgagor gives another mortgage on the same property for $950,000 to Bank A. The second loan given by Bank A can be tacked to the first mortgage so that the second loan has higher priority than the intervening mortgages given to Bank B and Bank C.

A mortgage may be given over a freehold estate or over a leasehold estate. Two types of mortgage exist: legal and equitable.[1] These are now discussed below.

B. Legal Mortgage

Prior to the *Conveyancing and Property Ordinance*, a mortgage was made by conveying the interest in land to the mortgagee. This assignment of the title to the land would be subject to re-assignment of the property to the mortgagor upon the repayment of the loan. At law, the mortgagor had to repay strictly in accordance with the mortgage terms. Failure to do so would result in the mortgagee keeping the property, and ending the mortgagor's right to redemption. For example, if a mortgagor was one day late in repaying the loan, the right of getting back the mortgaged property could be forfeited.

Equity dealt with this situation by recognising that a mortgagee intended only to hold the premises as security for the loan, and conferring an equitable right of redemption to the mortgagor. Under this equitable right, the mortgagee is to return the land to the mortgagor upon repayment of the loan, even if payment was made late. Equity thus allows the mortgagor a reasonable extension of time to repay the loan. Equity would not help the mortgagor where the loan repayment was delayed too long or if the limitation period for bringing a redemption action had expired.

Presently, all legal mortgages are created by a charge, which is in the form of a deed stating it is a legal charge. A *charge* is a hypothecation that allows the property (i.e., the subject of the charge) to be taken when the chargor (i.e., the debtor) defaults on the repayment of a debt.[2] Pursuant to section 44(1) of the *Conveyancing and Property Ordinance*, "a mortgage of a legal estate, including any second or subsequent mortgage of that legal estate, may be effected at law only by a charge by deed expressed to be a legal charge."

The same remedies are available to a chargee for a charge created under this section as to a mortgagee holding a mortgage. According to section 44(2) of the *Conveyancing and Property Ordinance*, a charge is in substance a mortgage:

> Under a mortgage effected by a legal charge, the mortgagor and the mortgagee shall, subject to this Ordinance, have the same

protection, powers and remedies (including but not limited to those relating to foreclosure and the equity of redemption but excluding the power of the mortgagee to enter into possession before any default by the mortgagor) as if the mortgage had been effected by way of assignment of the legal estate before the commencement of this section.[3]

If a document is in substance a mortgage, it will be treated as a mortgage by the courts regardless of its title or its form. In the case of *Ng Shou Chun v Hung Chun San* [1994] 1 HKC 155, the parties entered into a main contract for the "sale" of the property with a collateral contract for its repurchase. The court stated at that:

> equity looks at the substance of the transaction, not the form. . . . a sale, with a collateral agreement for repurchase by the vendor within a stipulated time, has been held by the courts to be . . . a transaction by way of mortgage. The undervalue, and the highly unusual provisions of the agreement here, suggest that this was just such a transaction. . . . but the circumstances seem to me . . . to be consistent more with a transaction by way of charge to secure the repayment of [the loan] than with a genuine transaction of sale and purchase.[4]

There is an essential difference between a mortgage and a charge. A mortgage involves the conveyance of property to the mortagee in order to secure repayment of a debt or the performance of an obligation. With a charge, there is no conveyance of property subject to a debtor's right of redemption. Rather, the legal estate remains with the mortgagor, who is capable now of creating subsequent legal mortgages. The charge grants the chargee (i.e., the lender) certain rights over the property as security for the repayment of a loan or the performance of an obligation.

The change created by the *Conveyancing and Property Ordinance* is that a mortgagee is no longer the sole legal owner of the mortgaged property and a mortgagor's rights over the property are no longer limited to the equitable right of redemption. Under the legal charge created by the Ordinance, a mortgagor retains ownership in the property, subject to a mortgagee's rights to use the property as security for repayment of the loan. A mortgagee can now no longer claim to be a holder of a leasehold estate. Today, a mortgagee's interest is an encumbrance upon the land, which gives the mortgagee certain rights over that property which may be exercised should the mortgagor fail to repay the loan.

C. Equitable Mortgage

An equitable mortgage is created by the transfer of the entire equitable interest to the mortgagee, subject to an agreement to return this interest to the mortgagor upon repayment of the loan.[5] The mortgagor's right in equity to redeem the property represents the mortgagor's equitable interest in the property. Under the common law, the mortgagee held the legal estate in the land. In other words, the mortgagee was the legal owner, holding the legal title. Equity, however, recognised the mortgagor as the real owner of the land subject to a mortgage. The mortgagor's equity of redemption could be transferred to the mortgagee. Prior to the 1984 implementation of the *Conveyancing and Property Ordinance*, all subsequent mortgages took effect by an assignment of the mortgagor's equity of redemption, i.e., equitable mortgages. An equitable mortgage can also be created by a charge.[6]

An equitable mortgage is where the mortgagee only receives an equitable interest in the land.[7] The equitable mortgagor has the equity of redemption.[8] Examples of equitable mortgages include a beneficiary under a trust of land or a purchaser under an agreement to buy land.[9] There are several reasons for a mortgagee acquiring only an equitable interest in land. First, the mortgagor's interest in the land may only be an equitable interest. Second, the mortgage may have been informally prepared and thus does not meet the formal legal requirements of a legal mortgage.[10] Because equity treats as done that which ought to be done, equity will still consider the mortgage agreement to be enforceable.

Equitable mortgages may be created by:
- a written agreement which is not accompanied by the deposit of the title deeds
- the deposit of only title deeds without the agreement, if such deposit amounts to part performance of the agreement to give security
- the written agreement and the deposit of documents of title
- a conveyance to a second mortgagee of the mortgagor's interest in the land. As the holder of the first mortgage has the legal interest, any subsequent mortgagees can only acquire an equitable interest.

Equitable mortgages can be registered in the Land Registry. Under section 3 of the *Land Registration Ordinance* (Cap 128), a registered equitable interest in land is effective over prior unregistered interests in this land and interests which are subsequently registered.

The most common type of equitable mortgage found in Hong Kong occurs where a mortgage is given on land held under a Government lease granted with a set of *Conditions of Sale*, which are conditions or requirements not yet satisfied. Until the conditions or requirements have been fulfilled, the grantee does not enjoy any legal estate under the Government lease. The grantee only enjoys an equitable interest in an agreement to grant a lease. Section 46 of the *Conveyancing and Property Ordinance* provides that an equitable mortgage under these circumstances will be converted to a legal charge upon compliance with the conditions and the mortgagor's legal estate is deemed granted.[11]

Following implementation of the *Conveyancing and Property Ordinance*, the mortgagee of an equitable mortgage by deed is given the same powers as a legal mortgagee.[12] An equitable mortgagee cannot deal with the legal estate unless authorised by a power of attorney under seal contained in the mortgage. Where an equitable mortgage is not made by deed, the mortgagee has no power:

• to take possession without a court order
• to sell
• to appoint a receiver

Further, no covenants for title are implied in an equitable mortgage under section 35 of the Ordinance. An equitable mortgagee may apply to an appropriate court for foreclosure upon default.

D. Landholding in Hong Kong – Leasehold Mortgage

As title to land in Hong Kong is by leasehold, focus will now turn to the creation of such mortgages. There are three ways to create a leasehold mortgage. The first method is by assignment. *Assignment* traditionally meant the mortgagor transferred the interest in the land to the mortgagee, placing ownership in the mortgagee. Thus, by an assignment, the leaseholder transfers the entire remainder of the lease term to the mortgagee with the provision for re-conveying upon repayment of the loan by the mortgagor. In an assignment, the mortgagee is effectively substituted for the mortgagor in the landlord-tenant relationship and becomes personally liable to the landlord for the covenants contained in the lease.

The second method of creating a mortgage over a leasehold interest is by sub-demise. *Sub-demise* is where the mortgagor grants a sub-lease to the mortgagee for a term of years which must be at least one day less than the mortgagor's lease. However, in practice, the term is approximately ten days less than the term remaining in the main lease. This practice is to allow time to the mortgagor to grant a subsequent mortgage if desired.

Additionally, the sub-lease will end in accordance with its terms or upon the repayment of principal and interest by the mortgagor. Finally, the mortgagee is not personally liable to the landlord for the provisions of the lease because there is no privity of contract and no privity of estate between the lessor and the mortgagee.

The third manner in which a leasehold mortgage may be created is by a charge. A charge is the security for payment of a debt where the creditor has a right to receive payment out of some specific fund or out of the proceeds of the sale of realty. A charge is preferred over the other two methods as a charge does not require the landlord's consent.

i. Mortgagee's Rights and Remedies

In a mortgage relationship, the parties have certain rights and certain remedies in the event of default. A *right* is a privilege to which a person has a lawful claim. This privilege or interest is recognised and protected by law. A *remedy* is the means provided by law to recover rights, or, to obtain compensation. The general rights and remedies of a mortgagee include several alternatives in the event of a default by a mortgagor.

a. Damages

One choice is to sue for the debt owed under the loan. Suing on the debt is a common law right based on contract as the mortgagor promised to repay the loan. If the mortgagor fails to repay the loan, the mortgagee may sue for the breach of the promise to repay. This remedy is appropriate where the value of land has dramatically increased.

b. Entry into Possession

Another alternative is for the mortgagee (or receiver, as explained below) to take possession of the defaulting debtor's premises:

> At common law, if the legal mortgage is by assignment, the ownership of the legal estate is vested in the lender, who is thus entitled to take possession as soon as the mortgage is executed, even if the mortgagor is not in default. In practice, the mortgage usually states that the mortgagor has quiet possession until default. In fact, this remedy of taking possession is seldom resorted to because the mortgagee is strictly accountable to the mortgagor for any loss occasioned by his own default. He is accountable not only for such rents and other incomes from

the property which he receives, but also for those rents and incomes which he ought to have received had he exercised due diligence and proper management. Under the statutory legal mortgage, the mortgagee does not have possession before default.[13]

Usually, however, the mortgagee would first seek a court order in accordance with Order 88, Rules of the High Court. Courts have restricted the mortgagee's exercise of this right to instances of breach by the mortgagor and in order to protect the security. Section 44(2) of the *Conveyancing and Property Ordinance* has preserved this right.[14] An equitable mortgagee has no right to possession.

Where a tenant lawfully occupies the property, the mortgagee takes possession by notifying the tenant to pay rent directly to the mortgagee. The priority of a mortgagee's and a tenant's interests determine whether the mortgagee is able to secure a possession order against the tenant.

As mentioned above, a mortgagee in possession of the property becomes liable to the mortgagor under lease covenants and is liable to the mortgagor for defaults. The mortgagee is accountable to the mortgagor for the income which should have been received from the property due to the mortgagee's negligence. The mortgagee must take care to maximise the return from the property.[15]

The mortgagee may avoid liability by appointing a receiver to take possession of the defaulting mortgagor's premises. Under section 50(2) of the *Conveyancing and Property Ordinance*, the receiver is "deemed the agent of the mortgagor and the mortgagor will be solely responsible for the receiver's acts and defaults." Where the mortgagor is a company, section 87 of the *Companies Ordinance* requires a notice of possession be filed in the Companies Registry.

c. Foreclosure

The third option is foreclosure, which is an equitable right.[16] Foreclosure allows a mortgagee to obtain a court order ending the mortgagor's right to redeem the property and transferring the legal estate to the mortgagee. This right arises as soon as the contractual date for redemption has passed, but usually is not exercised unless the mortgagor fails to repay for an unreasonable time. The right to foreclosure is available to all legal and equitable mortgagees. The foreclosing mortgagee's rights are subject to any prior mortgagee's rights.[17] The right to foreclose and the right of a prior mortgagee are preserved in the *Conveyancing and Property Ordinance*.[18]

The procedure for foreclosure is set out under Order 88, Rules of the High Court. This Order provides for issuing an order *nisi* to account for the money owed and for its payment within a fixed period, failing which the order *nisi* becomes final.[19] Unlike other jurisdictions, foreclosures are infrequent in Hong Kong. Generally, a Hong Kong mortgagee prefers to exercise its power of possession and sale; or, its power of appointing a receiver.[20]

d. Exercise of the Power of Sale

Another option available to a mortgagee is a sale. In theory, a mortgagee:

> has no implied power to sell the mortgagor's property free from the equity of redemption. In practice, the mortgage deed may contain an express power of sale enabling the mortgagee to sell the property out of court and free from the equity of redemption.[21]

Under the *Conveyancing and Property Ordinance*, a mortgagee can sell the defaulting mortgagor's mortgaged property subject to prior interests, but free from the claim of the mortgagor's right to redeem and free from the claims of subsequent mortgages and all other estates, interests and rights to which the mortgage has priority.[22]

Section 51 of the *Conveyancing and Property Ordinance* and paragraph 8 of Schedule 4 give the mortgagee the power to conduct a sale. Powers of the mortgagee are provided in paragraph 11 of Schedule 4.[23] Section 51(4) permits modifying these powers:

> The powers implied by subsection (1), and the provisions of the Fourth Schedule relating to the exercise of those powers may be varied or extended by the mortgage deed and, as so varied or extended, shall have effect as if contained in this Ordinance.

A mortgagee may be appointed as the attorney of the mortgagor to sell the realty. However, the general practice is for the mortgagee or its appointed receiver to repossess the premises to sell under the statutory power of sale. A mortgagee exercising the power of sale must use due care to secure a proper price for the premises.[24] Should the sale price be less than market price, the mortgagee must make up the difference to the mortgagor or a second mortgagee. A guarantor of the loan is also owed this obligation by the mortgagee.

Section 52 of the *Conveyancing and Property Ordinance* is intended to protect the purchaser at a foreclosure sale:

> Where a sale is made under a mortgage, the title of the purchaser shall not be affected by the fact that no case had arisen to authorize the sale or that due notice was not given or that the power was otherwise improperly or irregularly exercised; but any person who suffers loss through an unauthorized, improper or irregular exercise of the power of sale shall have a remedy in damages against the person exercising the power.

Section 54 of the *Conveyancing and Property Ordinance* regulates the distribution of the sale proceeds. This section states:

> Any money received by a mortgagee or a receiver from the sale . . . shall be applied according to the following priority –
>
> (a) in discharge of all rent, taxes, rates and other outgoings due and affecting the mortgaged land;
>
> (b) unless the mortgaged land is sold subject to a prior encumbrance, in discharge of that prior encumbrance;
>
> (c) in payment of the receiver's lawful remuneration, costs, charges and expenses and all lawful costs and expenses properly incurred in the sale or other dealing;
>
> (d) in payment of the mortgage money, interest and costs due under the mortgage,
>
> and any residue shall be paid to the person who, immediately before any sale or other dealing, was entitled to the mortgaged land or authorized to give a receipt for the proceeds of the sale of that land.

Under section 55(1) of the *Conveyancing and Property Ordinance*, a mortgagee's receipt is a good discharge of the debt:

> A receipt in writing of a mortgagee or a receiver shall be a sufficient discharge for any money arising under a power of sale or for any money or security comprised in the mortgage or arising under it; and a person paying that money or transferring that security shall not be concerned to inquire whether any money remains due under the mortgage.

e. Receivers

The fifth alternative is to appoint a receiver. A *receiver* is an individual appointed either by a court or by a mortgagee to take possession of the property. A receiver is to hold the realty for the purpose of paying the creditors. Pursuant to section 50 of the *Conveyancing and Property Ordinance*, a mortgagee may appoint a receiver when the mortgage money has become due.[25] *Due* refers to the time after the date for repayment or when an instalment is overdue. If payment is on demand, the authority to appoint a receiver arises at the mortgage's creation. This authority is to be in writing. As previously mentioned, the receiver is considered to be the mortgagor's agent. The provisions concerning the appointment of a receiver may be varied or extended by the express terms of the mortgage.

The authority to appoint a receiver is implied in all mortgages by deed, unless expressly contradicted, according to section 51(1) of the *Conveyancing and Property Ordinance*. In practice, the mortgage deed usually provides for the mortgagee to appoint a receiver who has extensive management powers.[26]

> A mortgagee under a mortgage by deed, whether it is legal or equitable, has a statutory power to appoint a receiver provided the mortgage was entered into after 1 November 1984. A mortgage created prior to that date, or an equitable mortgage created otherwise than by deed, must contain an express power to appoint a receiver if the mortgagee is to avoid having to apply to court for the appointment of a receiver under the court's general equitable jurisdiction.[27]

In summary, the appointment of a receiver gives a mortgagee all the advantages of possession without any of the liabilities.

Generally, the first mortgagee has both a common law and statutory right to hold the title deeds of the property until redemption. The mortgagee has the right to transfer the mortgage, e.g., the mortgagee can sell its rights under the mortgage to another party without the consent of the mortgagor. The transfer must be by deed and registered. Another privilege which the mortgagee or its appointed receiver may exercise is lease and surrender, i.e., to grant leases, surrender leases and/or accept the surrender of leases. Insurance may be required by the mortgagee from the mortgagor at its expense in order to insure against damage or loss of the mortgaged property.

ii. Mortgagor's Rights and Remedies

The mortgagor, like the mortgagee, possesses certain rights and remedies. Foremost of these rights is the right of redemption. Under the right of redemption, the mortgagor can redeem or take back the mortgaged property by repaying the loan along with any interest. This right of redemption may be legal or equitable. Legal redemption is provided in the mortgage deed with a set date.

An equitable redemption must be exercised according to the rules of equity. A mortgagor must give prior notice to the mortgagee of the intent to redeem, usually six months' notice or six months' interest in lieu of notice. The mortgage deed may state a shorter notice period. There can be no agreement that disallows redemption as this would be inequitable and therefore would be void.

The mortgagor may take action in order to protect its possessory rights. Under both legal mortgages and equitable mortgages, the mortgagee has no legal right to possession of the property under the *Conveyancing and Property Ordinance*; otherwise, the mortgagor has the right to bring an action for trespass. If the mortgagee takes possession without giving notice to the mortgagor, the latter can sue for possession. Under a legal charge, the mortgagor retains the legal estate and the right to possession until default. The mortgagor is entitled to sue for the recovery of possession of the land, trespass, or other wrong done to the land. The mortgagor may also keep any rental or other profits that may come from the use of the land and may sue for the recovery of such rent or profits.[28]

The mortgagor has the right to lease the land or dispose of the land, but subject to the mortgagee's interests. Thus, the mortgagor has a right to grant a sub-lease, accept surrender of a lease, convey the property to a third party, or, grant a subsequent mortgage unless a contrary agreement is contained in the mortgage deed.

The mortgagor may commit waste so long as the waste does not render the security interest deficient:

> A mortgagor is not under a duty to refrain from committing waste unless the act of waste is so serious as to endanger the security itself. It is common practice, however, for the mortgage to contain both an express covenant from the mortgagor that they will keep the property in good repair, and a right for the mortgagee to enter the property to inspect the state of repair.[29]

Another right available to the mortgagor is to inspect the title deeds. "The mortgagee has a right to hold the title deeds to the mortgaged land to protect his security, but s. 47 of the *Conveyancing and Property Ordinance* gives the mortgagor a right to inspect the title deeds."[30]

PART 3
Conveyancing

In this part, matters relating to Hong Kong conveyancing are presented in the general order in which the typical conveyancing process proceeds: sale and purchase agreement, nature of title, proof of title, assignment, completion and post-completion activities, remedies in the event of breach, mortgages and charges, and landlord-tenant.[1]

However, before proceeding to conveyancing matters, two related subjects, Government leases and the use of deeds of mutual covenants for multi-storey building management, will be reviewed to provide some background information to the material presented in the following chapters.

9

Leasehold Ownership in Hong Kong

In Hong Kong, the Government disposes of land by granting long leases. These were known as *Crown leases* prior to 1997 and as *Government leases* after 1997. With one exception all land held by private persons in Hong Kong in essence are leasehold.[1] Under a Crown or Government lease, the Hong Kong Government is the landlord. For the purposes of this chapter, leasehold estates are treated as realty.[2]

Although a tender system is used occasionally,[3] Government land is usually sold by auction, in which the highest bidder becomes the lessee. The agreement between the Government and the lessee sets out the provisions of the lease.[4] This agreement is known as the *Conditions of Sale*.[5] The amount of the premium payable is the auction bid price.

A certificate of compliance is issued by the Government when satisfied that the requirements under the Conditions of Sale have been met.[6] To encourage performance of these requirements, the Government usually does not allow the lessee to sell or otherwise dispose of the property until the conditions are met.

Signing a Conditions of Sale, rather than the Government lease itself, allows the Government to regulate land development and to avoid unnecessary expense and delay. In fact, despite the terms of the Conditions, which require the lessee to enter into the lease, it is the Government's policy not to issue a lease unless specifically requested.[7] Section 14(1)(a) of the *Conveyancing and Property Ordinance* (Cap 219) considers the Conditions of Sale with the Certificate of Compliance to be the equivalent of a formal Government lease.[8]

Most Crown or Government leases in Kowloon and in Hong Kong Island are granted for seventy-five years, with a right of renewal for a further seventy-five years, with the exception of the early 999-year leases granted between 1849 and 1898. The Crown lease with an option to renew can be renewed at a rent which is fixed by reference to the land's rental value without payment of a further premium. The *Government Leases Ordinance* (Cap 40) sections 3 to 5 automatically extend all renewable seventy-five-year or ninety-nine-year Crown or Government leases in Hong Kong. Articles 121 to 122 of the *Basic Law* now provide for the grant of leases for fifty-year terms.[9]

Leases in the New Territories were formerly granted for a seventy-five-year-term from 1 July 1898, renewable for another term of twenty-four years, less three days. From 1959, New Territories leases ran for ninety-nine years from 1 July 1898, meaning that they expired on 1 July 1997. Section 6 of the *New Territories Leases (Extension) Ordinance* (Cap 150)[10] extended all the leases in the New Territories to 30 June 2047, unless the lessee chose otherwise under section 5 of this Ordinance.[11]

Some Crown leases do not include an option to renew. Upon expiry of these leases, one of the following may occur:

- the land reverts back to the Crown, now the HKSAR Government
- the Government resells the land by auction to the highest bidder
- the Government resells the land to the last lessee at market price or
- the Government grants a new lease or the lessee renews the lease[12]

Non-renewable Government leases due to expire before 1997 may be extended without the payment of any premiums until 30 June 2047 at an annual rental of 3% of the land's rateable value.[13]

As previously stated, pursuant to either section 4 or section 5 of the *Government Leases Ordinance*, the right of renewal contained in the lease shall be considered to have been chosen for renewable Government leases, and under section 9 at an annual rate of 3% of the rateable value of the land.[14] The Government of the Hong Kong Special Administrative Region has stated that it will grant new leases for a term of fifty years without any premium, but at the annual rental of 3% of the rateable value of the land.

A Crown or Government lease is different from the usual landlord-tenant leases in that the former:

- is longer in duration
- has lower rent but a large premium
- contains terms giving the Crown or Government greater control over the development and/or use of the land
- allows the Crown or Government to *resume* (i.e., to take back) land if required for public purposes[15]

Government leases usually contain provisions regulating assignments and sub-letting. If a tenant enters into an agreement to sub-let or under-lease all of the remaining interest in the tenancy, the transaction is referred to as an *assignment*.[16] In an assignment of a lease, only the parties to the lease have changed. There remains only one lease on the estate. In effect, the party receiving the assignment (referred to as the *assignee*) from the original tenant (referred to as the *assignor*) is substituted for the original tenant. A lessee who makes an assignment transfers the remainder of the term to the purchaser (the assignee).

Land sold in Hong Kong is actually the residue or balance of the term of the Government lease that is being assigned by the lessee to the buyer. For instance, an owner who holds a Government lease of land for seventy-five years, of which there are sixty-five years remaining, sells that land by assigning the sixty-five years remaining in this lease to the purchaser. The owner then has no further interest in the land. The assignment of short-term leases is less common. Such leases usually contain a covenant prohibiting the tenant from assigning its interest without the landlord's consent. An assignor remains liable for the performance of the covenants in the lease.[17]

Sub-letting differs from assignment in that the original lessee maintains the original landlord-tenant relationship. The original lessee also creates a new landlord-tenant relationship with original lessee as the landlord and with the new lessee as the sub-tenant. Note that in many cases, the original lease contains a covenant against sub-letting without the original landlord's written consent.

A disposal for a period shorter than the residue of the term of the lease creates a new lease that is a separate interest or estate from the lease out of which it is created. The rental, term and covenants are distinct and need not be the same as the terms of the head lease. For instance, if a lessee holding a lease of seventy-five years wishes to allow another to have possession of the land for only five years of the seventy-five-year term, the lessee will create a sub-lease giving the right to exclusive possession of the land for five years. At the end of the five-year term, the right of possession of the land will go back to the lessee who may take up possession or grant another sub-lease.

10
Multi-storey Buildings in Hong Kong

Multi-storey buildings are the most common type of structure in Hong Kong. Multi-storey buildings are constructed on land held from a Government lease, and can be used for residential, commercial, or industrial purposes, or a combination of these purposes.[1] In relation to multi-storey buildings, one authority has observed:

> There were three main problems with early high-rise developments. First, the regulation of the management of the building had to be provided for. Usually this was done in the form of a deed of mutual covenant (DMC) which was not executed by all purchasers; under the DMC there were difficulties in ensuring that the benefit and the burden of covenants, especially positive covenants, affected all present and future owners of units. The rights of the owners were often subsidiary to the rights of the manager under the DMC; one way to avoid this was to incorporate. Secondly, the developer often wished to retain an interest in the land despite selling all units in the building, thereby disposing of all his rights; this was obtained by reserving rights for himself but without having any obligation to contribute to the upkeep of the building. The terms of the Building Management Ordinance now require the developer to contribute to the various charges associated with ownership of units in the building, or to have retained shares in the development to which an obligation to pay appropriate fees and charges has attached. The third problem concerned the sale of the units prior to completion of the building; this was not lawful by reference to the building covenant. Consequently purchasers could not protect their interests by registration.[2]

This section will discuss the management of multi-storey buildings in Hong Kong by reviewing the schemes of ownership in multi-storey buildings, a review of management of a multi-storey building through incorporated owners, and finally, a review of management of a multi-storey building through a deed of mutual covenant.

A. Ownership Schemes

Ownership schemes seek to address the sale of units prior to completion of a multi-storey building so that buyers may protect their interests by registration of a memorial at the Land Registry.[3] Registration normally would not be possible due to a covenant in the Government lease prohibiting the sale of units prior to completion.

Two schemes exist to achieve this purpose of protection of a buyer's title by registration: the Consent Scheme and the Non-consent Scheme.[4]

i. Consent Scheme

Under the Consent Scheme, a developer may sell units in an uncompleted residential, commercial or industrial development with the consent of the Director of Lands. Once consent is obtained, the sale and purchase agreement between the developer and the buyer can be registered, thus giving the buyer some protection.[5] Certain requirements must be met before the Director of Lands will give consent. Only a brief summary of the points which seem relevant to potential owners of units in a multi-storey building are set out below.

- Consent to sell will be given no more than 12 months prior to the estimated completion date.
- The right to buy a unit will be by ballot.
- The preliminary agreement shall not be a binding contract.
- The formal sale and purchase agreement must be a standard form contract and must be signed by the buyer within three days and by the developer within seven days.
- Only those signing the preliminary agreement are allowed to sign the formal sale and purchase agreement.
- A buyer may not resell, or otherwise deal with the benefit of the sale and purchase agreement, prior to completion and assignment.
- The preliminary deposit will be between 8% and 12% and a further payment up to 20% of the purchase price must be paid within fourteen days of signing the sale and purchase agreement.

- The sales brochure used to advertise the development must be approved by the Legal Advisory and Conveyancing Office of the Lands Department and must contain certain information in a particular form. This information includes details of fittings, finishes, terms of the Government lease, typical floor plan, etc. Additionally, the recent *Residential Properties (First-hand Sales) Ordinance* (Cap 621) has set out further requirements concerning the contents of the sales brochure, e.g., saleable area, cross-section plan, etc.

ii. Non-consent Scheme

The Non-consent Scheme affords protection for buyers of residential units in uncompleted buildings to which the Consent Scheme does not apply, but where the same solicitor represents both the developer and the buyer. This scheme is regulated by the Solicitors' Practice Rules, Rule 5C.[6]

B. Incorporated Owners

Owners' meetings to discuss a building's management under a deed of mutual covenant did not lead to efficient management due generally to a lack of co-operation between the owners. As a result, the owners' committee could not function as a legal body acting on behalf of all owners. Under the former *Multi-Storey Buildings (Owners Incorporation) Ordinance*, owners of a building could incorporate, giving the owners' corporation the authority to act on behalf of all owners in matters of common interest, particularly the management of the building.[7]

Incorporation transfers the owners' powers, rights, duties and privileges in the common property to the corporation.[8] The building's management is controlled by the incorporated owners acting through a management committee.[9] The management committee is responsible for the maintenance of the common areas and the corporation's property, the employment of tradesmen and professionals, insurance of the property and other similar matters.[10]

Owners may incorporate ownership of the building by registering a memorandum of incorporation with the Land Registry. Section 8 of the *Building Management Ordinance* (Cap 344),[11] sets out the procedures for incorporation and regulation of the incorporated owners' conduct.[12] This Ordinance also provides for the dissolution or winding up of the owners' corporation.[13]

C. Deed of Mutual Covenant

A deed of mutual covenant provides for the maintenance and management of the common parts of a multi-storey building.[14] A deed of mutual covenant ensures that the benefit and burdens of the rights and obligations are imposed upon all parts of the land and buildings and go with the ownership so that subsequent owners will be equally bound.[15]

A deed of mutual covenant works like this. A multi-storey building is divided into undivided shares by a document usually known as a deed of mutual covenant.[16] No separate leaseholds are issued to each individual owner. A purchaser buys the undivided shares of and in the building but not in the flat. This buyer does, however, receive the right of exclusive possession of the flat, and perhaps car parking space(s), through the assignment. Each assignee becomes a co-owner (a tenant in common) with the other owners. As tenants in common, they enjoy unity of possession of the land and the building.

On a new development, the first buyer of a unit in the building of undivided shares will, usually at the same time as the signing of the assignment, enter into the deed of mutual covenant with the developer – the owner of the rest of the whole building and, perhaps, the management company.[17] Subsequent buyers of units within the building do not need to enter into the deed of mutual covenant themselves. The assignments to them by the developer will incorporate provisions giving those buyers both the burdens and benefits of the deed of mutual covenant.[18] Subsequent buyers are bound by the deed of mutual covenant by their assignments which incorporate the now registered deed and by several sections of the *Conveyancing and Property Ordinance*.[19] "The most effective way to make the proprietary covenants in the deed of mutual covenant (DMC) enforceable against successors in title to the original parties to the deed, is by registration of the DMC in the Land Registry . . ."[20]

Thus, the rights and obligations of the developer and owners of undivided shares of property are regulated by the deed of mutual covenant. It should address: the owners' shareholding, covenants, personal rights and other matters pertaining to the management of land owned by many parties, and the covenants in the Government lease to which all owners are subject.[21] A deed of mutual covenant is thus a substantial document, typically referring to:[22]

- Regulation of ownership rights
  The allocation of shares and exclusive-use areas are set out. Each owner is given the exclusive right to hold, use, occupy and enjoy the

unit and the enjoyment of the common parts. This right is assigned to subsequent purchasers. The allocation of shares reflects each owner's share in the proceeds of sale of the land if, for example, the building is demolished and the land is sold. The number of shares allocated to a buyer may also determine the responsibility for payment of a proportion of the management and maintenance expenses of the building, but there may be a different division based on management shares.[23] Each owner's voting rights may also be related to the allocated undivided shares.

A developer may retain certain rights under a deed of mutual covenant if some units remain unsold. It is very common for a developer to retain the exclusive right to use some common areas, the right to name the building, the right to advertise on outside walls, and the right to designate common areas.

Other than the parties to a deed of mutual covenant, who have privity of contract, not every right reserved in a deed of mutual covenant is enforceable against the owners of undivided shares. Only those rights attached to the land are enforceable.[24] For example, in the case of The Incorporated Owners of Viking Garden v Golden Brains Ltd [1991] 1 HKC 353 the developer had reserved in the deed of mutual covenant the right to use the roof space of a building and to erect illuminated advertising signs. The Incorporated Owners contended that it had the right to the control, management and administration of the common parts, including the roof structure. The court agreed with the Incorporated Owners, that the developer had no right to place the advertising sign on the roof without the Incorporated Owners' consent.

In Lamaya Ltd v Supreme Honour Development Ltd [1991] 1 HKC 198 the court denied the respondent's right to name the building, a right reserved in the deed of mutual covenant. The court decided that such a right could not be enforceable because the right was a personal covenant rather than a right attached to the land.

- Management and maintenance
  The deed of mutual covenant will also provide for a manager or management company to be appointed and specify any powers and duties, which are usually quite broad. The management agreement, which is a personal agreement, does not confer any rights in the land. In practice, most management agreements are incorporated into the deeds of mutual covenant. Thus the deed binds all co-owners, the developer, and the property manager.

- Owners' representation
  A deed of mutual covenant may contain provisions for an owners' meeting to elect an owners' committee to coordinate with management on policy decisions. In the absence of such provisions, the Eighth Schedule of the *Building Management Ordinance*,[25] formerly known as the *Multi-Storey Buildings (Owners Incorporation) Ordinance*, provides for the collective representation of owners.[26] As explained by one authority:

  > The provisions of the Eighth Schedule . . . unless inconsistent with the terms of the deed of mutual covenant (DMC), are implied into all DMC's and bind the owners and manager. The implied clauses may then be amended, deleted, or re-incorporated into the DMC by a resolution of the owners. The terms in the Eighth Schedule deal mainly with the calling and conduct of meetings of the owners' committee and owners.[27]

  In accordance with section 34E of the *Building Management Ordinance*, the Ordinance's Seventh Schedule[28] has mandatory application in all deeds of mutual covenant, regardless of their commencement date. The Seventh Schedule aims to rectify unfair terms in existing deeds of mutual covenant by regulating the determination of management expenses and the removal of the manager.

  Prior to the commencement of the *Building Management Ordinance*, if any provisions of a deed of mutual covenant were inconsistent with the *Multi-Storey Buildings (Owners Incorporation) Ordinance*, the former prevailed, subject to any express statutory exceptions. The *Building Management Ordinance* now expressly provides that the Seventh Schedule prevails over any inconsistent provisions in the deed of mutual covenant.[29]

Lastly, one should note that a deed of mutual covenant is a contract and as such may be changed or ended under certain circumstances.[30]

11
Sale and Purchase Agreements

A sale and purchase agreement is a written contract for the transfer of an interest in realty, i.e., sale of land. A valid sale and purchase agreement is a legally binding agreement between the parties. In Hong Kong, there are several types of sale and purchase agreements:

- a preliminary agreement
- a formal sale and purchase agreement
- an oral contract, provided there is a written document of some kind recording the contract terms to comply with section 3 of the *Conveyancing and Property Ordinance*.

A formal sale and purchase agreement may be in a standard form, in order to comply with the Consent and Non-Consent Schemes requirements, or the formal sale and purchase agreement may be in the form suggested in Part A of Schedule 2 to the *Conveyancing and Property Ordinance*.[1]

A. General Legal Considerations

As a contract, a sale and purchase agreement requires the elements of a legally binding agreement to be present: agreement or consent, capacity, consideration, certainty of terms and the intent to be legally bound. Disputes arising from the transfer of realty generally involve a party's intention to be legally bound in a formal contractual relationship. This will be reviewed in the next section.

The transfer of an interest in real estate is required to be in writing. The *Conveyancing and Property Ordinance* section 3(1) provides that:

> Subject to section 6(2), no action shall be brought upon any contract for the sale or other disposition of land unless the agreement upon which such action is brought, or some memorandum or note thereof, is in writing and signed by the party to be charged or by some other person lawfully authorised by him for that purpose.

Similarly, section 5(1)(a) of this Ordinance provides that:

> (1) Subject to section 6 –
>> (a) no equitable interest in land can be created or disposed of except by writing signed by the person creating or disposing of the same, or by his agent thereunto lawfully authorized in writing, or by will, or by operation of law.

In Hong Kong, the transfer of realty generally involves a preliminary agreement, followed by a formal sale and purchase agreement. As the *Conveyancing and Property Ordinance* applies to both agreements, these agreements ought to be in writing. An oral contract may be enforced if there is a subsequent document which complies with the requirements of section 3(1).[2] Without anything in writing, an oral contract for the transfer of realty would not be enforceable in the courts, even though the contract may not be illegal or void.

In order to meet the requirements of section 3(1), the document must contain details of the parties, the property, the price and the completion date.[3] Further, any particular terms which the parties intend to include must be placed in the document. The document must be created after the parties made the agreement,[4] and must contain the parties' names or provide an adequate description. A description referring merely to *vendor* would be insufficient, but a description using terms such as *owner*, *proprietor* or *mortgagee* would be sufficient to identify the party.[5] Likewise, the document must sufficiently describe and identify the property, e.g., the address of a flat or the lot number of the parcel of land.

The document must provide the selling price (i.e., the consideration) or a method for determining the price. A court has enforced a sale and purchase agreement as being sufficiently clear where the consideration was to be:

> at such price not being less than £12,000 as may be agreed upon by two valuers one to be nominated by the lessor and

the other by the lessee or in default of such agreement by an umpire appointed by the said valuers.[6]

In contrast, another court held that there was no method for determining the price where an option to renew a lease provided the consideration to be "at such rental as may be agreed upon between the parties."[7] Similarly, a court found that a sale and purchase agreement providing for an agreement to "negotiate a fair and reasonable" price was too vague to be enforceable.[8]

The document must reflect the terms of the oral agreement. If any significant agreed oral terms are omitted from the document, the agreement will be unenforceable. A court decided that a document did not qualify as a note or memorandum where the parties orally agreed upon instalment payments of the purchase price but the document omitted this particular term.[9] Another court reached a similar result where an oral agreement was for the sale of both land and chattels but the document made no reference to the chattels.[10]

Courts will imply terms into an agreement in order to give effect to the contract.[11] However, courts will not re-write an agreement for the parties. Courts will not imply certain terms into an agreement; thus, these terms must be expressly included in the document if they are to be enforceable. In the case of *Kwan Siu Man Joshua v Yaacov Ozer* [1999] 1 HKC 150, CFA the agreement contained only the parties involved, the price and the property. The Court of Final Appeal held that, due to the volatile property market in Hong Kong at the time, the date of completion should be an essential term of any contract. Without such an essential term, there could be no binding agreement. Thus, this open contract was void.

The document must be signed. If only one party signs the document, it may only be enforced against that party. A note signed by an authorised agent may be sufficient to bind the principal. A solicitor, however, has no general authority to enter into contracts on behalf of the client. When expressly authorised, an estate agent can sign an agreement which binds the estate agent's principal.

Wisecal Ltd v Conwell International Ltd [2011] HKEC 967 is a Court of Appeal case which considered the extent of an agent's authority to enter into a preliminary sale and purchase agreement. Conwell, the seller, disputed that it has authorized a friend of Conwell's director and sole shareholder to enter into an agreement with the buyer. Conwell contended that the purported agent was to negotiate a sale but had exceeded the agent's authority by signing the preliminary agreement. The court decided that the agent acted reasonably and in good faith relying on one interpretation of vague instructions which is subject to several interpretations, even if the agent's interpretation is not the one intended by the principal.

The document is to record an agreement. The document must thus be subsequent to the agreement. If the term *subject to contract* appears on the document, the term would prevent a binding agreement. The term *subject to contract* would show that the document was merely a record of negotiations, the terms of which could change, i.e., be *subject to* a later agreement. Thus, the document would not be a note or memorandum for the purposes of section 3(1) of the *Conveyancing and Property Ordinance*.

Generally, the *parol evidence rule* provides that oral evidence will not be considered where it contradicts the terms of a written agreement.[12] An exception is found in collateral contracts where one party makes a promise in exchange for the other party entering into the main agreement. In the case of *De Lassalle v Guildford* [1901] 2 KB 215, the buyer refused to complete the contract until he received a statement that the property's drains were in order. In the case of *Otto v Bolton* [1936] 2 KB 46, the buyer refused to complete the transaction until he received a statement that the house was well built.

Section 3(2) of the *Conveyancing and Property Ordinance* states that nothing in subsection (1) shall affect the law relating to part performance. The courts will enforce an oral agreement for the sale of land by ordering specific performance – but no order for damages – where one party has partially performed the contract. The acts of part performance must, however, be clearly referable to the contract.

Part performance may be found by the payment of money, provided the performance is clearly related to the contract. A husband's payment of money in return for a promise by his wife to transfer the house to him as part of their divorce settlement is an example of part performance. Partial performance of an oral contract may also be found by a party's entry into possession or by the commercial tenant of leased premises installing machinery on the property.

B. Preliminary Agreements/Provisional Agreements

Preliminary agreements, also referred to as provisional agreements, are very common in Hong Kong and are usually prepared by an estate agent and signed by the vendor, purchaser and estate agent. (The estate agent signs the agreement to enable recovery of the agent's fee as part of the contract.)

i. Role of the Estate Agent

An estate agent can serve as the agent for both the seller and buyer in a sale, receiving a commission from both parties. An agent acting for two parties with potentially conflicting interests can only do so with the express agreement of the two parties with full knowledge of the situation.[13] Whether an estate agent will be the seller's agent for the purposes of making representations will depend upon the facts of each case.[14]

For example, a court found an estate agent liable in damages to a buyer where the agent had, whilst acting for the seller, failed to convey a purchase offer from a prospective buyer.[15] In another case, the estate agent's employee informed the buyer that certain illegal structures could be ignored because the management committee would take no enforcement action. The court found that: the estate agent acted as agent for the seller; the seller failed to give good title as the estate agent did not notify the buyer that the Building Authority had issued a removal order relating to the illegal structures; and the seller was liable to the buyer but could be reimbursed by the estate agent.[16]

In most cases, an estate agent will use its own preliminary agreement which will be signed by all the parties: the seller, buyer and estate agent. The terms of this preliminary agreement are generally unfavourable to a buyer. For example, there will often be a clause permitting the seller to withdraw from the agreement upon the payment of twice the preliminary deposit as damages to the buyer.

ii. Contents of Preliminary Agreements

A typical preliminary agreement would include the following items:
- the parties' details
- a description of the property
- the sale price
- payment of the initial deposit, normally 1% of the purchase price
- payment of the main deposit, usually 9% of the purchase price which, when combined with the initial deposit, will equal 10% of the purchase price
- payment of the residue of the purchase price and completion date
- the date for signing the formal sale and purchase agreement
- payment of the expenses of the conveyance and stamp duty
- the purchaser's liability on failure to perform the agreement
- the vendor's right to withdraw upon payment of a liquidated sum to the purchaser[17]

- payment of the estate agent's commission

At times, a provisional agreement's contents, i.e., the terms or words used, raise the issue of whether the parties intend to be legally bound by the document.

iii. Enforceability of Preliminary Agreements

An important issue concerning preliminary agreements is their legality. Whether a preliminary agreement is a contract is often disputed where market conditions might cause one of the parties to wish to withdraw from the agreement. As an example, if the property market rises, the seller might wish to cancel the agreement in order to obtain a higher price for the property from another buyer. If the property market falls, the buyer might wish to withdraw from the agreement as the property would be worth less than the purchase price. Most preliminary agreements are drafted allowing the seller to withdraw from the agreement upon payment of a sum as liquidated damages. In most standard form preliminary agreements, there will be no such provision in favour of the buyer.

Whether a preliminary agreement is binding depends upon the parties' intention as shown by the agreement's terms. The issue is whether signing of a formal agreement is a precondition before the parties become legally bound; or, whether signing of the formal agreement is the method by which the preliminary agreement, which already binds the parties, will be carried out. In Hong Kong:

> . . . whether parties have entered into contractual relationships with each other essentially depends upon the proper understanding of the expressions they have employed in communicating with each other, considered against the background of the circumstances in which they have been negotiating . . . Where they have expressed themselves in writing, the proper construction of the writing against that background will answer the question. The purpose of the consideration is to determine whether the parties intend presently to be bound to each other or whether . . . they do not so intend until the occurrence of some further event, including the signature of some further document or the making of some further arrangement. The question is one as to expressed intention and is not to be answered by the presence or absence of any particular form of words.[18]

If the signed preliminary agreement states that "the vendor agrees to sell and the purchaser agrees to buy," the agreement is likely to be binding. In the case of *Yeung Siu Hong v Chan Siu Mee Sandie* [1992] 2 HKC 559, the court interpreted a preliminary agreement which omitted this phrase as an "agreement to agree" rather than as a binding agreement.

Branca v Cobarro [1947] 2 All ER 101 is a case where the language in the agreement provided that "this is a provisional agreement until a fully legalised agreement drawn up by a solicitor and embodying all the conditions herein stated is signed." There was a provision requiring payment of a deposit. The court determined the agreement to be legally binding, noting that the required payment indicated the intent to be legally bound.

The case of *Chan Yock Kwong v Wong Hee Mao* [1962] HKLR 480 involved a Chinese-language agreement stating that the formal agreement was to be signed within one week and that a deposit was payable by the buyer upon signing this document. The agreement also provided that if the buyer defaulted, the deposit would be forfeited. Should the seller default, twice the amount of the deposit is to be paid as compensation to the buyer. The court stated that:

> both the parties were clearly determined to hold themselves . . . bound, but realized the desirability of a formal document . . . it was a provisional agreement to last until superseded by the formal agreement . . . [The clauses] contained provisions for the manner in which the transaction, already agreed to was to go through, and they do not . . . suggest that the fully legalized agreement is in any sense to be a condition to be fulfilled before the parties are bound. . . . the full terms of the transaction were agreed . . . which agreed terms were to be reduced into a more formal shape, and it is to be noted that the parties themselves admitted that the agreement accurately set out what they agreed . . . as the formal agreement, which was to supersede the present agreement, has never been signed, the present agreement remains operative . . . it is a binding contract.[19]

In a complicated case involving the seller, buyer and estate agency, the court determined that the preliminary sale and purchase agreement was not a contract. In *Phoneyork Co Ltd v Chesson International (Holdings) Ltd* [2012] HKEC 751, the court concluded that an undated preliminary sale and purchase agreement signed by Chesson along with cheque was not legally binding. An endorsement on the back of the cheque stated: "This cheque is only to be used and valid for the sale of the Building at the asking price of HK$158 million. This cheque, if not successful after exceeding 30 days, shall be returned within 10 days." A third document, a memorandum prepared before the preliminary sale and purchase agreement along with the cheque, was presented to the seller, Phoneyork, stated in part:

3. Our Company [Chesson] requests to see the vendor as soon as possible, to specifically discuss the matters in relation to the purchase.

4. This cheque is only to be used and valid for the sale of the Building at the asking price of HK$158,000,000.

5. The cheque was handed over [to the estate agency] on 29 September 2007, if the transaction is not successful after 30 days, the cheque shall be returned within 10 days.

Chesson argued that the cheque's endorsement was to ensure the cheque was not presented to a bank by Phoneyork. The memoranda was intended to ensure a face-to-face meeting between the seller and buyer to negotiate the sale price, as until this time, all communications were made through the estate agency. Chesson also argued that the estate agency made misrepresentations.

After rejecting the testimony of the estate agency's three staff members involved in this case, the court made the following decisions:

63. . . .

. . . it is conceivable that Mr Kai [of Chesson] was so confident in his own ability to persuade the owner to reduce the price . . . that he was prepared to sign the [preliminary sale and purchase agreement] and write the [cheque] for the initial deposit . . . He was prepared to do so because that was the only way, so he had been told by the estate agents, for him to secure a meeting with the owner. And he sought to protect his own position by requiring the estate agents to sign the . . . [memorandum] and even to bring the [cheque] back to him a few days later to add . . . [the endorsement] on the back . . .

. . .

68. . . . considering the circumstances . . . the only reason for making . . . [the memorandum and the cheque's endorsement] is that Mr Kai did not regard the . . . [preliminary sale and purchase agreement] as

> binding, and that he wanted to have something in writing
> so as to protect the defendant before he had a chance to
> meet the plaintiff. . . .

Chinese-language agreements, often headed *lum see hip yee* or *lum see* (臨時協議或臨時), have also raised similar difficulties in interpretation. The courts have applied the same criteria – determining the parties' intentions – to these agreements as to preliminary agreements. In the case of *Lam Wa Leung v So Chung Shek* [1983] 2 HKC 630 the court interpreted the term *lum see* as meaning temporary or provisional; yet the court held that naming an agreement *lum see* would not automatically preclude a legally binding agreement. In another case, *Lam Mean-soon v Luk Fuk Enterprises Ltd* [1980] HKLR 741, the court found a *lum see* agreement to be binding, where the translation stated, "This order is only of temporary nature. Both parties must attend and sign a separate formal Sale and Purchase Agreement."[20] The judge stated that the court:

> should not rivet its attention on one word and determine the
> nature of the document on that word alone, but that no matter
> how unambiguous that word may be when used in isolation, it
> should regard the whole document so as to see the context in
> which the word was used and thence to perceive the intention
> of the parties.[21]

Thus, the same test of intention will apply to *lum see* agreements as to other preliminary agreements.

If the preliminary agreement is not binding, the buyer will be entitled to the return of the deposit. If the preliminary agreement is binding, the general principle is that the initial deposit will be returned to the buyer if the agreement is not completed, unless stated otherwise in the preliminary agreement. A seller should ensure a provision in the preliminary agreement for forfeiture of the deposit in the event of breach by the buyer. The deposit may not be forfeited if the forfeiture is a penalty rather than a genuine pre-estimate of loss.

A conditional agreement expressly states that the agreement is *subject to* or *conditional upon* a particular event, e.g., subject to contract or subject to the securing of a mortgage. If the condition is a condition precedent, there will be no binding agreement until the condition is met, e.g., the contract is signed or the mortgage is secured.[22] If the condition precedent is too vague, the agreement might be void for uncertainty. This would be the situation where the contract's validity is based upon the condition precedent. Thus if the condition precedent is void, the contract does not come into effect.[23]

A general principle states that a conditional contract is not binding until the condition precedent is fulfilled. In the case of *Lung Yuk-lun v Gratefulfit Industrial Ltd* [1992] 1 HKLR 1, the mortgagee's consent to the sale of the realty was a condition precedent. The seller failed to obtain the mortgagee's consent. Consequently, the court held the agreement to be unenforceable by the buyer, even though the buyer was prepared to redeem the equitable mortgage "and that would have ensured . . . that the lender would have given its consent . . .".[24]

Another general principle is that the phrase *subject to contract* in a preliminary agreement constitutes a condition precedent. The parties will not be bound until the formal agreement has been signed. However, there are two exceptions to this general rule.

The first exception is where the words are determined to be meaningless in the context of the agreement or in the factual situation. For example, where the parties are already bound by a preliminary agreement and the term *subject to contract* is used in subsequent correspondence, the words will have no effect.[25] The term might also have no effect in the factual circumstances. For example, in a case involving a tender, the letter of acceptance used the term *subject to contract*. The court found these words to be meaningless since all the terms of the agreement were already contained in the documents.[26]

The second exception to the general rule is where the parties to the agreement have subsequently waived the effect of *subject to contract*. The Court of Appeal held in *Law v Jones* [1973] 2 All ER 437 that the parties could subsequently agree to waive the term *subject to contract* and thereby create a binding contract. The court in *Cohen v Nessdale Ltd* [1981] 3 All ER 118 recognised that this exception applies in a limited number of cases and that the waiver could be either expressed or implied from the parties' conduct.

Occasionally, after entering into a binding preliminary agreement or an *open contract* (a contract containing only the essential terms: parties, property and price) the parties fail to agree the terms of the formal sale and purchase agreement. The parties therefore proceed upon the basis of either the preliminary agreement or the open contract. The courts will imply all the necessary terms in order to implement the agreement.[27]

For example, courts have implied the following terms:

- that the seller will assign its full interest in the property
- that the seller will show and give good title to the property

- that the subject property will be free from encumbrances except for those specifically set out in the contract
- that time is of the essence for the completion of the contract
- that where no date for completion of the contract is specified, completion will be effected within a reasonable time of the seller showing good title
- that the buyer has the right to inspect the property prior to completion
- that the buyer may raise requisitions on title[28] within a reasonable time after the receipt of the title documents
- that the seller will give a good title in the assignment[29]
- that the seller will give vacant possession upon completion
- that the seller will deliver all relevant title deeds relating exclusively to the property to be assigned to the buyer upon completion

Because the parties are legally bound by the preliminary agreement, insertion of clauses in the formal sale and purchase agreement inconsistent with the terms of the preliminary agreement requires the other party's consent. A court stated thus:

> Where a party presses for a term which does not properly . . . reflect a provision agreed as part of the provisional agreement . . . [and] where the other party rejects inclusion of that term, then it is clear that the original party is able to fall back upon the provisional agreement and enforce it as an open contract . . . The intended subsequent agreement was to make formal and express what had been informal and perhaps only implied. Failure to achieve the desired formality does not affect the contractual rights and obligations already in place by virtue of the underlying provisional agreement.[30]

Another court reached the same conclusion where the seller wanted to put into the formal sale and purchase agreement restrictions upon the buyer's right to raise requisitions on title.[31] The same principle applies to the inclusion of new terms by the buyer.[32] The courts will allow those terms or conditions which would be implied into an open contract to be included in the formal agreement.

C. The Formal Sale and Purchase Agreement

The formal sale and purchase agreement replaces the preliminary agreement. The formal sale and purchase agreement contains the detailed provisions governing the sale. Only provisions consistent with the terms of the binding preliminary agreement may be inserted in the formal sale and purchase agreement unless the other party agrees to the inclusion of other provisions.

i. Generally

In cases where the parties have separate legal representation, the agreement is drafted by the seller's solicitor and approved by the buyer's solicitor. Joint representation of parties to a conveyancing transaction by a solicitor is generally prohibited because of the potential conflict of interest. However, there are exceptions to this general prohibition. Rule 5C of the Solicitors' Practice Rules provides that a solicitor may not represent more than one party to a conveyancing transaction except:

- where the Consent Scheme applies and its regulations are followed, e.g., use of the approved sale and purchase agreement
- where the Non-Consent Scheme applies and its regulations are followed, e.g., inclusion of the required mandatory terms in the sale and purchase agreement
- where there is a first sale of a completed development, provided the mandatory agreement is used
- where there is a sub-sale in any of the above three situations (confirmatory sale)
- where the parties are relate parties
- where the consideration is less than $1 million
- mortgages
- leases[33]

The form of the formal sale and purchase agreement may be:
- in the standard form required for agreements made concerning sales of realty governed by the Consent Scheme
- in the standard form and containing the mandatory clauses prescribed for agreements made in relation to sales of realty governed by the Non-Consent Scheme
- in the approved form and containing the clauses required for first sales of property where the parties are jointly represented
- in the approved form and containing the mandatory clauses in respect of a sub-sale of property in the above three cases where there is joint representation of the parties
- in compliance with Form 2 of Schedule 3 of the *Conveyancing and Property Ordinance* (The parties may choose to incorporate by reference the clauses in Part A of Schedule 2 to the Ordinance.[34] This

form and the incorporated clauses may be varied or amended by
agreement of the parties.)
- in the form and with the contents decided upon by the parties and
their solicitors

ii. The Contents of the Sale and Purchase Agreement

This section reviews the terms and conditions of a sale and purchase
agreement. The sale and purchase agreement selected for this discussion is
Form 2, set out in Schedule 3 to the *Conveyancing and Property Ordinance*.
This document is titled *Agreement for Sale of a Residential, Commercial,
Industrial or Other Unit in a Completed Building* (hereinafter referred to as
the "Form"). This agreement is in two parts: the terms or the conditions
of the agreement and a Schedule containing the property description.
Identified below and briefly discussed are some of the more common
clauses found in the Form.

Also reviewed is the document titled *Covenants and Conditions Which
May Be Incorporated by Reference*, which is set out in Part A of Schedule
2 of the *Conveyancing and Property Ordinance* (hereinafter referred to as
"Part A"). Section 36 of the Ordinance provides that the terms in Part
A may be incorporated into the parties' agreement. Consequently, the
conditions will not apply unless the parties have expressly incorporated
the terms in full or in part.

Clause 1 of the Form is the agreement by the vendor to sell and the
purchaser to buy the property described in the Schedule and the property
interest to be sold. Clause 1 states that "The Vendor sells and the Purchaser
purchases the land described in the Schedule hereto ("the Property") for
the residue of the term of years created by the Government lease referred
to in the Schedule."

This language is appropriately used where the seller holds the legal
estate and is conveying it to the buyer. If the seller holds an equitable
estate, the seller can only sell what it has: the equitable interest.[35] In this
instance, the wording should be "The Vendor sells and the Purchaser
purchases all the former's estate, right and interest in the land described in
the Schedule hereto ("the Property")".

Clauses 2 and 3 of the Form concerns to the sales price, the deposit
and its disposition. The purchase price, stated in Clause 2, is usually
payable in three stages. The first stage is the initial deposit, usually 1%
of the purchase price payable on signing the preliminary agreement. The
second stage is the main deposit, normally 10% of the purchase price

payable on signing the formal sale and purchase agreement. This amount is reduced to 9% if the initial 1% deposit has already been paid at the signing of the preliminary agreement. The third and final stage involves payment of the remainder of the purchase price on completion.

Pursuant to Clause 3 of the Form, the main deposit is to be paid to the seller's solicitor, not as agent for the seller, but as stakeholder. The purpose is to safeguard the deposit money. Should the seller's solicitor receive the buyer's deposit, as agent for the seller, the seller can require its agent (i.e., the seller's solicitor) to pay the deposit over to the seller:

> The task of a stakeholder, when paid a deposit by the parties to a contract of the sale of property . . . is to hold the stake upon the happening of the events that are specified in the contract. Thus, if in due course the sale of the property is completed or for any reason the deposit is forfeited, it would be his duty to pay over that money to the vendor. Alternatively, if for any other reason the sale is not proceeded with, he must pay the money to the purchaser.[36]

Failure by the buyer to pay the deposit will allow the seller to cancel the contract and sue for damages.

Clause 4 of the Form provides for completion and payment of the remainder of the purchase price. Matters relating to completion, e.g., apportionment of expenses, rents and outgoings, are found in Part A. Clause 4 of the Form provides for completion in person (known as *formal completion*) where the seller, buyer and their solicitors, and where appropriate, the solicitor of the parties' mortgagees, meet together in the seller's solicitor's office and the seller signs the assignment in the presence of the purchaser and receives the remainder of the purchase price. Instances of formal completion are rare in Hong Kong. More commonly, completion is accomplished by *undertaking* in Hong Kong. The parties' agreement to completion by undertaking must be stated in the sale and purchase agreement. This right to complete by undertaking will not be implied by the courts.[37]

Clause l of Part A provides:

> The rents and profits shall be received and all outgoings shall be discharged by the vendor up to and inclusive of the actual day of completion, and as from but exclusive of that day all outgoings shall be discharged by the purchaser. All such rents, profits and outgoings shall, if necessary, be apportioned between the vendor and the purchaser and paid on completion.

This provision stipulates that outgoing items, e.g., Government rent, rates, management fees, electricity fees, water charges and telephone charges, will be paid by the seller up to and including the day of completion and all subsequent charges shall be the buyer's responsibility. The seller, as a rule, sends the buyer a completion statement identifying these charges and their apportionment. The buyer typically pays what is owed to the vendor at the date of completion.

The parties should agree and stipulate the method of payment of the remainder of the purchase price, e.g., by cashier order or bank certified cheque. Unless agreed beforehand, payment by personal cheque will not be acceptable.

Clause 5 of Part A governs conveyances subject to tenants. A seller generally will give vacant possession of the property. If the premises are sold subject to a tenant, reference should be made to Part A's Clause 5. Vacant possession is interpreted to mean that there are no occupants of the property; and, that there is no physical item left in the premises which might interfere with the purchaser's enjoyment of the property.[38] The buyer should also seek an express provision by the seller that no other interests exist in the property, e.g., tenant's interests.

Clause 6 of the Form provides that: "Time shall in every respect be of the essence of this Agreement." Should a party desire time to be of the essence, this provision should be inserted in the agreement. Inclusion of this provision in a formal sale and purchase agreement is important in relation to the buyer's obligation to complete in a timely manner. The seller can consider any delay by the buyer as a breach of the agreement and the deposit can be forfeited.[39]

If the parties agree that completion shall take place on or by a certain date, the midnight rule will apply – the parties have until midnight on the specified date to complete the transaction. There will be no flexibility where the parties have specified in the agreement the precise time by which completion must take place. "When the parties appoint a specific time by which acts are to be performed, they have said by implication that those acts cannot be performed beyond that time, in accordance with the contract."[40]

Clause 8 of Part A provides:

> Such of the documents of title as are required for the purpose of giving title to the property shall be delivered to the purchaser. All other documents of title in the possession of the vendor shall be retained by the vendor who shall, if so required on

completion of the sale, give to the purchaser a covenant for safe custody thereof and for production and delivery of copies thereof, such covenant to be prepared by the purchaser.

If this condition is not included in the sale and purchase agreement, the courts will require the seller to deliver to the buyer at completion all the title documents relating exclusively to the property assigned.[41]

Clause 7 of Part A, concerning requisitions on titles, states:

(1) Any requisition or objection in respect of the title shall be delivered in writing to the vendor's solicitors as soon as practicable after delivery of the title deeds and, in any event, not later than 14 days prior to the date of completion.

(2) If the purchaser shall make and insist on any objection or requisition either as to title or any matter appearing on the title deeds or otherwise which the vendor shall be unable or (on the grounds of difficulty, delay or expense or on any other reasonable ground) unwilling to remove or comply with, or if the title of the vendor shall be defective, the vendor shall notwithstanding any previous negotiation or litigation be at liberty to annul the sale in which case the purchaser shall be entitled to the return of the deposit but without costs or compensation and, if that return is made within 7 days, without interest.[42]

The first section of this clause provides for the raising of requisitions on title.[43] The time limitation will not prevent the buyer from raising requisitions of which it was unaware from the title deeds supplied, even after the agreed period has expired if the requisitions go to the root of the seller's title.[44] Where the buyer should have known of a title defect from the documents provided, the requisition must be made within the agreed time limit. However, the buyer may not, simply because the requisition goes to the root of title, raise the requisition later where the defect could have been uncovered within the agreed time limit through due diligence.[45]

The second section allows a seller to cancel the agreement when unable or unwilling on certain specified grounds to give a good title. Four elements are required:

• the buyer's objection or requisition
• the seller's reasonable inability or unwillingness to remove the objection

- the seller's communication to the buyer of this inability or unwillingness
- despite this communication, the buyer insists upon the objection[46]

The second section of Clause 7 of Part A does not apply where a seller has bad title, or, has acted in bad faith or recklessly in entering the contract. This exception will apply if the seller knew of the defect when entering the contract.

Clause 3 of Part A reinforces the common law principle concerning the condition of the property: "The purchaser purchases with full knowledge of the physical condition of the property and takes it as it stands." Thus, the buyer bears the risk of the property being defective and requiring repair. The seller has no obligation to notify the buyer of known defects.[47]

There might be liability if a seller or its agent misrepresents facts or warrants the condition of the property. In this case, the buyer may recover damages but cannot rescind the contract. Clause 6 of Part A provides, in part, that:

- No error, omission or misstatement herein or in any plan furnished or any statement made in the course of the negotiations leading to the contract shall annul the sale or entitle the purchaser to be discharged from the purchase
- Any such error, omission or misstatement shown to be material shall entitle the purchaser to proper compensation, provided that the purchaser shall not in any event be entitled to compensation for matters falling within clause 3 or 5(3) hereof
- No immaterial error, omission or misstatement (including a mistake in any plan furnished for identification only) shall entitle either party to compensation
- The *Misrepresentation Ordinance* (Cap 284) applies to this agreement

Clause 11 of the Form provides that the "stamp duty and land registration fees payable on the assignment made pursuant to this Agreement shall be borne by . . ." In order to avoid doubt, the parties should make clear in the sale and purchase agreement which party or in what proportions will be responsible for the legal costs, the stamp duty and the registration fees. Responsibility for payment of these fees is subject to negotiation. This is discussed in more detail below.

Legal fees for the drafting and for the approval of a sale and purchase agreement are usually paid by the party incurring the fees, i.e., the seller pays its own solicitor's fees for drafting the agreement and the buyer pays its own solicitor's charges for approving the agreement. Legal fees incurred by the buyer's solicitor for drafting and by the seller's solicitor for approving the assignment are to be paid by the buyer according to the agreement. However, section 34A of the *Conveyancing and Property Ordinance* stipulates that where the parties are separately represented, any term in the sale and purchase agreement requiring the buyer to pay the seller's legal costs will be invalid in the following situations:[48]

- the sale of a flat in an uncompleted development
- the first sale of a flat in a completed development by the developer
- the sub-sale of the flat in either of the above situations

A buyer might consider including the following terms in the sale and purchase agreement concerning the property's condition and the enjoyment thereof:

- there are no illegal structures on the premises and that any structure in or on the premises has been erected in accordance with the *Buildings Ordinance* (Cap 123) and its regulations[49]
- the seller has received no notice requiring the demolition, repair or reinstatement of the premises or the surrounding slopes
- the seller has received no notice from the co-owners or manager of the building to carry out repairs or improvements of a substantial nature to the common parts of the building
- the seller has received no notice under the *Lands Resumption Ordinance* (Cap 124) or any similar notice relating to the resumption of the property

If the buyer wishes to enter the premises before the completion date for purposes such as renovation or decoration, the parties should make express provision in the agreement and the buyer should be permitted to enter as a licensee.[50] The agreement should provide:

- for the buyer to observe the covenants and conditions in the Government lease and in the deed of mutual covenant
- for the buyer to pay the outgoings for this period
- for the buyer to indemnify the seller in respect of any liability the seller might suffer as a result of this early occupation

The buyer should also consider including a related clause that early entry or use of the premises does not imply acceptance of the title.

A seller is entitled to recover the management deposit paid pursuant to the deed of mutual covenant. The parties might agree that the buyer repays the management deposit to the seller and the seller agrees to ensure that the manager will repay the deposit to the buyer when the buyer sells the property. In such an agreement, a buyer is at risk because the promise to repay the management fees is a personal one. If the seller or the mortgagee conveys the property to a third party, the buyer will be unable to compel that third party to refund the management fees.[51]

A sale and purchase agreement should deal with the matter of fixtures and fittings. Fixtures and fittings to be sold as part of the property should be specified in a separate schedule to the agreement. As fixtures pass with the land, theoretically fixtures need not be listed separately. However, to prevent a dispute whether an item is a fixture, the parties should include the item as part of the sale. As fittings are not considered to be part of the land, they are not subject to stamp duty. Therefore, the sale of fittings would best be included in a separate clause or schedule in the sale and purchase agreement which would include a separate price for the fittings. The seller should state that the fittings are not subject to claims by other parties.

To ensure a trouble-free transaction, a buyer should include in the sale and purchase agreement the right to inspect the property prior to completion. Although this is an implied contractual right, an expressed provision to this effect should be considered for inclusion in the agreement.

Stamp duty is paid on the sale and purchase agreement for residential property. The *Stamp Duty Ordinance* (Cap 117), section 29B(5) provides, in part, that the following information be provided in all sale and purchase agreements:[52]

- whether the property is residential or non-residential
- that the agreed consideration is set out in the agreement
- that the completion date is stated in the agreement
- that any other payments made in respect of the sale are set out in the agreement, e.g., commissions to estate agents

The parties should explicitly agree the available remedies in the event of a breach of the sale and purchase agreement. Clause 10 of Part A pertains to a buyer's default and provides in part:

> If the purchaser shall fail to comply with any of the terms and conditions of the agreement the deposit money shall be absolutely forfeited as and for liquidated damages (and not as a penalty) to the vendor who may (without being obliged to tender an assignment to the purchaser) rescind the agreement and either retain the property the subject of the agreement . . . or resell the same . . . Any deficiency arising

> from such resale and all expenses attending the same . . . shall
> be made good and paid by the purchaser . . .

This clause provides that the buyer's breach would result in forfeiture of the deposit to the seller and possible liability for any difference, i.e., any loss in the subsequent re-sale of the property to another party. Unless justified as a genuine pre-estimate of loss, the forfeiture of a deposit would be considered as an unlawful penalty.[53] The conventional deposit of 10% of the purchase price, however, will be subject to forfeiture upon rescission even if there is no evidence that it is a genuine pre-estimate of loss. The deposit represents an earnest intention of performance, which was liable to forfeiture on rescission. "There is no principle of law to the effect that a genuine deposit may not be effected by more than one payment."[54] If the amount of the deposit is a conventional sum, its forfeiture has been held by the courts to be justified in the event of the buyer's breach.

> [The] court will uphold provisions for the forfeiture of a
> deposit, *inter alia*, where it is shown that the deposit did not
> exceed a conventional percentage of the purchase price even if
> it in no way represents a genuine pre-estimate of the vendor's
> loss.[55]

Clause 11 of Part A pertains to a seller's default, providing in part:

> In the event of the vendor failing to complete the sale in
> accordance with the terms of the agreement it shall not be
> necessary for the purchaser to tender an assignment to the
> vendor for execution before taking proceedings to enforce
> specific performance of the agreement or for damages for
> breach of the agreement.

Clause 12 of Part A provides that the seller and any other necessary parties will sign a proper assurance to the buyer. This means the seller will convey its interest in the property by the proper and effective means, i.e., an assignment.

D. Remedies

The contractual remedies available to the seller and buyer in the event of a breach of contract by the other party include:
- specific performance of the agreement by the breaching party
- the innocent party may accept the other party's repudiatory breach as discharging the innocent party from future obligations

- rescission by the innocent party
- an action for damages
- any remedies expressly provided in the sale and purchase agreement[56]

i. Specific Performance

A contract for the sale of land is specifically enforceable: A grant of specific performance by the courts compels a defendant to perform specifically the terms of the contract. This equitable remedy is for cases where the contract's subject matter is considered to be unique and land is considered to be unique.

Specific performance is available where one party fails to complete by the agreed date regardless whether time is of the essence. Specific performance may also be granted in favour of a sub-buyer against the seller even where the original buyer is uncooperative. Specific performance is a desirable remedy for a seller where the market is falling or for a buyer where the market is rising.[57] Note that this remedy is available only where the innocent party is able and willing to fulfil its own obligations under the agreement.[58]

Specific performance is discretionary. A court may refuse the remedy if:

- the party seeking specific performance has been guilty of delay, i.e., *laches*
- the contract is void or voidable, e.g., misrepresentation or mis-description is involved[59]
- specific performance is impossible, e.g., the property has already been assigned to another person who is an innocent third party entering into the contractual relationship
- prejudice or hardship to third persons are of such a nature as would result in an unjust outcome if specific performance is granted[60]
- there has been inequitable conduct on the part of the party seeking specific performance, e.g., fraud or undue influence
- constant court supervision is required

The remedy of specific performance can be expressly excluded in the sale and purchase agreement.

ii. Repudiation and Rescission

Where one party commits a repudiatory breach of the contract, the innocent party may consider the repudiation as ending its contractual obligations.[61] If the innocent party chooses to accept the repudiation, there is no requirement that this acceptance be made within a reasonable time, provided the innocent party shows no signs of continuing with the contract in the interim. In *Cox v Crook* [1981] ICR 823 the court said:

> If one party . . . commits a repudiatory breach of the contract, the other party . . . can choose one of two courses: he can affirm the contract and insist on its further performance or he can accept the repudiation, in which case the contract is at an end. The innocent party must at some stage elect between these two possible courses . . . But he is not bound to elect within a reasonable or any other time. Mere delay by itself (unaccompanied by any express or implied affirmation of the contract) does not constitute affirmation of the contract; but if it is prolonged it may be evidence of an implied affirmation . . . [62]

In Hong Kong, *Ford Joint Ltd v Keen Lloyd (Holdings) Ltd*, unreported (1999) HCA 21393/1998 applied this statement of law.

A party accepting the repudiation is discharged from further performance under the contract. The injured party may also seek damages. By waiving the right to rescind the agreement and thus continuing with the contract, the innocent party loses the right to be discharged. For example, in the case of *Hillier Development Ltd v Tread East Ltd* [1993] 1 HKC 285, CA a waiver occurred when the buyer, despite a defective title, sent a draft assignment and asked the seller as to the payment of the remainder of the purchase price.[63]

The innocent party may rescind the agreement. That party may rescind where the circumstances surrounding the making of the contract would allow the innocent party to treat the contract as void *ab initio*.[64] For example, where mistake, undue influence or fraud affected at least one party during negotiations leading to the formation of a contract, rescission is possible. To rescind, it is essential that the parties can be placed in the same position they were in prior to the making of the contract, in other words *restitutio in integrum* must be possible. Because the parties are put back in the position they were in before the contract came into being, there is no damage and thus there will be no award court of damages.

iii. Action to Recover Damages

Damages may be awarded for breach of contract:
- independently of any other remedy

- in place of or in addition to an order for specific performance
- upon the innocent party's acceptance of the repudiation of the contract

Damages are not available as a remedy where the innocent party has rescinded the contract.

A buyer may seek damages for a breach of the sale and purchase agreement while choosing to complete the contract. This situation might arise where the property's value is less than the contract price, e.g., as a result of the seller's mis-description of the realty. In *Watson v Burton* [1957] 1 WLR 19 the court awarded damages because of the seller's mis-description as to the land's saleable area. In *Citilite Properties Ltd v Innovative Development Co Ltd* [1997] 2 HKC 74, the seller declared the property's saleable area to be approximately 1,000 square feet more than it actually was. The court concluded that the claimant did not receive the benefit of its bargain and awarded damages for the lower value of the premises. In the case of *Santani Ltd v Shum Shuk Fong* [2013] HKEC 104, the plaintiff paid approximately HK$2.5 million above the value of the flat in anticipation of continued use of leased government land which Ms. Shum had converted into a garden. The court decided that Ms. Shum committed fraudulent misrepresentation by saying that the plaintiff could continue use of the garden when Ms. Shum was aware of government notices to her to remove illegal structures in the garden. Consequently, the court ordered Ms. Shum to repay approximately HK$2.1 million to the plaintiff, i.e., the value of the flat without the garden.

On a related matter, in a move towards consumer protection in relation to the sale of new flats, the government has imposed the *Residential Properties (First-hand Sales) Ordinance* (Cap 621). To avoid misstatements of the kind discussed in the preceding paragraph or other "sharp" or questionable practices in relation to newly constructed flats, this new law regulates such matters as: the contents of sales brochures, price lists, saleable areas, show flats, etc.[65]

Section 17 of the *High Court Ordinance* (Cap 4) provides that the court may award damages in addition to or in substitution for the remedies of an injunction or specific performance. Monetary damages, in addition to specific performance, may be awarded where the innocent party has suffered losses which the remedy of specific performance could not compensate, e.g., the purchaser lost rental income for the period completion was delayed.

Upon the wrongful repudiation by one party, the innocent party may choose to accept the repudiation, rescind the contract and sue for damages. This might be the only remedy available for the injured party if, for whatever reason, specific performance is unavailable.

The innocent party may recover damages in respect of loss that flows from the breach or which was within the knowledge or contemplation of the parties. This principle is stated in the case of *Hadley v Baxendale* (1854) 9 Ex 341:

> [such damages may be recovered] as may fairly and reasonably be considered arising naturally, i.e., according to the usual course of things, from such breach of the contract itself, or such as may reasonably be supposed to have been in the contemplation of both parties, at the time they made the contract as, the probable result of the breach of it.[66]

The case of *Victoria Laundry (Windsor) Ltd v Newman Industries Ltd* [1949] 2 KB 528 clarified this test: reasonable foreseeability or predictability depends upon the parties' knowledge at the time they enter into the contract. For example, in *Haw Hong International Ltd v Kei Oi Wah Linia*, unreported, (1990) HCA 3582/1989, the tenants of the property repudiated the agreement. The landlord accepted the repudiation and relet the premises at approximately 30% lower rent as a result of the intervening Tiananmen massacre on 4 June 1989 which created uncertain social and economic conditions. In determining the damages to be awarded to the landlord, the court found that the events in Beijing were not totally unpredictable to the public in Hong Kong. Hence, the damages were foreseeable.

Should a buyer fail to complete, the seller will be able to obtain damages calculated as the difference between the contract price and the market price at the time of the property's resale less any forfeited deposit. Hence, if property market values fall in the interim, damages may be considerable; if the market rises, damages, if any, will be nominal.

The actual sale price is often the best evidence of the market price. As the court noted in *Hee Tak Lee Co Ltd v Keen Lloyd (Holdings) Ltd*, unreported (1999) HCA 20799/98:

> The price at which the seller has resold is strictly not to be taken in preference to the market price, but it has been taken in most cases on the ground that the resale price affords good evidence of the market [price].

The seller can also recover any costs of the resale. Repair expenses or reinstatement expenses may be recoverable where the buyer was allowed early occupation and damaged the property. The seller cannot recover legal costs paid for the failed transaction or the estate agent's fees paid.[67]

A buyer may rescind the agreement and seek damages where a seller commits a breach of the contract, other than by failing to give good title. A buyer's damages would be the difference between the contract's purchase price and the costs of purchasing a similar property on the open market, i.e., the market value.[68] A court will admit the sale/purchase prices of comparable property in order to assist in determining market value. The buyer may also recover as damages any deposit paid and costs involved in the new purchase.

Certain expenditures will not be recoverable by a buyer as damages where a seller breaches the contract other than by failing to provide good title. These unrecoverable expenditures include any stamp duty paid on the sale and purchase agreement, estate agent's fees and legal costs incurred in the failed transaction.[69]

Damages are usually determined or assessed as of the date of the breach. For a seller, this application will determine the seller's damages by ascertaining the property's market price at the date of the buyer's breach. For a buyer, this application will determine the buyer's cost of acquiring a similar property in the open market at the time of the seller's breach.

The exception is where, at the court's discretion, justice requires the amount of damages to be assessed at another time. The date of assessment is important where the property market is experiencing wide fluctuations. Where a seller is in breach and the market is rising, the buyer may be awarded damages assessed at a later date than the date of the breach.[70] Where a buyer is in breach and the market is falling, damages may be awarded in favour of the seller as at the date of the actual resale of the property, provided the seller does not unreasonably delay the sale.[71] Where a seller fails to minimize its loss, the courts may decline to award the difference between the contract price and the actual sale price obtained.[72] The courts will also look to a later date than the date of the breach for the assessment of damages where the innocent party attempts, although unsuccessfully, to obtain specific performance of the contract.[73]

Where a seller is in breach of contract by failing to give good title, the buyer's damages are limited[74] to recovery of the deposit with interest, conveyancing costs (e.g., fees for approving the sale and purchase agreement, and, drafting the assignment), and, stamp duty.[75] There are three exceptions to the rule. The first exception involves a fraudulent seller.[76] The second exception involves a defect in title which arose after the signing of the sale and purchase agreement but prior to completion.[77]

The third exception is where the seller has failed to take reasonable steps to remove the defect in title.[78]

iv. Other Remedies

The parties may agree the remedies available either in the preliminary agreement or in the formal sale and purchase agreement. If properly worded, these remedies in the event of breach may exclude any other remedies or damages to the innocent party. The following provisions are commonly found in such agreements.

a. Forfeiture of Deposit

Clause 10 of Part A provides:

> If the purchaser shall fail to comply with any of the terms and conditions of the agreement the deposit money shall be absolutely forfeited as and for liquidated damages (and not as a penalty) to the vendor who may (without being obliged to tender an assignment to the purchaser) rescind the agreement and either retain the property the subject of the agreement or any part or parts thereof or resell the same . . .

Thus this statutory provision provides for the forfeiture of the deposit to the seller upon the buyer's breach.[79] A deposit of 10% or less of the agreed purchase price will usually be treated as a genuine pre-estimate of loss. In *Sung Wai Kiu v Wong Mei Yin* [1997] 1 HKC 288, the court found that the forfeiture of a 35% deposit to be a penalty. An exception can, however, be found in *Polyset Ltd v Panhandat Ltd* [2000] 4 HKC 203, where the court allowed forfeiture of a 35% of the purchase price deposit, finding it to be a genuine pre-estimate of loss considering the lengthy period between contract formation and completion as well as the property market's volatile fluctuations.

Another exception concerns confirmors where a sum exceeding 10% is considered to be a proper deposit.[80] Generally, forfeiture will depend on the terms in the contract. In *Wan Moon Ling Wandy v Sino Gain Investment Ltd* [1997] 2 HKC 592, the buyer gave two deposits which together amounted to 10% of the total price. Upon default, the buyer claimed that the second payment should not have been forfeited because the second payment was part of the purchase price. The court stated that both payments were intended by the parties to be a deposit to secure or guarantee performance of the contract because the agreement described the first payment "as an initial deposit and the second payment . . . as 'further deposit and part-payment of purchase money.'"[81]

In the event of the buyer's breach, the seller can keep any part payments and the deposit by the buyer only if the sale and purchase agreement so provides. In the case of *Goldspeed Investment Ltd v Easy Success Enterprises Ltd* [2000] 2 HKC 183 the buyer paid a HK$2,520,000 deposit along with two instalment payments of HK$2,520,000 each towards the purchase price of HK$25.2 million for a floor of a commercial building under construction. The buyer failed to complete, resulting in the seller keeping the monies paid. The buyer sued for the return of the two instalment payments. The seller eventually sold the premises for HK$10,200,000 along with another floor for a total of HK$35.3 million. The court determined, in relation to the seller's right to keep the instalment payments, that:

> payments in the event of determination of the agreement could only have arisen from the terms of the agreement. . . . [Absent] such term, the defendant [vendor] would not be entitled, on the termination of the agreement, to retain the part payments as security for any loss it might sustain on a resale.[82]

The court concluded that the contract clause did not allow the seller to deduct unliquidated damages from the part payments; however, the seller's counterclaim:

> is sufficient to extinguish the plaintiff's [buyer] claim for return of the part payments . . . As against a claim arising out of a transaction between the parties, there could be set-off in equity a cross claim arising under the same transaction whether sounding in debt or unliquidated damages . . . [83]

b. Liquidated Damages – Payable by Seller

Commonly in preliminary agreements, there is a clause allowing the seller to pay the buyer double the initial deposit as liquidated damages if the seller fails to complete. This clause would also specify that the buyer shall have no other remedy, either for specific performance or for damages. The courts have held that this clause, if clearly drafted, is enforceable and would thus limit the buyer to only an award of liquidated damages.[84]

The clause will be construed *contra proferentem*.[85] Should a seller fail to make prompt repayment of the deposit together with an equal sum as stipulated in the agreement, specific performance would remain available to the buyer. The clause is required expressly to exclude specific performance. The court granted the remedy of specific performance in *Cheung Bing Sum Juana v Lee Leo* [1994] 3 HKC 132 where the provision stated, "[i]n the event of a breach, I [the vendor], apart from compensating the deposit in double, shall also be liable for the losses incurred by the purchaser, Mr. Leo Lee."[86] Likewise, in *The Thompsett Mind Ltd v Triumph Field Ltd*, unreported (1993) HCA 1826/1992 the court allowed specific performance where the clause stated that if the seller failed to complete, "the vendor shall immediately compensate the purchaser with a sum equivalent to the amount of the initial deposit as liquidated damages together with a refund of the initial deposit." Both clauses did not exclude specific performance.

c. Liquidated Damages – Payable by Buyer

The parties may agree to include a clause in the sale and purchase agreement that the buyer, upon breach, will pay the seller liquidated damages in the amount of the difference between the contract sum and the sum obtained by the seller upon eventual sale. The Court of Appeal enforced such a clause in *Bestech Development Ltd v Fu Wai Loi*, unreported (1992) CACV 121/1992 where the court stated that a calculation for damages did not include the expenses arising from the letting of the property prior to resale to another buyer after the original buyer's default or the interest paid by the second buyer for the delay in completion. The court stated:

> On those facts the question for decision on the appeal is this: Is the purchaser entitled to be credited against his liability to the vendor for the deficiency on the resale with the sums received by the vendor which, but for the purchaser's breach of contract in failing to complete the original sale, the vendor would not have received? The answer is that the purchaser is not so entitled. It is clear law that the intention of the parties in the case of liquidated damages is to be implemented by holding the plaintiff entitled to recover the stipulated sum on breach without requiring proof of the actual damage and irrespective of the amount of the actual damage . . . [87]

A sale and purchase agreement may contain a provision that the buyer may cancel the agreement by paying double the preliminary deposit. The Court of Appeal upheld such a clause in *Cheong Pik Shan v Lee Bun*, unreported (1994) HCA 3113/1992.

d. Exclusion of Common Law Remedies

Similar to the rules governing exclusion of the remedy of specific performance, common law remedies, e.g., damages, can be excluded by including a specific provision in the sale and purchase agreement. In *Goldspeed Investment Ltd v Easy Success Enterprises Ltd* [2000] 2 HKC 183, the parties had a contract provision that the buyer, if in default, should pay any deficiency in the resale price if the premises were resold within six months. The realty was not resold within that time period. The court found that the contract provision did not replace the common law right to damages.

E. Assignment

The function of an assignment is to transfer title from a transferor (the seller) to a transferee (the buyer). An assignment is given effect by a legal document known as a *deed*. The required form of the assignment is determined by whether the transferor possesses a legal or equitable interest in the estate.

i. Formal Requirements and Practices

Section 4(1) of the *Conveyancing and Property Ordinance* provides that a legal estate in land can be created, extinguished or disposed of only by deed.[88] Section 4(2) of the Ordinance provides the exceptions to the general rule found in section 4(1).[89] These exceptions involve the:

- assent by the personal representative(s) of a deceased
- surrender, e.g., of a lease
- grant, disposal or surrender of a lease taking effect in possession for a term not greater than three years at the best rent which can be reasonably obtained
- creation or disposal of a legal estate by operation of law; e.g., a deceased's property vesting in the Official Administrator by operation of law (*Probate and Administration Ordinance* (Cap 10))

Where an assignment is in writing but does not amount to a deed, the courts may exercise equitable jurisdiction by construing the assignment as a contract to assign.[90] If the contract can be specifically enforced and if no discretionary bars prevent such action, the assignee (the person receiving the assignment) could enforce the contract of assignment.[91] Before specific enforcement of the contract, the assignee is regarded as having equitable title to the property.[92]

Section 5(1)(a) of the *Conveyancing and Property Ordinance* states in part, "no equitable interest in land can be created or disposed of except by writing signed by the person creating or disposing of the same . . . "[93] The exceptions to this general rule include the following situations:

- leases for less than three years can be created orally pursuant to section 6(2) of the *Conveyancing and Property Ordinance*
- possessory titles acquired without any written document[94]
- partial performance of an oral agreement to sell land may make the agreement enforceable
- proprietary estoppel[95]

An assignment is usually prepared by the buyer's solicitor. An exception involves the assignment of a flat in a large development, where all the assignments are usually drafted by the developer's solicitor to ensure uniformity.[96] A sample form, *Assignment of a Lot or Section of a Lot or of a Residential, Commercial, Industrial or Other Unit in a Completed Building*, is provided in Form 1 of Schedule 3 to the *Conveyancing and Property Ordinance*. The use of this form is not mandatory.

The date to be inserted in the assignment should be the deed's delivery date, i.e., the date on which the assignment takes effect as the obligation to stamp and register the document is calculated from the date of the deed.

All the required parties to the transaction must be included in the assignment. It is no longer necessary to make successors in title parties to an assignment as section 39(1) of the *Conveyancing and Property Ordinance* states: "A covenant relating to any land of the covenantee shall be deemed, unless the contrary intention is expressed, to be made with the covenantee and his successors in title and persons deriving title under or through him or them." Section 40(1) provides the same for the covenantor:

> A covenant relating to any land of a covenantor or capable of being bound by him, shall be deemed, unless the contrary intention is expressed, to be made by the covenantor on behalf of himself, his successors in title and persons deriving title under or through him or them.

A buyer's failure to sign an assignment for the sale of realty does not invalidate the document. In *Choi Hung Investment Co Ltd v Chinco Investment Ltd* [1995] 1 HKC 203 the court found that, "the absence of a valid execution of an assignment by the assignee does not affect title to the property. It might affect the enforceability of the covenants . . . but not his title . . . "[97]

A mortgagor or chargor is a required party to a mortgage or charge. Therefore, this party should sign the documents in order to give them effect. The mortgagee or chargee is a necessary party to the reassignment or to the discharge. Therefore, the mortgagee or chargee needs to sign in order to have a valid document.

For deeds of gift, the only necessary or required party is the donor, who must sign the deed.

ii. Confirmations

A confirmation occurs where the seller agrees to sell property to Buyer₁ but, before completion, Buyer₁ agrees to sell the same property to Buyer₂. In this scenario, assignment of the legal estate will be directly from the seller to Buyer₂. Because Buyer₁ has an equitable interest in the subject property under the sale and purchase agreement, Buyer₁ signs the assignment in order to convey its equitable interest in the property to Buyer₂. Therefore, the necessary parties are: seller, confirmor (Buyer₁) and, where covenants are given, the ultimate owner, Buyer₂.[98]

At present, the Hong Kong Government has prohibited certain confirmation sales in an attempt to cool an over-heated property market.

> The Lands Department will disallow confirmor transactions of first-hand uncompleted flats which are granted pre-sale consent by the department . . . In other words, purchasers of those flats will not be allowed to re-sell, sub-sell or transfer the benefits of the agreements for sale and purchase before completion of the transaction.[99]

Should confirmation sales be permitted in the future, an example of a confirmation gone wrong is the case of *Qualihold Investments Ltd v Bylax Investments Ltd* [1991] 2 HKC 589 where the court decided that in order to be an effective confirmation, a corporate confirmor must sign the deed in accordance with its articles of association. In this case, the claimant rejected an earlier conveyance of the property made by Fullway Ltd as a corporate confirmor. The claimant refused to complete the sale because of a defective title. Fullway's corporate Memorandum of Association and Articles of Association provided that every document be considered as properly signed if sealed with the company seal and signed by any two directors or the managing director. Only one director had signed the document on behalf of Fullway and this person was not the managing director at the time and was not authorised by a vote of the board of directors to sign the document. The court decided the claimant need not proceed with the purchase of the property because:

- Fullway failed to assign such interest as it had in the property by a duly executed assignment
- Fullway's purported request and direction to the vendor to assign the property to Purchaser$_2$ was ineffective
- Fullway's purported covenant that it had not created a defect or encumbrance affecting Purchaser$_2$'s title to the property was also ineffective

The principles of *Qualihold* are very limited today unless a company's Articles of Association completely exclude the operation of the *Conveyancing and Property Ordinance*.

iii. Nominations

A similar procedure occurs with nominations.[100] A sale and purchase agreement may contain a provision that the seller agrees to sell to the buyer or to its nominee. The buyer may then in writing nominate Buyer$_2$ to take the assignment. The necessary parties to the assignment will thus be the seller and Buyer$_2$ if giving any covenants. Buyer$_1$ should relinquish any interest it may have in the property to ensure that Buyer$_2$ receives an unencumbered title.

The full names of the parties, both English and Chinese, signing the document should be given together with their Hong Kong identity card numbers and addresses. Depending upon the facts of each case, difficulties might arise over the use of names. In *Tsang Bing Kwan Andes v Korea Marvel Co* [1997] 3 HKC 565 the court noted:

> Amongst those deeds was a confirmation dated 12 October 1996 stating that Korea Marvel Co Ltd had changed its name to Hansol Electronics Inc as of 31 October 1995. . . . the confirmation was executed almost a year after the change of name and that notwithstanding the change of name, the provisional agreement was entered into by the vendor under its old name. A requisition was raised, inter alia, relating to this change of name. . . . The vendor does not only have to make good title at completion but is also under an obligation to show good title by properly answering the requisitions raised by the purchaser at a reasonable time before completion is due to take place.

In the present case, by supplying documents in a foreign language after the close of business on 23 December, the date for completion, the defendant had clearly not discharged its obligations.[101]

The court decided that the buyer could cancel the contract. On the other hand, in *Sunluck International Development Ltd v Hing King Development Ltd* [1997] 4 HKC 134, the court held that two errors in the Chinese characters of the seller's name presented no real risk, on the facts, to the buyer.

iv. Covenants and Obligations

The covenants for title are regulated by section 35(1) of the *Conveyancing and Property Ordinance*.[102] The provisions of the sale and purchase agreement will determine which covenants of title should be incorporated into the assignment. Covenants for title are important because the doctrine of merger provides that the terms of the sale and purchase agreement merge into the conveyance upon execution of the assignment. In order to remain valid after the assignment is signed, the terms contained in the sale and purchase agreement must be specifically stated in order to provide further protection for the buyer.

Where a seller assigns as beneficial owner, the following covenants are incorporated:

(a) that the Government lease exists and is valid

(b) that so far as the same relates to the land assigned:
1. the premium and Government rent have been paid
2. the covenants, terms and conditions contained in the Government lease and any deed of mutual covenant have been observed and performed up to the date of the assignment

(c) that the covenantor/seller has good right and title to assign the land free from encumbrances except as specified in the assignment. This covenant replaces the sale and purchase agreement's provision that the seller will give good title

(d) that the land may be entered and enjoyed by the assignee without any lawful interruption or disturbance. This is the covenant for quiet enjoyment of the property. The seller must give the buyer possession of the assigned land and this possession must be free from physical disturbance by the seller, its agents or its servants[103]

(e) a covenant for further assurance at the buyer's cost. (The covenant for further assurance provides that, at the buyer's expense, the seller will correct any defect(s) in title after completion.)[104]

The liability of a seller who assigns as beneficial owner does not amount to absolute legal responsibility. The seller's liability extends only to a breach committed by:

- the seller
- any person through whom the seller has derived title other than by purchase, e.g., liability for the acts of anyone who gave the property to the seller as a gift
- any person assigning by the direction of the seller
- any person claiming through the seller otherwise than by purchase, e.g., mortgagees, lessees and licensees who obtain an interest in the property from the seller

On the part of the assignor assigning as a donor, there is only an implied covenant on the part of the donor for further assurance under section 35(1)(c) of the *Conveyancing and Property Ordinance*. Under section 35(1)(d), involving situations where the assignor assigns as a trustee, confirmor, mortgagee under power of sale, legal chargee under power of sale, or personal representative, the only covenant for title is that the person assigning has not encumbered the title.

v. Mortgages

Where a mortgagor/chargor charges the property as beneficial owner, the covenants implied in the legal charge are the same as for a seller who assigns as owner, except that:

- the covenant for quiet enjoyment applies only if the mortgagee/chargee takes possession of the premises
- the covenant for further assurance is at the borrower's cost
- the chargor also covenants that it will continue to pay Government rent and perform the covenants in the Government lease during the duration of the mortgage or charge

vi. Co-ownerships and Multi-storey Buildings

Land held by tenants in common requires a seller to assign its right to exclusive occupation along with simultaneously assigning some of its undivided shares.[105]

A property developer may assign a fixed number of shares to a buyer and keep the remainder. The developer may allocate the remaining shares as it desires, provided the total number of shares is not increased. Unless prohibited in the deed of mutual covenant, a subsequent owner of undivided shares may divide those shares and sell them to different buyers. A seller is not required to show the share allocation to the other flats. The seller is only required to show the number of shares allocated to the flat to be assigned.

In order to sell shares in a multi-storey building, the number of shares allocated to the seller needs to be accurately set out. The case of *Lee Tak Chun v East Weal International Ltd* [1994] 1 HKC 722 involved the allocation of 227 shares to a building's 35th floor which the owner then divided into twelve separate units. The court held that the seller could not pass good title as there was no clear allocation of the shares to each of the units by the sub-deed of mutual covenant. The case of *Marking Ltd v Cheerifat Investment Ltd*, unreported (1995) HCMP 2727/1995 had the opposite outcome. In this case, there were 138 shares in the building allocated to the whole ninth floor where the owner partitioned the space into separate units. The shares were then allocated to each unit in a control card and the share apportionment instrument was registered. The court held that the seller had good title as there was a clear allocation of shares to the units, even though there was no sub-deed of mutual covenant. Likewise, in *Goldjet International Investment Ltd v Ling Ki Wai* [1997] 3 HKC 503, the subdivision registers had been opened based upon assignments of flats and the control card showed the allocation of shares. Thus, good title had been shown.

F. Completion

Completion involves the payment of the purchase price by the buyer in return for the seller signing the assignment. Post-completion involves the stamping and registration of the assignment. Completion is frequently made more complicated by the involvement of a purchaser's mortgagee. The seller's mortgagee may also be involved in this process where the seller intends to pay off the outstanding mortgage from the funds received from either the buyer or the buyer's mortgagee.

i. Completion Practices

As mentioned earlier, completion may either take place in person, known as *formal completion*, or by way of *solicitors' undertakings*. With formal completion, which is infrequent in Hong Kong, all the involved parties' solicitors attend, usually at the office of the seller's solicitor. The purchase money is given to the seller and, where appropriate, to its mortgagee. Any outstanding mortgage(s) is paid in full, following which the seller signs the assignment.

Completion is more commonly accomplished in Hong Kong through solicitors' undertakings.[106] Completion by way of mutual undertakings consists of the cheque for the purchase money being sent to the seller's solicitor in return for a promise by the seller's solicitor to return the documents within a specified time. If the property is subject to a mortgage which will be paid in full before completion, there ought to be separate cheques: the amount of money required to discharge the mortgage will be paid in one cheque made payable to the mortgagee, and the remaining amount in another cheque made payable to the seller's solicitor.[107]

Each method of completion has advantages and disadvantages. The advantages of formal completion include:

* safe procedure for vendors and purchasers
* relatively expeditious procedure
* safety for the purchaser's mortgagee and the purchaser in that the assignment and mortgage can be registered almost immediately and in time to comply with the backdating provisions of the *Land Registration Ordinance* (Cap 128)

A disadvantage of formal completion is the logistical arrangements required to enable all the parties and/or their solicitors to be present. Also multiple sales of high-rise buildings make formal completion impracticable.

The advantage of completion by undertaking is that it is convenient for solicitors and mortgagees. This is particularly applicable in the sales of multiple units in high-rise buildings. There are several disadvantages to completion by undertaking:

* time delay; particularly by a vendor's mortgagee in signing documents. This delay adversely affects the stamping and registration for priority purposes, as documents should be registered within one month of execution. Penalties for late stamping may also be incurred. It is improper to misdate intentionally a document for the purposes of gaining priority in registration.
* the solicitor provides the undertaking whereas the client signs the documents. The solicitor cannot require the client to honour the undertaking.

ii. Stamp Duty

Stamp duty[108] is payable upon every conveyance on sale,[109] including the sale of property but not gifts of property or mortgages of property. If the sale of property is below market value, the Stamp Office will assess the true value of the property and charge duty on the true value.[110]

Residential property sales require the sale and purchase agreement, rather than the assignment, to be stamped.[111] The stamp duty on the sale and purchase agreement is assessed on an *ad valorem* basis.[112] Where the full stamp duty has been paid on the sale and purchase agreement, the assignment is only stamped with a nominal $100 stamp. This would not apply where a nominee of the purchaser is involved, because the assignment is made to a person other than the purchaser named in the sale and purchase agreement. In this circumstance, the *ad valorem* stamp duty must be paid again.

The stamp duty normally is due within 30 days of the signing of the sale and purchase agreement or the assignment. If a preliminary agreement is replaced by a formal agreement between the same parties on the same terms within the first 14 days allowed for stamping, the time for stamping the subsequent agreement is 30 days from the date of its signing. Stamp duty should be paid promptly so that the stamped document can be registered.[113]

iii. Land Registration

The *Land Registration Ordinance* creates a system of public record for the registration of deeds, conveyances, judgments and other instruments affecting realty. This type of land registration system is called a deeds registration system. In order to protect one's property interests, the holder of that registerable interest in land must register an instrument which shows that interest. Priority is given to registered instruments either in accordance with the date of registration or as otherwise provided by law.[114] Registration also makes easy the tracing of title and determining whether there are any defects in that title.

Under this registration system, the doctrine of notice has been modified. As explained by one authority:

> The terms of the Land Registration Ordinance operate to preclude a registering party being affected by notice of a prior unregistered, [but] registrable interest except perhaps in cases where the conduct of the registering party has amounted to

actual fraud. This is contradictory to the terms of section 4 of the Ordinance. So it would require the court to accept that the elements of "bona fide" cannot allow protection to a purchaser who is "mala fide". The consequence is that although notice is irrelevant – the conduct of the purchaser has been such that the court cannot overlook the deceit or "moral turpitude" of his actions. The ability to ignore the prior interest even extends to those prior interests under which the interest holder is in occupation of the land at the time the registering party enters into his contract. However, if the occupier's interest is not in writing, then section 4 is inoperable, and the incoming purchaser may find he takes subject to the prior interest of which he had notice. Further, the Ordinance provides that an unregistered interest in writing is null and void against the registering party even if he had constructive notice of it, prior to registration.[115]

Section 2(1) of the *Land Registration Ordinance* provides:

> The Land Registry shall be a public office for the registration of deeds, conveyances, and other instruments in writing, and judgments; and all deeds, conveyances, and other instruments in writing, and all judgments, by which deeds, conveyances, and other instruments in writing, and judgments, any parcels of ground, tenements, or premises in Hong Kong may be affected, may be entered and registered in the said office in the prescribed manner.

The following documents, also referred to as *instruments*, should be registered: sale and purchase agreements, assignments, deeds of mutual covenants, mortgages and charges, discharges of mortgages, certificates of compliance, occupation permits, *lites pendentes*,[116] charging orders, covenants, powers of attorney affecting land and long term leases.[117] The exceptions to this rule include:

- short-term leases (i.e., for less than three years) do not have to be registered[118]
- floating charges are not registrable, but should be registered upon crystallisation (浮動押記具體化)[119]
- licences do not affect land and therefore may not be registered
- wills cannot be registered

Regulation 5 of the Land Registration Regulations (Cap 128A) states that registration is made by delivering the instrument together with a memorial of the instrument in the prescribed form to the Land Registry.[120] Under Regulation 7 of the Land Registration Regulations, the memorial must be prepared and verified by a solicitor. Regulation 8 requires that any plan mentioned in or attached to an instrument delivered for registration must be colour coded as specified in the Second Schedule so that the colour can be identified, e.g., R (red), Y (yellow), etc.

Registration of property instruments does not confer ownership rights but does affect priority of the instruments. Under section 3(1) of the *Land Registration Ordinance*, all instruments shall have priority according to their respective registration dates. The exception is found in section 5 of the Ordinance which provides that all instruments registered within one month of the date of execution shall have priority according to their execution dates.

Another exception, also found within section 5, pertains to charging orders and *lites pendentes*.[121] A duly registered charging order or *lis pendens* will have priority from the commencement of the day following the date of registration of the order *nisi*.[122] The case of *Wong Kam Wing v Cyril Murkin (HK) Ltd* [1989] 2 HKC 603 states that the priority of charging orders depends on the order of registration of the orders *nisi* rather than dates of the orders absolute.

In another case, two banks were seeking priority of their charging orders. *Incorporated Owners of Century Centre v Bank of China* [2011] HKEC 864 involved the following time line:

- Bank of China [hereinafter BOC] registers its charging order *nisi* on 14 June 2001
- BOC then registers the above which has now become a charging order absolute on 23 July 2001
- HSBC registers its charging order *nisi* on 17 August 2002
- HSBC then registers the above which has now become a charging order absolute on 18 October 2002
- BOC re-registers its charging order absolute on 13 August 2005
- HSBC re-registers its charging order absolute on 7 September 2007
- BOC re-registers its charging order absolute on 27 September 2010

The court determined that the BOC charging order absolute had priority over HSBC's charging order. Consequently, the funds were to be paid first to BOC with any remainder to be paid to HSBC.

Example I[123]

An assignment is signed on 1 July and registered on 10 August. A charging order *nisi* was registered on 2 August. *Prima facie* the effective date of the assignment is 10 August. The provision in section 5 relating back to date of execution provision does not apply as the assignment was not registered within 30 days of its execution. The charging order takes effect the day after the registration of the order *nisi*, i.e., that is 3 August. Therefore, the charging order should take priority over the assignment and the assignee is bound by the charging order. However in *Yau Siu Yeung v Wing Sum Lo* [1988] HKC 693 and *Ng Kam Ha v Vincent Sina Traders* [1987] HKLR 1193 the court held that the seller had conveyed all its interest in the land at the date of the assignment's execution, regardless whether the assignment was registered. As the assignment predated the charging order, the property is not affected by the charging order.

Example II

A sale and purchase agreement is signed on 1 July and registered on 20 July. A charging order *nisi* is registered on 10 July. The assignment is signed on 15 July and registered on 20 July. The charging order binds the land as, at the time of its registration, the seller still holds the bare legal estate, as the equitable interest in the property has passed to the buyer. The charging order binds the property and the buyer must pay the purchase money to the chargee to the extent that is necessary to discharge the order. Coming to a similar conclusion, the court in *Tse Fook Choy, Joey Callan v Kwong On Bank Ltd* [1999] 3 HKC 126 at page 131 held that "no charging order created after the date of the contract could gain priority to the interest of the purchaser or his successors in title" Section 3(2) of the *Land Registration Ordinance* stipulates that all documents relating to land, which are not registered shall be absolutely void as against a subsequent *bona fide* purchaser or mortgagee for valuable consideration. This does not apply to interests exempt from registration, such as short-term tenancies.

iv. Title Registration[124]

As discussed in the previous section, the Land Registry provides a record of interests in real estate by registering deeds relating to each property and establishes the priority of each document. The register does not make any representation concerning the ownership or the validity of documents that have been registered.

Approximately a decade ago, Hong Kong sought to replace the current deeds registration by title registration. Under a title registration system, each time there is a transaction concerning a particular property, the Land Registry makes a determination of the new ownership. The act of registration conveys the title to the new owner and the title register gives a clear statement as to the owner. The historical documents are no longer needed to prove title. As a general rule, unless a matter is recorded on the title register it will not affect the title of an owner.

The Legislative Council enacted the *Land Titles Ordinance* (Cap 585) in 2004. However, for various reasons, this legislation has not come into effect. In the past few years, changes to the law have been considered in order to overcome perceived shortcomings in the law's implementation and operation. Consultations are ongoing as of mid-2013. Upon conclusion of the consultations, the Land Titles (Amendment) Bill will be drafted by the Land Registry for submission to the Legislative Council.[125]

As this law is not yet finalized due to the amendments and as this law has not come into being, nothing further needs to be discussed at this time.

Notes

Chapter One

1. The Hong Kong Government's Bilingual Laws Information System's *The English-Chinese Glossary of Legal Terms* [hereinafter *BLIS Glossary*] translates *common law* as "普通法" and *common law jurisdiction* as "普通法司法管轄區". See the *BLIS Glossary* website at: http://www.legislation.gov.hk/eng/glossary/homeglos.htm

2. For a general introduction to personal property, see, e.g., Bruce Welling, Property in Things in the Common Law System (1996); Michael Bridge, Personal Property Law (3rd ed. 2002); Sarah Worthington, Personal Property Law: Text, Cases and Materials (2000); and Simon Gleeson, Personal Property Law (1997).

3. *Interpretation and General Clauses Ordinance* (Cap 1), section 3. The *Official Solicitor Ordinance* (Cap 416), section 2(6) translates *property vested in* as "轉歸予 . . . 的財產".

4. See 20 Halsbury's Laws of Hong Kong para. 295.027 (2010) [hereinafter 20 Halsbury's].

5. L.B. Curzon & P.H. Richards, The Longman Dictionary of Law 560 (8th ed. 2011) [hereinafter Curzon] defines *succession*:
   (1) The order in which persons succeed to property, or some title.
   (2) Term applied to the estate of a deceased person.
   (3) Process of becoming entitled to property of a deceased by the operation of law or will.

6. *Wills Ordinance* (Cap 30), section 2 provides: "'will' (遺囑) includes a codicil and any other testamentary instrument or act, and 'testator' (立遺囑人) shall be construed accordingly."

7. See generally *Intestates' Estates Ordinance* (Cap 73). *Id.* at section 2(1) translates *intestate* as "無遺囑者".

8. The *BLIS Glossary* translates the term *succession* as "死亡繼承". See also the Law Reform Commission of Hong Kong, Report on Law of Wills, Intestate Succession and Provision for Deceased Persons' Families and Dependents (Topic 15) (1990).

9. "Abandonment of goods takes place when possession of them is quitted voluntarily without any intention of transferring them to another." 20 HALSBURY'S at para. 295.025.

10. Defined as *occupancy*. See *id.* at para. 295.036.

11. See also *id.* at paras. 295.037–295.039.

12. *Id.* at para. 295.011. This section also states:
    'Possession' may mean legal possession: that possession which is recognised and protected . . . by law. The elements . . . of legal possession are an intention of possessing together with that amount of occupation or control of the entire subject matter of which it is practically capable and which is sufficient to exclude strangers from interfering.

13. BLACK'S LAW DICTIONARY 412 (9th ed. 2009) [hereinafter BLACK'S LAW DICTIONARY]. The *BLIS Glossary* translates the term *custodian* as "保管人".

14. JOHN N. ADAMS & HECTOR MACQUEEN, ATIYAH'S SALE OF GOODS 11–12 (12th ed. 2010). See CURZON at 51. The *BLIS Glossary* translates *bailment* as "委託保管"; *bailee* as "委託保管人"; and *bailor* as "受寄人".

15. DEREK MENDES DA COSTA, RICHARD BALFOUR & EILEEN GILLESE, PROPERTY LAW: CASES, TEXT AND MATERIALS para. 4.1 (2nd ed. 1990) [hereinafter PROPERTY LAW: CASES, TEXT AND MATERIALS].

16. JUDITH SIHOMBING, GOODS: SALES AND SECURITIES 2 (3rd ed. 1997).

17. *Common law* is defined in the *Interpretation and General Clauses Ordinance*, section 3: "(普通法) means the common law in force in Hong Kong."

18. For further analysis of this topic, see 20 HALSBURY'S at para. 295.020.

19. For a detailed discussion see PROPERTY LAW: CASES, TEXT AND MATERIALS, chapter 3; 20 HALSBURY'S at para. 295.020. Under the *Limitation Ordinance* (Cap 347), sections 4(1)(a) and 5, the owner of goods must sue in court within six years to reclaim the goods.

20. See *Parker v British Airways Board* [1982] 1 QB at 1017–1018 discussing the finder's rights and obligations and the occupier's rights and liabilities.

21. *Conversion* is defined by BLACK'S LAW DICTIONARY at 356 as the: "wrongful possession or disposition of another's property as if it were one's own . . ."

22. This is known as the plea of *jus tertii*. As explained by 20 HALSBURY'S at para. 295.024:
    If the plaintiff was in possession of goods at the time of the act complained of, the defendant in an action for wrongful interference with goods is not entitled to show that a third party, under whom he did not claim, has a better right than the plaintiff . . .

23. *Id.* at para. 295.016.

24. *Id.* at para. 295.022.

25. Real property evolved because historically enforcement was by real actions which were only available to holders of freehold estates. Thus, leasehold estates are personal property, as they were regarded as a personal right and enforced by the leaseholder bringing a personal action against the lessor. As there is no freehold estate in Hong Kong (except St. John's Cathedral), there is virtually no realty. Nevertheless, in order to distinguish leasehold interests from other types of personal property, leaseholds are described as *chattels real*, as opposed to other personal property which are called *chattels personal*. Today, the distinctions between chattels real and realty have disappeared, and it is accepted in Hong Kong to describe land as real property. For further historical information see, e.g., 20 HALSBURY'S at para. 295.001 where it states in part:

> In England, the distinction between personal and real (or freehold) property was manifested in the early rule that freehold estates and interests in land were specifically recoverable, by a 'real' action, from a wrongful taker, whereas no action lay to compel restitution of other forms of property, the appropriate remedy for such cases being a mere 'personal' action for damages . . .

26. *Common law* and *equity* are conceptually two separate and parallel sets of law. In Hong Kong, there is a unified court system which applies both the common law and equitable rules. The UK's parallel but separate system was not introduced here. There are thus no separate courts of common law and courts of equity (i.e., Chancery) in Hong Kong. The rules and remedies of both are available from the same judiciary in Hong Kong.

    The *BLIS Glossary* translates *rules of the common law* as "普通法規則" and *rules of equity* as "衡平法" or "衡平法規則". See also explanation at *supra* note 17.

27. That is, without any evil intent or purpose, fraud, conspiracy or collusion.

28. JUDITH-ANNE MACKENZIE & MARY PHILIPS, TEXTBOOK ON LAND LAW 18–19 (14th ed. 2012) [hereinafter MACKENZIE & PHILIPS]. The essential characteristic of the trust is the separation of the property's title from the right to use and enjoy the property. The trustee is the owner of the property but holds this property for the beneficiary. *Id.* at 271. See also, SARAH NIELD, HONG KONG LAND LAW 28 (2nd ed. 1997) [hereinafter NIELD].

29. The law of trusts may be considered as a separate area of law due to its complexity. Thus, the law of trusts will not be discussed further. See, e.g., S.H. GOO AND ALICE LEE, LAND LAW IN HONG KONG chapter 4 (Trust) (3rd ed. 2010) [hereinafter GOO & LEE]; 26(2) HALSBURY'S LAWS OF HONG KONG (2009); JOHN THURSTON & DEBORAH ANNELLS, A PRACTITIONER'S GUIDE TO TRUSTS – HONG KONG EDITION (2007); LAWRENCE MA, EQUITY AND TRUSTS LAW IN HONG KONG (2nd ed. 2009).

Part 1

1. See, e.g., 16 HALSBURY'S LAWS OF HONG KONG para. 230.043 (2010) [hereinafter 16 HALSBURY'S].

2. *Interpretation and General Clauses Ordinance*, section 3.

Chapter Two

1. MACKENZIE & PHILIPS at 590. See also GOO & LEE at chapter 1 (Tenures, Estates, Land and Property).

2. The *BLIS Glossary* translates *grant, grantor* and *grantee* as "授予", "授予人" and "承授人" respectively.

3. MACKENZIE & PHILIPS at 588.

4. *Id.* at 162.

5. *Id.* at 163; See also MEGARRY'S MANUAL OF THE LAW OF REAL PROPERTY 42 (A.J. Oakley, ed., 8th ed. 2002) [hereinafter MEGARRY'S MANUAL]; SIR ROBERT MEGARRY & WILLIAM WADE, THE LAW OF REAL PROPERTY para. 3–056 (8th ed. 2012) [hereinafter THE LAW OF REAL PROPERTY].

6. See M.P. THOMPSON, CO-OWNERSHIP (1988); MEGARRY'S MANUAL at chapter 8 (Co-Ownership). See also GOO & LEE at chapter 10 (Co-Ownership).

7. See NIELD at 228.

8. The *BLIS Glossary* translates the term *joint tenancy* as "聯權共有".

9. NIELD at 230. See also GOO & LEE at 532–534.

10. NIELD at 230.

11. *Id.* at 231.

12. (1861) 1 John & H at 557.

13. *Conveyancing and Property Ordinance* (Cap 219), section 8 provides:
    (1) A joint tenancy of an estate or interest in land may be severed at law only by –
        (a) a notice served by a joint tenant on the other joint tenants; or
        (b) an instrument.
    (2) A joint tenancy of an estate or interest in land may be severed in equity by a notice served by a joint tenant on the other joint tenants or by any other method that is effective in equity or that would, but for subsection (1), be effective at law.

14. The notice must be served by a joint tenant on the other joint tenants. However, the case of *re 88 Berkeley Road, London NW9, Rickwood v Turnsek* [1971] 1 All ER 254 held that written notice of severance is effective once delivered even if not received by the addressee(s). See also the case of *Ho Nga Sheung v Ma Fook Leung* [1993] 2 HKC 647 (joint tenancy severed by divorce proceedings).

15. See the following section on the creation of co-ownership.

16. The *BLIS Glossary* translates the term *tenancy in common* as "分權共有".

17. *Estate* in this sense refers not to an estate in land, but, rather, to the assets of a deceased person's total property, the realty as well as the personalty. See BLACK'S LAW DICTIONARY at 586. The *Intestates' Estates Ordinance*, section 2 provides that: "*estate* (遺產) means real and personal estate."

18. *Conveyancing and Property Ordinance*, section 9.

19. The *BLIS Glossary* translates the term *vest in* as "歸屬".

20. In the case of *Mole v Ross* (1951) 24 ALJ 356, the court decided that it was unnecessary to use the precise words *as joint tenants* to create a joint tenancy, but that any clear and plain language expressing an intention to do so will suffice. See GOO & LEE at 542–545; MEGARRY & WADE at paras. 13-015–13-021. The *BLIS Glossary* translates the term *legatee* as "受遺贈人".

21. GOO & LEE at 532–542; MACKENZIE & PHILIPS at 284; MEGARRY'S MANUAL at 308; THE LAW OF REAL PROPERTY at para. 13–017.

22. GOO & LEE at 544. See, e.g., *Lake v Gibson* (1729) 1 Eq Ca Abr 290, 291.

23. MEGARRY & WADE at para. 13–022; MEGARRY'S MANUAL at 314.

24. In the case of *Bull v Bull* [1955] 1 QB 234, the claimant and his mother, the respondent, together purchased a house with the son contributing a larger part of the purchase price than his mother. The property was taken in the son's name. The parties agreed that the mother should occupy two rooms of the house and that the son and his wife occupy the rest of the house. Differences arose between the parties and the son sued for possession of the rooms occupied by the mother. The court decided in favour of the mother, an equitable tenant in common who should be entitled to share the proceeds of sale of the property. The court ordered that the house be sold and the proceeds be divided between them in the proper proportions:

> The son is, of course, the legal owner of the house; but the mother and son are, I think, equitable tenants in common. Each is entitled in equity to an undivided share in the house, the share of each being in proportion to his or her respective contribution . . . My conclusion, therefore, is that, when there are two equitable tenants in common, then, until the place is sold, each of them is entitled concurrently with the other to the possession of the land and to the use and enjoyment of it in a proper manner: and that neither of them is entitled to turn out the other.

[1955] 1 QB at 236–238.

NIELD at 241–242 states that:

> while co-owners may be joint tenants at law, they may hold that legal estate on trust for themselves as either joint tenants or tenants in common in equity. The reverse result does not, however, follow. Co-owners who hold as tenants in common at law will hold as

tenants in common in equity, for equity leans in favour of a tenancy in common and will follow the law in this respect.

25. *Morley v Bird* (1798) 3 Ves Jun 628, 631. See GOO & LEE at 545.

26. GOO & LEE at 545. The Privy Council held in the case of *Malayan Credit Ltd v Jack Chia MPH Ltd* [1986] 1 All ER 711, 715 that there was an equitable presumption in favour of a tenancy in common where the co-owners held for their various business purposes: "where premises are held by two persons as joint tenants at law for their several business purposes, it is improbable that they would intend to hold as joint tenants in equity."

27. See, e.g., the preceding section on joint tenancy and MACKENZIE & PHILIPS at 296–300; GOO & LEE at 547–559.

28. The *BLIS Glossary* translates the term *partition* and *partition of property in land* as "分劃" and "分劃土地財產" respectively. See GOO & LEE at 559–575.

29. *Partition Ordinance* (Cap 352), section 4.

Chapter Three

1. DANIEL P. MCLOUGHLIN, PRINCIPLES OF REAL ESTATE LAW 30 (1992). See also 17(1) HALSBURY'S LAWS OF HONG KONG para. 235.483 (2007) [hereinafter 17(1) HALSBURY'S] as to the definition of *tenancy*. See also GOO & LEE at chapter 9 (Licences).

2. 17(1) HALSBURY'S at para. 235.001.

3. [1985] AC at 818. See also 17(1) HALSBURY'S at para 235.001; MALCOLM MERRY, HONG KONG TENANCY LAW 1–10 (5th ed. 2010) [hereinafter MERRY].

   17(1) HALSBURY'S at para. 235.008 provides that:

   . . . an agreement creates the relationship of landlord and tenant and not that of licensor and licensee where there is the grant of exclusive possession for a fixed or periodic term at a stated rent.

4. 17(1) HALSBURY'S at para. 235.007 states that there:

   . . . can be no tenancy without the grant of exclusive possession. Exclusive possession enables the tenant to exclude strangers and to exclude also the landlord unless the landlord is exercising rights to enter the land granted to him under the tenancy agreement.

5. NIELD at 487.

6. Chancery Practice, Inns of Court 1990/91.

7. See I.J. DAWSON & ROBERT A. PEARCE, LICENCES RELATING TO THE OCCUPATION OR USE OF LAND (1979) [hereinafter DAWSON & PEARCE], for a detailed discussion. See also MERRY at 4–10.

8. (1673) Vaugh at 351. See also 17(1) HALSBURY'S at para. 235.010.

9. NIELD at 487.

10. See also the case of *Attorney General v Chiu Pak Yue* (No. 2) [1963] HKLR 544.

11. *Hounslow London Borough Council v Twickenham Garden Development Ltd* [1971] Ch 233, 243.

12. DAWSON & PEARCE at 44. See also 17(1) HALSBURY'S at para. 235.014; GOO & LEE at 492.

13. NIELD at 489. See also 17(1) HALSBURY'S at para. 235.011; GOO & LEE at 493–511.

14. As discussed in more detail later in this section, a lease is considered to be a transaction affecting land. See 17(1) HALSBURY'S at paras. 235.050–235.054. See also GOO & LEE at chapters 7 (Leases) and 8 (Leasehold Covenants).

15. The *BLIS Glossary* translates the term *exclusive possession* as "獨有管有".

16. 17(1) HALSBURY'S at para. 235.007. See also GOO & LEE at 386–408.

17. [1977] 1 WLR at 1185.

18. *Id.* See also GOO & LEE at 378–384.

19. [1944] KB at 370. *Lace v Chantler* is frequently quoted as authority. A more recent case is *Ashburn Anstalt v Arnold* [1988] 2 WLR 706.

20. E.g., yearly, quarterly or monthly. See also GOO & LEE at 410–412; THE LAW OF REAL PROPERTY at para. 17–072 and MEGARRY'S MANUAL at 346–349.

21. 17(1) HALSBURY'S at para. 235.160 observed:

    A tenancy from year to year arises either by express agreement or by implication of law. It differs from a tenancy at will in that it may be determined only by notice duly given except where there is a stipulation for determination without notice. The appropriate words for the express creation of the tenancy are 'from year to year' . . .

    See also MERRY at 43–44; MEGARRY'S MANUAL at 347. The *BLIS Glossary* translates the term *tenancy from year to year* as "按年計算的租賃".

22. See *Conveyancing and Property Ordinance*, section 6 which provides:

    (1) All interests in land created by parol and not put in writing and signed by the persons creating the same, or by their agents thereunto lawfully authorized in writing, have, notwithstanding any consideration having been given for the same, the force and effect of interests at will only.

    (2) Nothing in section 3 or 5 or in subsection (1) shall affect the creation by parol of leases taking effect in possession for a term not exceeding 3 years (whether or not the lessee is given power to extend the term) at the best rent which can be reasonably obtained without a premium.

23. For further information, see 17(1) HALSBURY'S at paras. 235.166, 235.169, 235.176–235.178; GOO & LEE at 411, 425.

24. The *BLIS Glossary* translates the term *tenancy at will* as "隨意終止的租賃".

25. 17(1) HALSBURY'S at para. 235.003; NIELD at 277.

26. NIELD at 277. See also GOO & LEE at 412–413; 17(1) HALSBURY'S at para. 235.003; MERRY at 41–43.

27. [1952] 1 KB at 296.

28. THE LAW OF REAL PROPERTY at para. 17–075; MEGARRY'S MANUAL at 349.

29. An implied tenancy is addressed in 17(1) HALSBURY'S at para. 235.151:
    A tenancy at will is implied where a person is in possession by the owner's consent, and his possession is not as employee or agent or as a licensee holding under an irrevocable licence, and is not held in virtue of any freehold estate or of any tenancy for a certain term. Such a tenancy is implied accordingly in cases of mere permissive occupation without payment of rent.

30. As explained in *id.* at para. 235.153, this situation arises when:
    A tenant who, with the landlord's consent, remains in possession after his lease has expired is a tenant at will until some other interest is created, either by express grant or by implication by the payment and acceptance of rent. . . . The terms of a tenancy at will which arises in this way will be those of the expired lease unless inconsistent with the nature of a tenancy at will and unless there is evidence of a contrary intention.

    Note the effects of the amendments in the *Landlord and Tenant (Consolidation) (Amendment) Ordinance 2004* which came into effect 9 July 2004. These amendments removed the security of tenure provisions from the *Landlord and Tenant (Consolidation) Ordinance.*

31. See 17(1) HALSBURY'S at para. 235.154 states:
    A tenancy at will is determinable by either party on his expressly or impliedly intimating to the other his wish that the tenancy should be at an end. Until the intimation is thus given, the tenant is lawfully in possession . . . the landlord may not recover the premises . . . without a previous demand of possession or other determination of the tenancy. A demand for possession by the landlord which determines the tenancy at will is not a notice to quit. The issue of a writ claiming possession is a sufficient demand for possession to bring the tenancy to an end.

32. *Id.* at para. 235.004; GOO & LEE at 413 (citations omitted).

33. NIELD at 278. See also MERRY at 45–47.

34. As explained by one authority:
    A person who enters on land by a lawful title and, after his title has ended, continues in possession without statutory authority and without obtaining the consent of the person then entitled, is said to be a tenant at or on sufferance, as distinct from a tenant at will who is in possession with the landlord's consent. This is so whatever the nature of the tenant's original estate, whether he was tenant for

years, or the subtenant of a tenant for years, or a tenant at will. A tenancy at sufferance arises by implication of law and may not be created by contract between the parties.

There can be no tenancy at sufferance against the Government. In such a case, the person holding over is a mere trespasser. . . .

17(1) HALSBURY'S at para. 235.158.

35. See, e.g., Tenancy (Notice of Termination) (Exclusion) (Consolidation) Order (Cap 7A), para. 2:

Tenancies held from–
(a) the Hong Kong Housing Authority,
(b) the Hong Kong Housing Society, and
(c) (Repealed L.N. 164 of 1992)
(d) the Hong Kong Settlers Housing Corporation Limited,

are excluded from the further application of Part V of the Landlord and Tenant (Consolidation) Ordinance (Cap 7).

36. The *BLIS Glossary* translates the term *deed* as "契據".

37. See *Landlord and Tenant (Consolidation) Ordinance* (Cap 7), section 6(1).

38. See *Stamp Duty Ordinance* (Cap 117), Schedule 1. The *BLIS Glossary* translates the term *ad valorem* as "從價費" and *stamp duty* as "印花稅".

39. *Land Registration Ordinance* (Cap 128), section 5, the text of which is set out *infra* Chapter Eleven note 121.

40. *Land Registration Ordinance*, at section 4.

The *BLIS Glossary* translates *bona fide purchaser* as "真誠買方" and *bona fide purchaser for value* as "付出價值的真誠購買人".

41. For more details on options to renew, see, e.g., 17(1) HALSBURY'S at paras. 235.106–235.107.

42. *Conveyancing and Property Ordinance*, section 3(1).

43. Tenancies where the premises are let wholly or primarily as a residence. MERRY at 45. See also *Landlord and Tenant (Consolidation) Ordinance*, section 2.

44. See Note 9 of Form CR109; *Landlord and Tenant (Consolidation) Ordinance* (Cap 7), section 119L.

45. Covenants may be *positive* (e.g., a covenant to repair), or *negative* (e.g., a covenant not to assign). See 17(1) HALSBURY'S at para. 235.424.

The *BLIS Glossary* translates *covenant* as "契諾".

46. See *Conveyancing and Property Ordinance*, sections 4(1) and 4(2)(d) which state:

(1) A legal estate in land may be created, extinguished or disposed of only by deed.
(2) This section does not apply to–
. . .

(d) the grant, disposal or surrender of a lease taking effect in possession for a term not exceeding 3 years (whether or not the lessee is given power to extend the term) at the best rent which can be reasonably obtained without a premium;

   . . .

47. The *BLIS Glossary* translates the term *condition* as "條件".

48. This includes even the most fundamental of covenants, including the one to pay rent.

49. For further analysis on the topic of remedies for breaches of covenant or condition, see 17(1) HALSBURY'S at para. 235.100.

50. *Hamlyn & Co v Wood & Co* [1891] 2 QB 488, 491. In the Hong Kong case of *Hang Tak Co Ltd v Attorney General*, unreported, (1986) HCA 2567/83, the court applied the business efficacy test. See also JUDITH SIHOMBING & MICHAEL WILKINSON, A STUDENT'S GUIDE TO HONG KONG CONVEYANCING 91–100 (6th ed. 2011) [hereinafter STUDENT'S GUIDE] on Government leases.

51. GOO & LEE at 436–437. See *Landlord and Tenant (Consolidation) Ordinance*, section 119V which provides in part:

(1) Any person who unlawfully deprives a tenant or sub-tenant of occupation of any premises commits an offence . . .

(2) Subject to subsection (3), any person who, in relation to any premises–

(a) either–

(i) does any act calculated to interfere with the peace or comfort of the tenant or sub-tenant or members of his household; or

(ii) persistently withdraws or withholds services reasonably required for occupation of the premises as a dwelling; and

(b) knows, or has reasonable cause to believe, that that conduct is likely to cause the tenant or sub-tenant–

(i) to give up occupation of the premises; or

(ii) to refrain from exercising any right or pursuing any remedy in respect of the premises,

commits an offence . . .

52. But see the case of *Wise Stand Ltd v United Pentecostal Church of Hong Kong Ltd*, unreported, DCCJ 19369/2001. See, e.g., MERRY at 55–57.

53. See GOO & LEE at 437–438; MERRY at 57–60. The *BLIS Glossary* translates the term *derogation* as "減免" or "減損".

54. On the subject of habitability, 17(1) HALSBURY'S at para. 235.292 states:

. . . on the letting of an unfurnished dwelling house or flat there is no implied warranty on the part of the landlord that it is in a reasonably fit state for habitation . . . The intending tenant is presumed to make his own inquiries as to its condition . . . he takes the house as it stands . . . If the house is, in fact, uninhabitable, then, after accepting the lease, the tenant is without remedy except where he has obtained a warranty of fitness, or where he has been induced to take the lease by misrepresentation . . . [by] the landlord, in which case the tenant may be entitled to rescission or damages. The mere omission of the landlord to disclose defects is not such misrepresentation but the deliberate concealment of some defects may be conduct equivalent to a fraudulent misrepresentation. . . .

55. Regarding furnished premises:

On the letting of a furnished house, there is an implied condition that it is in a fit state for habitation . . . and, if this condition is not fulfilled, the tenant is entitled to repudiate the contract at once. . . . it is not enough that the landlord believes the house to be in a fit state for habitation; it must in fact be reasonably habitable. The implied condition may be treated also as a warranty, and the tenant may recover damages for the breach. The condition and warranty relate, however, only to the state of the premises at the commencement of the tenancy; and there is no implied condition or warranty that they are to continue fit for habitation throughout the term.

Id. at para. 235.294. See also GOO & LEE at 438–439; MERRY at 60–62.

56. See discussion below concerning repairs. For a discussion of a landlord's liability to make repairs, see 17(1) HALSBURY'S at paras. 235.289–235.290.

57. See MERRY at 63–65 and chapter 9 (Repairs).

58. GOO & LEE at 442–443. 17(1) HALSBURY'S at para. 235.298 states:

Waste consists of any act or omission which causes a lasting alteration to the nature of the land in question to the prejudice of the person who has the remainder or reversion of the land. The obligation not to commit waste is an obligation in tort, and is independent of contract or implied covenant.

59. MACKENZIE & PHILIPS at 222.

60. Voluntary waste:

occurs when the tenant does an, whether deliberate or negligent, act which tends to destroy or diminish the premises. A clear instance would be pulling down a building (even if it is replaced by a building of greater value). More common examples are the removal of fixtures and the alteration of the premises . . .

MERRY at 64.

61. On occasions, it is difficult to distinguish between voluntary waste and ameliorating waste where the alterations might be considered an improvement. The case of Cheung Yeung Kan v Lui Kwan [1973–1976] HKC 237 held the alteration of the character of the premises to be a decisive factor. See also 17(1) HALSBURY'S at para. 235.299.

62. See 17(1) HALSBURY'S at para. 235.298.

63. A tenant for a fixed-term of years is liable for permissive waste. Many fixed-term leases contain an obligation to repair that supersedes the duty not to commit waste. Yearly tenants must keep the premises wind-tight and water-tight but will not be liable for fair wear and tear (the gradual deterioration caused by normal use or the normal action of weather). Weekly or monthly tenants must keep the premises in "a tenant-like manner" by "doing the little jobs about the place that a reasonable tenant would do" like cleaning the windows, mending a fused light, clearing a blocked sink, etc. NIELD at 288.

64. MACKENZIE & PHILIPS at 222 provides:
    Generally the rule is that a weekly tenant is liable for voluntary waste but not for permissive waste: in other words he may not knock a wall down but he can let it fall down . . . The duty is increased . . . that he must use the premises in a 'tenant-like manner' . . . This means that the tenant must clean the premises, mend the electric light if it is fused, unstop blocked sinks, and generally 'do the little jobs about the place which a reasonable tenant would do'.

65. 17(1) HALSBURY'S at para. 235.301. *Id.* at para. 235.310 reviews "fair wear and tear." *Id.* at para. 235.302 reviews the remedies available for the failure to repair.

66. See, e.g., GOO & LEE at 442; MERRY at 63.

67. BLACK'S LAW DICTIONARY at 1237 defines *privity of contract* as "[t]he relationship between the parties to a contract, allowing them to sue each other but preventing a third party from doing so." LexisNexis, HONG KONG ENGLISH-CHINESE LEGAL DICTIONARY 1418 (2005) [hereinafter LEXISNEXIS] translates this term as "契約之相互關係".

68. BLACK'S LAW DICTIONARY at 1238 defines *privity of estate* as "[a] mutual or successive relationship to the same right in property, as between grantor and grantee or landlord and tenant." LEXISNEXIS at 1418 translates this term as "出租人與承租人的相互關係".

69. See, e.g., MERRY at 65.

70. See, e.g., *id.* at 63; GOO & LEE at 442.

71. See, e.g., MERRY at 65.

72. 17(1) HALSBURY'S at para. 235.333 states:
    [Absent an agreement], a tenant for years or a tenant from year to year or other term has the right to assign his term or tenancy, or to create underleases or subtenancies. A restraint on assignment or underletting is, however, valid, and may be created either by condition or by covenant. If it is created by a condition, the condition will express the lease to be void upon those events, but it will be construed as making the lease subject to re-entry at the election of the landlord. More usually the restraint will be imposed by the tenant's covenanting not to assign or underlet. An assignment

in breach of such a covenant or condition is not void but is effective
subject to the landlord's rights to forfeit the lease.

See *id.* at paras. 235.330–235.339.

73. See, e.g., *id.* at para. 235.055; GOO & LEE at 443–444.

74. *Damages* generally refer to monetary compensation. *Injunction* is a court order either ordering a person to or prohibiting a person from performing an act.

MERRY at 141 explains that:

A declaration of legal rights is really a polite alternative to an order for specific performance. Where the plaintiff is confident that the defendant will act on the decision of the court . . . he may ask that the court simply declare the legal position without the sanction of an order or an award of damages.

The *BLIS Glossary* translates *injunction* as "禁制令" or "強制令" and *declaration* as "宣告".

Chapter Four

1. For additional information on the topic of subleases/underleases, see 17(1) HALSBURY'S at paras. 235.075–235.077. See also GOO & LEE at chapter 7 (Leases).

2. For instances where a lease may confer upon the tenant an option to purchase the landlord's interest in the demised premises, see 17(1) HALSBURY'S at para. 235.101; STUDENT'S GUIDE at 897–898.

3. For discussion of the option to purchase the premises by the tenant, see 17(1) HALSBURY'S at paras. 235.101–235.104; and for the option to renew a lease, see *id.* at paras. 235.106–235.107.

4. See, e.g., MERRY at 159; Goo & Lee at 422–424.

5. See 17(1) HALSBURY'S at para. 235.165.

6. Alternatively at the end of the quarter or as the case may be.

7. See also GOO & LEE at 424 and 17(1) HALSBURY'S at paras. 235.108–235.110 for a discussion of an option to determine a lease before the expiration of the lease term.

8. See *Conveyancing and Property Ordinance*, section 62(1).

9. Concerning this procedure, see GOO & LEE at 425–427; 17(1) HALSBURY'S at para. 235.448. The *BLIS Glossary* translates the term *surrender* as "退回".

10. *Reversion* is defined by BLACK'S LAW DICTIONARY at 1345 as the:

interest that is left after subtracting what the transferor has parted with from what the transferor originally had; specif., a future interest in land arising by operation of law whenever an estate owner grants to another a particular estate, such as a life estate or a term of years, but does not dispose of the entire interest . . .

The *BLIS Glossary* translates the term *reversion* as "復歸權益".

11. For analysis, see, e.g., 17(1) HALSBURY'S at paras. 235.449–235.454; MERRY at 187–190.

12. CURZON at 221 defines *equitable lease* as a: "lease which does not satisfy the necessary requirements for a legal lease but is, nevertheless, valid in equity." The definitions of *equitable interest* and *legal estate* are set out in the *Conveyancing and Property Ordinance*, section 2.

13. This matter is discussed in further detail in 17(1) HALSBURY'S at para. 235.451.

14. *Id.* at para. 235.450.

15. *Id.* at para. 235.453.

16. As explained in greater detail:

    The grant by the landlord of a new lease to a third person, with the tenant's consent, operates as a surrender of the old lease, provided the old tenant gives up possession to the new tenant at or about the time of the grant of the new lease. The same effect is produced where the landlord, with the tenant's consent, accepts another person as tenant, and that other person takes possession . . .

    Id. at para. 235.454.

17. One should note:

    A merger occurs where the tenant acquires the landlord's reversion or a third person acquires both the lease and the reversion with the result that the two interests merge, being in the ownership of the same person. The principle underlying surrender and merger is the same, namely that the lease and the reversion become vested in the same person . . .

    Id. at para. 235.448 fn.1. See, e.g., GOO & LEE at 428; MERRY at 190.

18. NIELD at 299–300.

19. See, e.g., GOO & LEE at 427, 466–469; MERRY at 171–181. The *BLIS Glossary* translates the term *forfeiture* as "沒收租賃權".

    See, e.g., *Landlord and Tenant (Consolidation) Ordinance*, sections 117 and 126.

20. *Landlord and Tenant (Consolidation) Ordinance*, section 126 provides:

    In the absence of any express covenant for the payment of rent and condition for forfeiture, there shall be implied in every tenancy a covenant to pay the rent on the due date and a condition for forfeiture for non-payment within 15 days of the due date.

    See GOO & LEE at 469–471.

21. The *BLIS Glossary* translates the term *distress* as "扣押".

22. See, e.g., *High Court Ordinance* (Cap 4), sections 21F–21H, which provide that relief will be granted to the defaulting tenant if the rental arrears and costs are paid in full before the time for acknowledging service of the writ or before a possession order is executed. Similar provisions can be found in the *District Court Ordinance* (Cap 336), section 69. The *BLIS Glossary* translates the term *waiver* as "放棄" and *estoppel* as "不容反悔法".

23. *Conveyancing and Property Ordinance*, section 58(4).

24. See, e.g., MERRY at 199–201; 17(1) HALSBURY'S at para. 235.478; GOO & LEE at 486–487 for explanations of *mesne* profits.

25. NIELD at 294–295.

26. See, e.g., MERRY at 176–179.

27. For an in-depth discussion of estoppel in the context of Hong Kong property and conveyancing, see STUDENT'S GUIDE at 841–852.

28. For a more detailed explanation of this procedure, see, e.g., GOO & LEE at 465–466; 17(1) HALSBURY'S at paras. 235.236–235.254; MERRY at 99–117.

29. See 17(1) HALSBURY'S at para. 235.227.

30. *Landlord and Tenant (Consolidation) Ordinance*, section 75–114A.

31. The *BLIS Glossary* translates the term *ex parte application* as "單方面申請".

32. See *Landlord and Tenant (Consolidation) Ordinance*, section 93.

33. The *BLIS Glossary* translates *interpleader* as "互爭權利訴訟".

34. *Landlord and Tenant (Consolidation) Ordinance*, section 2 provides:
    "domestic premises" (住宅處所) means premises the subject of a separate letting (including any bed-space, cubicle, room, floor or portion of a floor or building) which are used wholly or primarily for human habitation:
        Provided that the following shall not be deemed to be domestic premises within the meaning of this definition–
    (a) any building or portion of a building which is used for habitation only by caretakers or watchmen not exceeding 2 in number;
    (b) any building or portion of a building which is used for habitation only by office attendants or their families;
    (c) any particular portion of an hotel or boarding-house which is let by the keeper of such hotel or boarding-house to a guest of such hotel or boarding-house . . .

35. *Id.* at section 115(1).

36. *Id.*

37. As explained by one authority:
    A tenancy means a tenancy entered into orally or into writing and includes an agreement for a tenancy and a sub-tenancy. . . . a tenancy arises when exclusive possession of premises are given for a term at a rent . . . A tenancy is to be distinguished from a licence to occupy premises. A tenancy at sufferance . . . creates no interest in land, [and thus] is not truly a tenancy.
    17(1) HALSBURY'S at para. 235.483. See, e.g., the case of *Street v Mountford* [1985] AC 809, HL. For more detailed discussion of the lease/licence distinction, see Chapter Three section B of this book.

38. *Landlord and Tenant (Consolidation) (Amendment) Ordinance*, section 5(2).

39. *Id.* at section 5(1).

40. *Id.* at section 6(1).

41. *Id.* at section 6(2).

42. *Id.*

43. *Id.* at section 5(7).

44. *Id.* at section 5(4).

45. *Id.* at section 119L.

46. *Id.* at section 117(3).

47. *Id.* at Part 4.

48. For a detailed review, see STEPHEN D. MAU, HONG KONG LEGAL PRINCIPLES: IMPORTANT TOPICS FOR STUDENTS AND PROFESSIONALS (3rd reprint 2010); 17(1) HALSBURY'S at paras. 235.479–235.504.

49. The *Landlord and Tenant (Consolidation) Ordinance* was divided into seven parts, of which certain sections affected the terms of tenancies between landlords and tenants of domestic premises [Part I which included sections 2–48]. Provisions concerning protected tenancies and permitted rents [Part I] and tenure and rent of domestic premises [Part II which included sections 49–74C], which had previously been extended in force for successive two-year periods were not renewed upon expiry in December 1998. Consequently, their effect will only continue for a limited time. Even before December 1998, the principal provisions were in effect those regarding new tenancies of domestic premises, since they apply to renting buildings occupied after 18 June 1981 and all new rentals after 9 June 1983. 17(1) HALSBURY'S at para. 235.480.

50. 17(1) HALSBURY'S at paras. 235.485, 235.493. For further analysis, see, e.g., MALCOLM MERRY, HONG KONG TENANCY LAW (4th ed. 2003), chapter 15 (Domestic lettings) and chapter 16 (Grounds of opposition) [hereinafter MERRY 2003].

51. *Landlord and Tenant (Consolidation) Ordinance*, section 116(5) mandates:
    (a) The benefits and protection afforded by this Part shall, in any tenancy to which it applies, be available to the widow, widower, mother, father or any daughter or son over the age of 18 years of the tenant where she or he was residing with the tenant at the time of the tenant's death; and, for the purposes of this Part, references to a tenant shall except in this subsection include a reference to such widow, widower, mother, father, daughter or son.
    (b) Only one person mentioned in paragraph (a) shall be entitled to the benefits and protection of this Part at one time and, in default of agreement by those persons, the Tribunal shall nominate that person on such grounds as appears to it to be just and equitable.

(c) The benefits and protection afforded by this Part shall not be available to a personal representative of a deceased tenant or, notwithstanding any will or the law of succession on intestacy, any other person who is not a person mentioned in paragraph (a) as entitled to those benefits and that protection.

52. See 17(1) HALSBURY'S at para. 235.493.

53. For a more detailed review of this procedure, see, e.g., 17 HALSBURY'S LAWS OF HONG KONG para. 235.469 (2000) [hereinafter 17 HALSBURY'S]; GOO & LEE at 429–432.

54. 17 HALSBURY'S at para. 235.469.

55. For more details concerning this procedure, see *id.* at para. 235.470.

56. *Id.*

57. *Id.*

58. *Lands Tribunal Ordinance* (Cap 17), section 10(2)(d). Subsection 2 states:
(2) Without prejudice to the generality of the powers vested in it under subsection (1), the Tribunal may–
. . .
(d) for good cause, enlarge the time, whether or not that time has already expired, fixed by any Ordinance–
(i) for the giving of any notice (and whether or not the notice relates to any proceedings);
(ii) for the taking of any step in any proceedings;
(iii) for the filing or lodging of any document in any proceedings.

59. See the case of *Speakman v Huang Investment Ltd* [1987] 1 HKC 258.

60. See *Landlord and Tenant (Consolidation) Ordinance,* former section 119M(2).
17 HALSBURY'S at para. 235.508 which notes:
In practice, the power of the tenant to give notice of refusal of the new tenancy provides to the tenant the opportunity to consider the terms of the new tenancy ordered to be granted by the Lands Tribunal and to elect not to accept the grant if he considers the Tribunal's determination of the rent is higher than he is prepared to pay or other terms of the grant are unacceptable.
See also 17 HALSBURY'S at paras. 235.471, 235.477.

61. 17 HALSBURY'S at para. 235.471 (citing *Landlord and Tenant (Consolidation) Ordinance*, former section 119A(4)).

62. I.e., the tenant has served Form CR103. See also 17 HALSBURY'S at para. 235.508. See MERRY 2003 at chapter 16 (Grounds of opposition).

63. Note that in accordance with *Landlord and Tenant (Consolidation) Ordinance* section 119L, a landlord is required to file a Form CR109 with the Commissioner of Rating and Valuation, failing which a landlord is not entitled

to maintain an action to recover rent under the lease or agreement, although the landlord may still forfeit the lease or tenancy for non-payment of rent, provided that there is a forfeiture clause in the agreement. 17 HALSBURY'S at para. 235.507 (citing *Fuk Lai Ling v Poon Shu-Wan* [1983] 1 HKC 126).

For a discussion of non-payment of rent and breach of covenant, see MERRY 2003 at 228–229.

64. 17 HALSBURY'S at para. 235.486.

65. See *id.* at para. 235.487. See, MERRY 2003 at 229–235 for a review of this ground.

66. 17 HALSBURY'S at para. 235.488.

67. For a review of these criteria, see 17(1) HALSBURY'S at para. 235.502; MERRY 2003 at 234–235.

68. For more information, see 17(1) HALSBURY'S at para. 235.503; MERRY 2003 at 231–232.

69. See the former section 119H(1)(a). One authority discusses this in greater detail:

> Where the Tribunal does not make an order for the grant of a new tenancy on the ground that the landlord requires the premises for his own use, or use of stipulated close relatives, the Tribunal may specify the name of the person for whom it is satisfied the premises are required. Furthermore, in such cases the landlord must not, for a period of 24 months after the decision of the Tribunal declining to make an order for the grant of a new tenancy, let the premises or any part of the premises or assign, transfer or part with possession of the premises or any part of the premises. Nor must the landlord use, or allow the use of the premises or any part of the premises other than as a residence for the person for whose occupation the Tribunal was satisfied that the premises were required.

17 HALSBURY'S at para. 235.497.

70. See the former section 119H(2); 17 HALSBURY'S at para. 235.497.

71. See the former section 119H(9); 17 HALSBURY'S at para. 235.497.

72. For a further discussion of this topic, see 17 HALSBURY'S at para. 235.498; MERRY 2003 at 235–238.

73. For further details, see 17 HALSBURY'S at para. 235.491.

74. See also *id.* at para. 235.498 which presents the restrictions upon landlords claiming possession of the premises upon the basis of rebuilding of the premises.

75. The former section 119F(4).

76. See, e.g., MERRY 2003 at 238–239.

77. 17 HALSBURY'S at para. 235.492.

78. See, e.g., MERRY 2003 at 240–241.

79. 17 HALSBURY'S at para. 235.493.

80. *Id.* at para. 235.494. See also MERRY 2003 at 241.

81. 17 HALSBURY'S at para. 235.473 (citing the *Landlord and Tenant (Consolidation) Ordinance* (Cap 7), former section 119D(3)(a)(ii)). See also 17 HALSBURY'S at para. 235.476.

82. See the former section 119D(3)(a)(iii) of the *Landlord and Tenant (Consolidation) Ordinance.*

83. *Lands Tribunal Ordinance,* former section 8(7) provides:
     The Tribunal shall have jurisdiction to make orders for possession or for ejectment in relation to premises to which Part I, or tenancies or sub-tenancies to which Part II, Part IV or Part V of the Landlord and Tenant (Consolidation) Ordinance (Cap 7) applies where the contractual period of a tenancy or sub-tenancy has been terminated by forfeiture, by surrender (including surrender under the former section 52A, or under section 117, of that Ordinance), by notice of termination within the meaning of Part IV or Part V of that Ordinance or by notice to quit given by the landlord to the tenant, the tenant to the landlord, the principal tenant to the sub-tenant or the sub-tenant to the principal tenant.

84. See 17 HALSBURY'S at para. 235.477.

85. *Landlord and Tenant (Consolidation) Ordinance,* former section 119J states:
     The terms of a tenancy granted by order of the Tribunal under this Part (other than terms as to the duration thereof and as to the rent payable thereunder) shall be such as may be agreed between the landlord and the tenant or as, in default of such agreement, may be determined by the Tribunal; and in determining those terms the Tribunal shall have regard to the terms of the current tenancy and to all relevant circumstances.

86. *Id.* at former section 119I.

87. *Id.* at former section 119.

88. See 17 HALSBURY'S at para. 235.503.

89. *Landlord and Tenant (Consolidation) Ordinance,* former section 119K.

90. *Id.* at former section 119M.

91. See, e.g., *Landlord and Tenant (Consolidation) Ordinance,* section 2 which also states: "'business premises' (商用處所) means premises which are not domestic premises." Part V states:
     (1) . . . this Part shall apply to every tenancy . . . whether the same be effected orally or in writing and notwithstanding any provision in such tenancy, including any provision purporting specifically to exclude the provisions of this Part.
     . . .
     Landlord and Tenant (Consolidation) Ordinance, section 121.

92. E.g., tenancies for a fixed term of three years or more which contain no provisions for early termination other than for breach of condition of the tenancy.

93. For in-depth analysis of this topic, see 17(1) HALSBURY'S at paras. 235.505–235.510 and MERRY 2003 at chapter 17 (Notice of termination for business premises) for detailed information concerning commercial tenancies in Hong Kong.

94. MERRY at 81, 85–86.

95. *Landlord and Tenant (Consolidation) Ordinance*, section 126.

96. See *Landlord and Tenant (Consolidation) (Amendment) Ordinance*, section 9:
    (1) Notwithstanding the repeal of section 122 of the principal Ordinance on the commencement date–
        (a) a notice of termination served under section 122(1) of that Ordinance before that date shall have effect in relation to which it applies; and
        (b) the definition of "notice of termination" in section 120A of that Ordinance shall continue to apply in relation to that tenancy.
    (2) On and after the commencement date, a tenancy to which Part V applies and which is in existence on the day before the commencement date, but in respect of which no notice of termination has been served before the commencement date under section 122(1) of the principal Ordinance–
        (a) may be terminated in accordance with its terms or as otherwise agreed between the parties; or
        (b) if it is a tenancy which was continued by virtue of section 122(4) of that Ordinance, may be terminated either as a month to month tenancy or as agreed between the parties.
    (3) Proceedings relating to Part V which are pending in the Tribunal on the commencement date, and decisions of the Tribunal relating to that Part which have not been given effect to on that date, may respectively continue and be given effect to on and after the commencement date notwithstanding the repeal of certain provisions of that Part by section 8 of this Ordinance.
    (4) Proceedings relating to provisions of Part V saved by this section may be commenced in the Tribunal on or after the commencement date.

97. MERRY 2003 at 250.

98. A notice to quit may also provide the tenant with an extended tenure. However, an extension does not, by its operation, end the tenancy agreement which continues in force except for those provisions which would be inconsistent with a month-to-month tenancy. *Id.* at 251.

99. *Id.*

100. *Id.*

101. In *Fujitsu Hong Kong Ltd v Kwan Sit-cham* [1991] HKDCLR 23 the judge implied a term that the landlord must give interest for the deposit.

Chapter Five

1. See STUDENT'S GUIDE at 78–80. The *BLIS Glossary* translates the term *fixture* as "固定附著物" and *fitting* as "裝置". See also GOO & LEE at 11–32.

2. See also the case of *Elitestone Ltd v Morris* [1997] 2 All ER 513; 17(1) HALSBURY'S at paras. 235.126–235.127; MERRY at 204–208.

3. See also 17(1) HALSBURY'S at para. 235.128.

4. *Goldful Way Development Ltd v Wellstable Development Ltd* [1998] 4 HKC 679.

5. *Deen v Andrews* [1986] 1 EGLR 262.

6. *Irene Loong v Pun Tsun Hang* [1959] HKDCLR 192. Yet, in *Yu Yiu Kong Samuel v Kobylanski Stephen Andre*, [2001] HKEC 821, the court stated:

   > If the item is intended to be permanent and to afford a lasting improvement to the land or building, it will be a fixture. If the attachment is intended to be temporary and no more than necessary for the use and enjoyment of the item, it remains a chattel . . . Applying these tests . . . the air-conditioning unit . . . a window-type air-conditioner, was not a fixture. Its attachment to the wall was only temporary. It could have been removed without much damage to the wall. Such an air-conditioner was no different in nature from a ceiling fan or wall-lamp. All of these items are . . . chattels rather than fixtures.

7. *Penta Continental Land Investment Co Ltd v Chung Kwok Restaurant Ltd* [1967] HKDCLR 22, 26.

8. *Orient Leasing (Hong Kong) Ltd v NP Etches* [1985] HKLR 292, 298.

9. For comments concerning lease provisions to leave fixtures, see 17(1) HALSBURY'S at para. 235.137. Concerning a landlord's remedies for the wrongful removal of fixtures, see *id.* at para. 235.138. Commenting further on trade fixtures, *id.* at para. 235.131 states:

   > A tenant may remove fixtures if they have been affixed for the purposes of trade or manufacture, so long as the lease does not provide to the contrary, and so long as they are capable of being severed from the land without irreparable injury to it . . .

   See also MERRY at 206–207.

10. 17(1) HALSBURY'S at para. 235.132. See also MERRY at 207–208.

11. 17(1) HALSBURY'S at para. 235.133.

Chapter Six

1. For a review of adverse possession in Hong Kong, see the Consultation Paper prepared by the Law Reform Commission, dated December 2012,

and available at: http://www.hkreform.gov.hk/en/docs/adversepossession_e. pdf. See also GOO & LEE at chapter 5 (Limitation Ordinance and Adverse Possession); KEVIN GRAY & SUSAN GRAY, ELEMENTS OF LAND LAW [9.1], [10.1] (5th ed. 2009).

2. For a discussion of the policy behind adverse possession, see HILARY LIM & KATE GREEN, CASES & MATERIALS IN LAND LAW 60–64 (2nd ed. 1995) [hereinafter LIM & GREEN].

3. P.J. DALTON, LAND LAW 153–154 (4th ed. 1996). In the context of Hong Kong, see *Limitation Ordinance*, in particular sections 7 and 8.

4. The *BLIS Glossary* translates the term *limitation period* as "時效期限".

5. *Wallis's Cayton Bay Holiday Camp Ltd v Shell-Mex & BP Ltd* [1975] QB 94, 103 CA.

6. [2007] 10 HKCFAR at 593, quoting *Powell v McFarlane* (1979) 38 P&CR 452, 470–472.

7. *Lee Theatre Realty Ltd v Tong Wah Jor* [2009] HKEC 1950, CFI; [2013] HKEC 646, CA. See also STUDENT'S GUIDE at 61–68; 16 HALSBURY'S at paras. 230.0829–230.0852 and 20 HALSBURY'S at paras. 285.129–285.130.

8. *Lam Che v Foung Sheu Kwun* [2010] HKEC 1252. A similar case is *Ho Yuet Po v Estate of Cheo Ho* [2013] HKEC 601 where the owner of the premises passed away and no one claimed the property as heir. After the appropriate passage of time and meeting the other requirements, Ho became the owner of the premises through adverse possession.

Chapter Seven

1. BLACK'S LAW DICTIONARY at 568.

2. LEXISNEXIS at 1747 translates *servitude* as "地役". For further information on easement, see GOO & LEE at chapter 14 (Easements).

3. LIM & GREEN at 170.

4. See GALE ON EASEMENTS (J. Gaunt & P. Morgan, 19th ed. 2012) and CHESHIRE AND BURN'S MODERN LAW OF REAL PROPERTY (E.H. Burn & J. Cartwright, eds., 18th ed. 2011).

5. [1956] 1 Ch at 140.

6. MACKENZIE & PHILIPS at 478 states:
   > It is not sufficient for the right to confer a merely personal advantage on the current owner. Such a personal right is said to be an interest 'in gross' and it is not possible to have an easement in gross. All easements must be 'appurtenant', that is, they must benefit identifiable land.

   Chan Sik Cheung v Director of Lands [1995] 3 HKC 199, 208 states that easements in gross are: "unknown to the common law and do not exist in Hong Kong."

7. *Bailey v Stephens* (1862) 12 CB (NS) 91, 115. See GOO & LEE at 666–668.

8. NIELD at 320.

9. BLACK'S LAW DICTIONARY at 941 defines *lie in grant* as "to be passable by deed or charter without the ceremony of livery of seisin." The term *livery of seisin* refers to the transfer of possession of the land. For an explanation of the ceremony, see http://legal-dictionary.thefreedictionary.com/livery+of+seisin

10. See GOO & LEE at 669–671.

11. [1892] 1 Ch at 484.

12. The *BLIS Glossary* translates the term *appurtenant* as "從屬" and "附屬於".

13. See, e.g., NIELD at 319–322 and 16 HALSBURY'S at paras. 230.616–230.635.

14. I.e., without any limitations.

15. MEGARRY'S MANUAL at 422–423; THE LAW OF REAL PROPERTY at para. 27–058.

16. As this is rare in Hong Kong, no further comments are made. For additional information, see, e.g., THE LAW OF REAL PROPERTY at para. 30–028; MEGARRY'S MANUAL at 422.

17. See the case of *Bettison v Langton* [2001] UKHL 24.

18. *Cross-Harbour Tunnel Co Ltd v Commissioner of Rating and Valuation* [1977–1979] HKC 81 uses the term "wayleave" while the *Electricity Networks (Statutory Easements) Ordinance* (Cap 357) refers to "statutory easements."

19. NIELD at 327. See also GOO & LEE at 677–679.

20. NIELD at 331. See also GOO & LEE at 692–699.

21. NIELD at 331.

22. (1879) 12 Ch D 31. As noted by NIELD at 333–334, the similarity between the *Conveyancing and Property Ordinance*, section 16 and the rule in *Wheeldon v Burrows* is striking, but there are a number of distinctions:

    – s 16 operates where there is diversity of occupation before the sale. It therefore does not apply to quasi-easements. *Wheeldon v Burrows*, by contrast, operates in just this situation.

    – s 16 operates only where there is a formal assignment or lease of the property but *Wheeldon v Burrows* will apply where there is an agreement to assign or lease. [citation omitted]

    – s 16 will pass rights that are not continuous or apparent or reasonably necessary for the enjoyment of the property. [citation omitted] In both cases, however, the right must be enjoyed at the time of the lease or assignment.

    – s 16 and the rule in *Wheeldon v Burrows* both give way to a contrary intention expressed by the parties. However, whereas *Wheeldon v Burrows* is based upon the presumed intention of the parties so that a right cannot arise unless it is within the implied contractual rights of the grantee, s 16 may operate to create an easement to which the grantee has no right under the contract by which he acquired his interest in the land.

23. (1879) 12 Ch D at 49 (emphasis added). See GOO & LEE at 697–700.

24. NIELD at 334. See GOO & LEE at 692–693.

25. [1965] 1 QB at 181.

26. MACKENZIE & PHILLIPS at 519.

27. *Id.* (emphasis in original). See GOO & LEE at 693–697.

28. *Pwllbach Colliery Co Ltd v Woodman* [1915] AC 634, 646–647.

29. NIELD at 334.

30. MACKENZIE & PHILLIPS at 519–520.

31. *Id.* at 519.

32. NIELD at 335. See GOO & LEE at 700.

33. NIELD at 335.

34. *Id.* at 337.

35. *The Statute of Westminster I* 1275 later fixed the time as 1189. See GOO & LEE at 703.

36. NIELD at 337.

37. *Id.* See the cases of *Bridle v Ruby* [1988] 3 WLR 191; *Tang Tim-fat v Chan Fok-kei* [1993] 2 HKLR 373 and see MACKENZIE & PHILLIPS at 535; GOO & LEE at 703–704.

38. See the case of *Neaverson v Peterborough RDC* [1902] 1 Ch 557 where a claim was defeated by proof that during the period of time when it was possible to have made the grant there was no person who could lawfully have made the grant.

39. NIELD at 341. An informal release will be effective provided it would be inequitable for the dominant tenant to claim that the right still exists. See GOO & LEE at 710.

40. NIELD at 341. See GOO & LEE at 710–711.

41. MACKENZIE & PHILLIPS at 547.

42. NIELD at 340 (citing *Crown Leases Ordinance* (Cap 40), section 15 and *New Territories Leases (Extension) Ordinance* (Cap 150), section 7).

43. This is a complicated area and is regulated in part by statute. A comprehensive discussion of covenants is outside the scope of this introductory work. The reader is referred to NIELD at chapters 14 (Leasehold Covenants) and 15 (Land Covenants). See also CLEMENT SHUM, GENERAL PRINCIPLES OF HONG KONG LAW 254 (3rd ed. 1998) [hereinafter SHUM].

44. LIM & GREEN at 192–193.

45. MACKENZIE & PHILLIPS at 512.

46. NIELD at 365.

47. MACKENZIE & PHILLIPS at 512 (emphasis in original).

48. Privity of contract means that only parties to a contract can sue based on that contract.

49. NIELD at 378.

50. *Id.*

Chapter Eight

1. See generally NIELD at chapter 17 (Mortgages); GOO & LEE at chapter 15 (Mortgages); STUDENT GUIDE at 1263–1308.

2. BLACK'S LAW DICTIONARY at 759 defines *hypothecation* as the "pledging of something as security without delivery of title or possession". The *BLIS Glossary* translates this term as "押貨預支".

3. *Foreclosure* is defined in BLACK'S LAW DICTIONARY at 674 as a "legal proceeding to terminate a mortgagor's interest in property, instituted by the lender (the mortgagee) either to gain title or to force a sale in order to satisfy the unpaid debt secured by the property". The *BLIS Glossary* translates *foreclosure* as "取消回贖" and *foreclosure action* as "止贖訴訟". The *Stamp Duty Ordinance*, section 2 translates *foreclosure order* as "止贖令".

4. [1994] 1 HKC at 158–159.

5. 16 HALSBURY'S at para. 230.640 defines *equitable mortgage*:

    An equitable mortgage is a contract which creates a charge on the property but does not convey any legal estate or interest to the creditor; such a charge amounts to an equitable interest. . . .

    As a general rule all property, whether real or personal, which may be the subject of a legal mortgage can equally be charged in equity.

    An equitable mortgage may be made either (1) by an agreement to create a legal mortgage; (2) by a mortgage of an equitable interest; (3) by a deposit of title deeds; or (4) by an equitable charge.

    See also STUDENT'S GUIDE at 1262–1271; JUDITH SIHOMBING & MICHAEL WILKINSON, HONG KONG CONVEYANCING, vol. 1(B), chapter XIII, paras. 1001–1051 (2009) [hereinafter HK CONVEYANCING]. The *BLIS Glossary* translates *equitable mortgage* as "衡平法上的按揭".

6. 16 HALSBURY'S at para. 230.641 defines *equitable charge* as follows:

    An equitable charge on land is a security which does not create a legal estate, but only confers upon the creditor an equitable interest in the land. It entitles the holder to have the property . . . sold by an order of the court to raise the money charged on it, but, in the absence of any express provision to that effect, or unless it is a mortgage by deposit of title deeds, it does not amount to an agreement to give a legal mortgage, although, it may, if registered, take priority over subsequent transactions. Even if the security provides for a legal mortgage to be granted, it is still an equitable charge as distinguished from a mortgage.

See also STUDENT'S GUIDE at 1262–1271; HK CONVEYANCING, vol. 1(B), chapter XIII, at paras. 754, 755–801.

7. SHUM at 258; Goo & Lee at 716–717.

8. BLACK'S LAW DICTIONARY at 580 defines *equity of redemption* as being the: right of a mortgagor in default to recover property before a foreclosure sale by paying the principal, interest, and other costs that are due. A defaulting mortgagor with an equity of redemption has the right, until the foreclosure sale, to reimburse the mortgagee and cure the default.

16 HALSBURY'S at para. 230.642 defines this right as follows:

Incident to every mortgage is the right of the mortgagor to redeem, a right which is called his equity of redemption, and which continues notwithstanding that he fails to pay the debt in accordance with the proviso for redemption a legal obligation for which time is of the essence. This right arises from the transaction being considered as a mere loan of money secured by . . . the estate. Any provision inserted in the mortgage to prevent redemption on payment of the debt or performance of the obligation for which the security was given or which allows the mortgagee to return the property encumbered is termed a clog or fetter on the equity of redemption, and generally is considered to be void against a consumer whereas as against a commercial party it will be void only if unreasonable. It is thought that the right to redeem is so inseparable an incident of a mortgage that it cannot be taken away by an express agreement of the parties . . . The right continues unless and until, by judgement for foreclosure or, in the case of a mortgage of land where the mortgagee is in possession, by the running of time, the mortgagor's title is extinguished or his interest is destroyed by sale either under the process of the court or under a power in the mortgage incident to the security.

GOO & LEE at 715 states:

The morgagor's right to redeem after the legal date of redemption is called the *equitable right of redemption*. It arises only when the legal date of redemption has passed. This must not be confused with the mortgagor's *equity of redemption*, a term which is used to describe the sum total of the mortgagor's right of ownership subject to the mortgage, ie the legal right to redeem on the date of redemption and to have the land reconveyed to him on redemption plus the equitable right of redemption. The equity of redemption arises as soon as the mortgage is created. It is an equitable interest in land which can be conveyed, devised, settled, leased or mortgaged, just like any other interest in land. 'The mortgagor's equitable right to redeem is, in the eyes of the law, an equitable estate.' As the mortgagor only has an equity of redemption, any subsequent mortgage he grants must necessarily be equitable. (citation omitted)

See also STUDENT'S GUIDE at 1266–1268; HK CONVEYANCING, vol. 1(B), chapter XIII, at paras. 1, 2, 5–50. The *BLIS Glossary* translates *equity of redemption* as "衡平法贖回權".

9.   NIELD at 445.

10. E.g., there is no mortgage deed, but the debtor/mortgagor deposits the title deed as security. The deposit is treated as evidence of an agreement to create a mortgage and as partial performance of that agreement.

11. NIELD at 445. See also GOO & LEE at 716–717; STUDENT'S GUIDE at chapter 13 (Security Transactions Over Land).

12. See, e.g., *Conveyancing and Property Ordinance*, section 50(1).

13. SHUM at 260.

14. *Conveyancing and Property Ordinance*, section 44(2) provides:
     Under a mortgage effected by a legal charge, the mortgagor and the mortgagee shall, subject to this Ordinance, have the same protection, powers and remedies (including but not limited to those relating to foreclosure and the equity of redemption but excluding the power of the mortgagee to enter into possession before any default by the mortgagor) as if the mortgage had been effected by way of assignment of the legal estate before commencement of this section.

15. *Palk v Mortgage Services Funding PLC* [1993] 2 WLR 415. See also GOO & LEE at 774–775; 16 HALSBURY'S at para. 230.0772; STUDENT'S GUIDE at 1310–1311; HK CONVEYANCING, vol. 1(B), chapter XIII, at paras. 1552–1604.

16. As defined in BLACK'S LAW DICTIONARY at 674, "to terminate a mortgagor's interest in property; to subject (property) to foreclosure proceedings to change".

17. SHUM at 260–261.

18. The *Conveyancing and Property Ordinance*, section 53(2) provides:
     (2) Where a mortgagee obtains an order of foreclosure absolute, that order shall (unless it otherwise provides) operate–
     (a) to assign to the mortgagee the mortgagor's estate in the mortgaged land, subject to any other mortgage having priority to the mortgage under which the foreclosure order was obtained; and
     (b) to discharge that land from the mortgage under which the foreclosure order was obtained and any subsequent mortgage.

19. An order *nisi* is a temporary order which will become final unless opposed by the other party. See *infra* Chapter Eleven note 122.

20. See 16 HALSBURY'S at paras. 230.790–230.792; STUDENT'S GUIDE at 1307–1310; HK CONVEYANCING, vol. 1(B), chapter XIII, at paras. 1451B and vol. 2(E), chapter XIII, at paras. 81–115.

21. SHUM at 259. Section 51 of the *Conveyancing and Property Ordinance* provides, among other things, that:

   (1) Unless the contrary intention is expressed, there shall be implied in any legal charge or equitable mortgage by deed, the powers, exercisable by the mortgagee, a receiver (acting personally or through their agents) and any person entitled to give a receipt for the mortgage money on its repayment, mentioned in the Fourth Schedule.

   (2) Any power exercisable under a mortgage shall be subject to any prior estates, interests and rights to which the mortgaged land is subject.

   (3) No power of sale shall empower a mortgagee or a receiver under an equitable mortgage, by virtue of that mortgage only, to assign the legal estate in the mortgaged land.

   (4) The powers implied by subsection (1), and the provisions of the Fourth Schedule relating to the exercise of those powers may be varied or extended by the mortgage deed and, as so varied or extended, shall have effect as if contained in this Ordinance.

   (5) This section shall not apply to any mortgage executed before the commencement of this section.

22. 16 HALSBURY'S at para. 230.777. See *id.* at paras. 230.776–230.787. See also STUDENT'S GUIDE at 1312–1313; HK CONVEYANCING, vol. 1(B), chapter XIII, at paras. 1554–1705; GOO & LEE at 781–795.

23. *Conveyancing and Property Ordinance*, Schedule 4, para. 11 provides:

   The powers mentioned in paragraphs 2 to 9 shall not be exercisable unless–

   (a) notice requiring payment of the mortgagee money has been served on the mortgagor, or on one of the several mortgagors, and default has been made in payment of the mortgage money or part thereof for one month after such service; or

   (b) interest under the mortgage is in arrear and unpaid for one month after becoming due; or

   (c) there has been a breach of a provision, express or under this Ordinance, of the mortgage other than a covenant for payment of the mortgage money and interest.

24. In the case of *Tse Kwong Lam v Wong Chit Sen* [1983] 3 All ER 54 the court held that the mortgagee had failed to take reasonable care to obtain market price where notice of the foreclosure auction was advertised only shortly

before the auction; the reserve price was determined arbitrarily without any advice from a qualified valuer; and only one bid was received, which came from a related company.

A receiver in these circumstances has the same duty to act in good faith.

25. *Conveyancing and Property Ordinance*, section 50 provides:
    (1) There shall be implied in any legal charge or equitable mortgage by deed, where the mortgage money has become due, a power exercisable in writing by the mortgagee . . . to appoint a receiver or receivers of the mortgaged land and the income thereof, to remove any receiver appointed and appoint another in his place.
    (2) Any receiver so appointed will be deemed the agent of the mortgagor and the mortgagor will be solely responsible for the receiver's acts and defaults.
    . . .
    (8) The provisions of this section are subject to contrary intention expressed in the mortgage deed and may be varied or extended by the mortgage deed, and, as so varied or extended, shall have effect as if contained in this Ordinance.

26. See GOO & LEE at 775–781; SHUM at 260.

27. NIELD at 477.

28. *Id.* at 464.

29. *Id.*

30. *Id.* at 463.

Part 3

1. As noted in 16 HALSBURY'S at para. 230.133:
    The types of contract for the sale of land in Hong Kong include:
    (1) sales under Conditions of Sale; most alienation of land by the Government is effected by a public auction, and the contract is called Conditions of Sale under which the purchaser receives a leasehold estate; Other [*sic*] forms of alienation include Conditions of Exchange, and Conditions of Regrant.
    (2) secondary sales where the Government lessee sells his land, or more correctly assigns his leasehold, to a purchaser where no estate agent is involved, in most of these cases the parties will instruct a solicitor to act prior to being bound;
    (3) secondary sales where the Government lessee sells his land, or more correctly assigns his leasehold, to a purchaser where neither party instructs a solicitor initially, but both sign a contract, referred to as a Preliminary or Provisional Agreement, drafted by an estate agent who is agent for both vendor and purchaser, and who also signs the contract; . . .

(4) sales of uncompleted units in multi-storey developments, which are regulated by the Lands Department under the Consent Scheme; and

(5) sales by mortgagees on the mortgagor's default.

See also *id.* at para. 230.004, where the main Hong Kong ordinances relating to land are presented.

Chapter Nine

1. The only freehold land in Hong Kong is St John's Cathedral which was granted in perpetuity but subject to the condition that the land continues to be used as a church. For a detailed history, see HK CONVEYANCING, vol. 1, chapters I (Land Tenure in Hong Kong) and II (System of Land Holding in Hong Kong).

2. This work will follow Hong Kong local practice where:

    the Government lessee is referred to . . . as the 'owner' of the land, despite the fact that he merely holds a leasehold estate. Then when that 'owner' grants a sub-lease, the sub-lessee's interest is referred to as that of a 'lessee'.

    16 HALSBURY'S at para. 230.002. See also HK CONVEYANCING, vol. 2, chapter II, at para. 52; STUDENT'S GUIDE at chapter 8 (Formation of Contract for Sale of Land); chapter 9 (Contract–Vitiating Factors); chapter 10 (Contract–Capacity, Status and Disabilities).

3. NIELD at 303–304:

    Occasionally Government leases are granted otherwise than by auction. Privately negotiated Conditions of Grant may be made for public purposes, for instance, for a school. Where land is exchanged for other land, which is quite common where an old site is being redeveloped, it may be convenient for the lessee to surrender his old Government lease and obtain a new grant where, for instance, he wishes to change slightly the boundaries of the site or where evidence of his title is rather fragmented. In this case, Conditions of Exchange are issued. . . . The Conditions of Extension may be issued where an additional area of land is granted as an extension to, and on the same terms as, an existing site. These other types of agreement for a Crown lease are also governed by s 14 of the *Conveyancing and Property Ordinance.*

    16 HALSBURY'S at para. 230.131:

    Letters A and Letters B are also called Land Exchange Entitlements. They were issued on the resumption of New Territories land, between 1960 and 1983, to entitle the holder to a grant of land in an urban New Territories development area at some future time. Both forms of Letters could be used to offset the price of land purchased from the Government by auction or tender. The New Territories Land Exchange Entitlements (Redemption) Ordinance, with effect from 27 June 1997, provides for the conversion of the Letters A and B into money payments at a prescribed value and for the extinguishment of their use for payment of land.

4. A tenant's rights and obligations are usually set out in the Government lease or by implication of law, e.g.:

- quiet enjoyment;
- exclusive possession;
- assignment or sub-lease; and,
- offensive trade

See, e.g., *supra* Chapter Three section F.

5. There are five kinds of conditions:

- Conditions of Sale – under which land is sold;
- Conditions of Exchange – under which the granted land is exchanged for other land;
- Conditions of Grant – under which land is granted for a particular purpose;
- Conditions of Regrant – under which a grantee applies for a new grant upon the expiration of the lease; and,
- Conditions of Extension – under which additional land is granted by the Government.

For a detailed discussion of these conditions, see 16 HALSBURY'S at paras. 230.108–230.114. See also STUDENT'S GUIDE at 86–103; HK CONVEYANCING, vol. 2(A), chapter II, at paras. 151–196 and paras. 251–311.

6. Various authorities may issue the certificate, including: the Director of Public Works, the Registrar of Titles or the Director of Lands. A certificate of exemption is issued in the New Territories for buildings which do not need to comply with the *Buildings Ordinance* (Cap 123). A certificate of exemption has the same effect as a certificate of compliance. See 16 HALSBURY'S at para. 230.108 fn.3 (citing *Chung Mui Teck v Hang Tak Buddhist Hall Association Ltd* [2001] 2 HKLRD 471, CA).

7. 16 HALSBURY'S at para. 230.420 fn.7 comments:

No Government lease has issued, since prior to 1970, on the completion of the building covenant in the conditions of sale . . . only the conditions of sale now represent the Government lease. The equitable interest of the purchaser becomes legal on the issue of a certificate of compliance from the Government indicating that the purchaser has observed the covenants in the conditions; there are usually two such covenants, namely the payment of the premium . . . and the building covenant . . . see the Conveyancing and Property Ordinance (Cap 219) s 14 as to the conversion from equitable interest to legal estate.

8. *Conveyancing and Property Ordinance*, section 14(1)(a) states:

(1) Where a person has a right to a Government lease of any land upon compliance with any conditions precedent, then, upon compliance with those conditions –

(a) the equitable interest under that right shall become a legal estate in that land as if held under a Government lease issued in accordance with that right . . .

9.   Article 121 of the *Basic Law* provides:

As regards all leases of land granted or renewed where the original leases contain no right of renewal, during the period from 27 May 1985 to 30 June 1997, which extend beyond 30 June 1997 and expire not later than 30 June 2047, the lessee is not required to pay an additional premium as from 1 July 1997, but an annual rent equivalent to 3 per cent of the rateable value of the property at that date, adjusted in step with any changes in the rateable value thereafter, shall be charged.

Article 122 of the *Basic Law* states:

In the case of old schedule lots, village lots, small houses and similar rural holdings, where the property was on 30 June 1984 held by, or, in the case of small houses granted after that date, where the property is granted to, a lessee descended through the male line from a person who was in 1898 a resident of an established village in Hong Kong, the previous rent shall remain unchanged so long as the property is held by that lessee or by one of his lawful successors in the male line.

10.   *New Territories Leases (Extension) Ordinance* (Cap 150), section 6 states:

The term of a lease to which this Ordinance applies is extended, from the date on which it would, apart from this Ordinance, expire, until the expiry of 30 June 2047, without payment of any additional premium.

11.   *Id.* at section 5(1) provides:

A lessee may exclude from the application of this Ordinance his interest under a lease, other than an undivided share in the land to which the lease relates, by registering in the Land Office register . . . a memorandum in a form specified by the Land Officer.

12.   For further discussion, see, e.g., 16 HALSBURY'S at paras. 230.102–230.104, 230.116; STUDENT'S GUIDE at 22–36; HK CONVEYANCING, vols. 2 & 2(A), chapter II, at paras. 52–270 and paras. 355–530.

13.   As summarized by one authority:

All leases of land granted, decided upon or renewed before the establishment of the Hong Kong Special Administrative Region which extend beyond 30 June 1997 and all rights in relation to such leases are recognised and protected under the law of the Hong Kong Special Administrative Region.

As to the leases of land granted or renewed where the original leases contain no right of renewal, during the period from 27 May 1985 to 30 June 1997, which extend beyond 30 June 1997 and expire not later than 30 June 2047, the lessee is not required to pay an additional premium as from 1 July 1997, but an annual rent equivalent to 3 per cent of the rateable value of the property at that date, adjusted in step with any changes in the rateable value after that date, is to be charged.

17(1) HALSBURY'S at para. 235.019. The *BLIS Glossary* translates *rateable value* as "應課差餉租值".

14. *Government Leases Ordinance* (Cap 40), section 9 states in part:

(1) Subject to subsection (9) the new Government rent payable under a new Government lease shall be an amount equal to 3 per cent of the rateable value of the lot or section held under new Government lease.

(2) . . . the rateable value . . . of a lot or section held under a new Government lease is the rateable value or interim valuation as set out on the relevant day in the list declared under section 13 of the Rating Ordinance (Cap 116), of the tenement . . .

. . .

(9) Where the person . . . entitled to exercise the right of renewal contained in a renewable Government lease paid . . . the new Government rent of a lot or section in an amount exceeding that which is specified in subsection (1) the new Government rent of the lot or section shall be –

(a) for the period from the expiration of the renewable Government lease to the 30 June 1973 the amount so paid . . . and

(b) for the period from the 1 July 1973 to the expiration of the term of the new Government lease the amount specified in subsection (1).

15. See GOO & LEE at 55–60.

16 HALSBURY'S at para. 230.969 notes: "The Government lease invariably has a clause entitling the Government to resume land for public purposes." For detailed analysis of the topic of Government resumption of land, see 16 HALSBURY'S at paras. 230.038, 230.969–230.1014. *Id.* at para. 230.038 provides an overview of this topic, stating in part that:

the form of acquisition, by the Government of the land held under a Government lease prior to the termination of that lease, is that of resumption except where land [is] being compulsorily acquired or purchased under the Land Acquisition (Possessory Title) Ordinance. This entitles the Government . . . to take back the land under . . . the Lands Resumption Ordinance. Compensation is payable on resumption similar to that payable for compulsory acquisition.

By contrast to resumption, the Government . . . does have a right to re-enter as lessor and forfeit the lease where the lessee has

> breached the covenants in the Government lease, or has failed to pay rent or premium due. Re-entry can be physically taking back the land or merely re-entry in principle. . . . No compensation is payable . . .
>
> The right to resume land is given to the Government where that land is needed for public purposes. Resumption and acquisition result in the early determination of the lease without fault on either party. Fair compensation must be paid . . .

Note, however:

> A statutory power to resume land is usually a power to resume compulsorily and to resume the whole land or interests in it; however, the statute . . . may specifically authorise the taking of an easement or statutory right. In some cases there is no resumption or the taking of interests or rights, but merely the imposition of restrictions on the use of alienated land, for which compensation can be payable.

Id. at para. 230.971. See also STUDENT'S GUIDE at 156–176 (resumption of land). See, HK CONVEYANCING, vol. 1, chapter II, at paras. 286–348 (statutory procedure for resumption and challenges thereto) and vol. 2(A), chapter II, at paras. 401–430 (resumption of land and its procedures) and paras. 431–440. (compensation).

16. The *BLIS Glossary* translates *assignment* as "轉讓" and *assignee* as "承讓人".

17. See, e.g., 17(1) HALSBURY'S at paras. 235.077, 235.337–235.342, 235.395.

Chapter Ten

1. 16 HALSBURY'S at paras. 230.419–230.423. See also MALCOLM MERRY & PAUL KENT, BUILDING MANAGEMENT IN HONG KONG (2nd ed. 2008); STUDENT'S GUIDE at 273–298; HK CONVEYANCING, vol. 1, chapter IV (co-ownership) and vol. 2(B), chapter IV, at paras. 1–52 (system of co-ownership); GOO & LEE at chapter 16 (multi-storey building management).

2. 16 HALSBURY'S at para. 230.422.

3. The *BLIS Glossary* translates *memorial* as "註冊摘要".

4. A detailed analysis of the consent and non-consent schemes is beyond the scope of this work. Further information on these schemes may be found at 16 HALSBURY'S at paras. 230.425–230.427; STUDENT'S GUIDE at 298–300. See HK CONVEYANCING, vol. 1, chapter IV, at paras. 35–60 (consent scheme) and paras. 61, 65–75 (non-consent scheme).

   Consent Scheme and Non-consent Scheme's web site: http://www.clic.org.hk/en/topics/saleAndPurchaseOfProperty/sale_and_purchase_of_property_under_construction/q1.shtml

5. An unregistered or unregistrable sale and purchase agreement might result in a developer's mortgagee(s) having priority interest over the purchaser(s) in

the development. This would be particularly relevant in a liquidation of the developer.

6. See *infra* Chapter Eleven section C where this is discussed. The link to this rule is set out *infra* Chapter Eleven note 33.

7. 16 HALSBURY'S at para. 230.453. See generally STUDENT'S GUIDE at 371–388.

8. 16 HALSBURY'S at para. 230.456. See also GOO & LEE at 826–839.

9. *Id.* at para. 230.430.

10. *Id.* at para. 230.456.

11. See *Building Management Ordinance* (Cap 344), section 8 discussing the duties of the Land Registrar and certificates of registration.

12. 16 HALSBURY'S at para. 230.430.

13. See *id.* at para. 230.462. The *Building Management Ordinance* states at section 33(1):

> A corporation may be wound up under the provisions of Part X of the Companies Ordinance (Cap 32) as if it were an unregistered company within the meaning of that Ordinance and the provisions of that Ordinance relating to the winding up of an unregistered company shall, in so far as they are applicable, apply to the winding up of a corporation.

14. The *BLIS Glossary* translates *deed of mutual covenant* as "公契".

15. HARTLEY BRAMWELL, CONVEYANCING IN HONG KONG 270–271 (1981). For an extensive review of DMCs, see HK CONVEYANCING, vol. 1, chapter IV, at paras. 76–260.

16. An undivided share is:

> an undivided share in the legal estate of the whole property. Without a Deed of Mutual Covenant (DMC), each co-owner of the property would be entitled to the full use and enjoyment of the whole property. The DMC governs the right of the co-owners amongst themselves and regulates, amongst other things, the portions of the property in respect of which each owner would have the exclusive right of enjoyment. That exclusive right of enjoyment cannot be assigned on its own, but has to be assigned by a vendor who was assigning that right of exclusive enjoyment together with an assignment of his right of exclusive enjoyment to some other part of the building with undivided shares . . .

16 HALSBURY'S at para. 230.438 fn.2. See also *id.* at para. 230.432, where it is stated:

> In general, the deed of mutual covenant will provide that the owner will not be able to deal separately with the elements which make up his rights as tenant in common; thus his right of exclusive use to his particular unit cannot be dealt with separately from any rights he may have over other parts of the building such as a parking space.

One owner may be treated as having exclusive rights over part of the common property due to his occupation of that common property; with this right comes the obligation to maintain that part of the common property.

17. The definition is provided in the *Conveyancing and Property Ordinance*, section 2, given in Part 1 of this book.

18. Unless the contrary intention is expressed in the assignment, Part 1 of Schedule 1 of the *Conveyancing and Property Ordinance* entitled "Implied Covenants in any Assignment of Land", is implied into every assignment by virtue of section 35(1)(a), and Part I(B) contains the provision relating to deeds of mutual covenant.

19. As one authority explains:

The Conveyancing and Property Ordinance [CPO] makes provision for the enforcement of the benefit and the burden of the covenants in the deed of mutual covenant (DMC), at least in so far as those covenants are proprietary and not merely personal . . . The provisions of the Ordinance:

(1) enable a person to take rights and liabilities under a deed, although not a party to it, subject to certain limitations; these limitations are that the party or his successor in title, must have been in existence at the time the covenant was entered into, that the person was clearly intended to benefit directly by the covenant, and is capable of enforcing it [CPO section 26],

(2) provide that certain implied covenants of due performance are included in assignments . . . these must be expressly excluded if they are not to be inserted [CPO section 35(1) and Schedule 1];

(3) provide that, unless a contrary intention is expressed, covenants are deemed to be made with successors in title of the covenantee and similarly in respect of the covenantor [CPO sections 39(1) and 40(1)];

(4) provide that covenants are enforceable against successors in title . . . this intention is implied unless the contrary is shown [CPO sections 39 and 41(2)(c)];

(5) enable a covenant to be enforceable despite the fact that the covenantor and covenantee own the same land; without this, the enforcement of the covenants in the DMC would be difficult as the parties are co-owners of the Government lease [CPO section 41(7)];

(6) provide for termination of liability in respect of the covenant when the covenantor no longer owns the subject land [CPO section 41(8)];

(7) provide that positive covenants will be enforceable against successors in title . . . [CPO sections 41(2) and 41(5)];

(8) reserve the operation of covenants in a DMC entered into at a time when conditions of sale affected the land, but which were later replaced by the Government lease on the issuance of the certificate of compliance; similar provision is made in respect of a DMC registered prior to the conversion of the conditions of sale into the Government lease [CPO sections 42(1) and 42(2)];

(9) provide that where the Government lease, having expired, has been renewed the pre-existing covenants are to continue in force under the new lease [CPO section 42(3)].

16 HALSBURY'S at para. 230.447. See also *id.* at para. 230.436, and fn.2 thereto which states:

To overcome problems with the enforcement of the covenants in the DMC against owners who were not parties to the DMC, the Law of Property (Enforcement of Covenants) Ordinance 1956 was enacted, the relevant provisions of which have now been subsumed into the Conveyancing and Property Ordinance (Cap 219) ss 39, 41 . . .

E.g., *Conveyancing and Property Ordinance*, section 41 provides in part:

(2) This section applies to any covenant, whether positive or restrictive in effect –
(a) which relates to the land of the covenantor;
(b) the burden of which is expressed or intended to run with the land of the covenantor; and
(c) which is expressed and intended to benefit the land of the covenantee and his successors in title or persons deriving title to that land under or through him or them.

(3) . . . a covenant shall run with the land and, in addition to being enforceable between the parties, shall be enforceable against the occupiers of the land and the covenantor and his successors in title and persons deriving title under or through him or them by the covenantee and his successors in title and persons deriving title under or through him or them.

. . .

(9) A covenant in an instrument registered in the Land Registry under the Land Registration Ordinance (Cap 128) against the land affected by the covenant shall bind the successors in title of the covenantor and the persons deriving title under or through him or them whether or not they had notice of the covenant.

20. 16 HALSBURY'S at para. 230.448. See also STUDENT'S GUIDE at 349–350.

21. 16 HALSBURY'S at para. 230.437.

22. See also the list of nine provisions typically addressed in a deed of mutual covenant presented in *id.* at para. 230.438.

23. As explained in *id.* at para. 230.431:

The land is notionally divided into a number of equal undivided shares, and each owner is allocated a number of these shares proportionate to his interest as set out in the deed of mutual covenant (DMC). In general, unless the owners agree these assigned values cannot be altered by the management. For the purpose of deciding the quantum of each owner's share in the land and his liability for various obligations, the undivided shares are given a value by the developer. These 'valued' shares are usually referred to as management shares. They are expressed to be a reflection of the purchase price paid, the size of the unit, the purpose of its use, and so on.

In some DMC's, the term 'management shares' is used in a different way to refer to either undivided shares in the common parts held by the manager as trustee for all owners, or undivided shares giving the manager the right to use parts of the common property for its commercial gain.

24. See *Conveyancing and Property Ordinance*, section 41(2), set out in *supra* Chapter Ten note 19.

25. *Building Management Ordinance*, Schedule 8 regulates the procedures for such matters as the meetings of the owner's committee and the meeting of owners.

26. As amended by the *Multi-Storey Buildings (Owners Incorporation) (Amendment) Ordinance* (No. 27 of 1993) which is derived from the results of the Government's consultative paper: "Proposals to Remedy Unfair Provisions in Existing DMCs".

27. 16 HALSBURY'S at para. 230.459.

28. For a summary of the mandatory provisions of Schedule 7, see 16 HALSBURY'S at para. 230.458.

Building Management Ordinance, section 34E provides in part:
(1) Subject to subsection (4), the provisions in Schedule 7 shall be impliedly incorporated –
   (a) into every deed of mutual covenant made on or after the material date; and
   (b) as from the material date, into every deed of mutual covenant made before that date.
(2) The provisions incorporated into a deed of mutual covenant by virtue of this section shall –
   (a) bind the owners and manager of the building; and
   (b) prevail over any other provision in the deed that is inconsistent with them.
   . . .

Schedule 7 of this Ordinance provides for the regulation of such matters as contained in the following headings:
1. Determination of total amount of management expenses

    2. Keeping of accounts

    3. Manager to open and maintain bank account

    4. Special fund

    5. Contracts entered into by manager

    6. Resignation of manager

    7. Termination of manager's appointment by owners' corporation

    8. Obligations after manager's appointment ends

    9. Communication among owners.

29. 16 HALSBURY'S at para. 230.455. See *Building Management Ordinance*, section 34E(2) which is set out in part in the preceding footnote.

30. As it is unlikely that most readers of this work will experience the alteration or termination of a deed of mutual covenant, no further comment is provided here. For further information, see 16 HALSBURY'S at para. 230.445; STUDENT'S GUIDE at 383–388; HK CONVEYANCING, vol. 2(B), chapter IV, at paras. 2151–2204.

Chapter Eleven

1. See *infra* section C.

2. An exception to the requirement for writing is contained in section 6 of the *Conveyancing and Property Ordinance* which provides that a lease for a term of less than three years, which takes effect in possession at the best rent available, does not need to be in writing so as to comply with section 3(1).

   The failure to comply with section 3(1) of the *Conveyancing and Property Ordinance* will make the contract unenforceable, but not void. Thus, if the parties choose to honour the agreement by an assignment, the buyer's title is not defective.

3. See 16 HALSBURY'S at paras. 230.162–230.164. No particular form or format is required for the writing. See, e.g., *id.* at para. 230.158.

4. See *id.* at para. 230.157. The exception is where a written offer which is accepted verbally may be enforced against the offeror, with the written offer serving as the note or memorandum. *Id.* at para. 230.158.

5. For other examples, see *id.* at para. 230.162.

6. *Sudbrook Trading Estate Ltd v Eggleton* [1983] 1 AC 444, 474–475.

7. *King's Motors (Oxford) Ltd v Lax* [1970] 1 WLR 426, 427.

8. *Courtney and Fairbairn v Tolaini Bros (Hotels) Ltd* [1975] 1 All ER 716.

9. *Tweddell v Henderson* [1975] 2 All ER 1096.

10. *Ram Narayan v Rishad Hussain Shah* [1979] 1 WLR 1349, PC.

11. On the topic of open contracts and implied terms, see, e.g., 16 HALSBURY'S at paras. 230.193–230.195. See also STUDENT'S GUIDE at 1052–1060 (open contract and implied terms) and 1044–1045 (implied terms). See generally, HK CONVEYANCING, vol. 2(E), chapter XI, at paras. 1–3.

12. See STUDENT'S GUIDE at 831–832.

13. *Richard Ellis Ltd v Van Hong Tuon* [1988] 1 HKLR 169, CA; *Chesterton Petty Ltd v Groeneveld*, unreported, CACV No. 69 of 2000 (Court of Appeal).

14. See, e.g., *Cheng Kwok Fai v Mok Yiu Wah Peter* [1990] 2 HKLR 440.

15. *Chan Yiu-ming v L & D Associates* [1992] HKDCLR 1.

16. *But Chung Yin v Billion Extension Development Ltd* [1997] 1 HKC 531.

17. The *BLIS Glossary* translates *liquidated sum* as "經算定款項".

18. *Daiman Development Sdn Bhd v Mathew Lui Chin Teck* [1981] 1 MLJ 56, 58; cited with approval in *Lam Tam Yi v Chak Wai Man* [1993] 1 HKC 537, 541. See also the case of *Kwan Lai Kit Eddie v Leung Muk Lan*, unreported, (2000) HCA 2179/1998.

19. [1962] HKLR at 492.

20. [1980] HKLR at 743.

21. *Id.* at 746.

22. In the case of *Regal Success Venture Ltd v Jonlin Ltd* [2000] 2 HKC 199, CA; on appeal [2000] 4 HKC 143, CFA, a clause in the sale and purchase agreement provided that the sellers must show good title to the satisfaction of specified solicitors, failing which the buyers could end the agreement. The court held that the agreement was a conditional contract.

23. For example, in the case of *Lee-Parker v Izzet* (No 2) [1972] 1 WLR 775 the agreement was made "subject to the purchaser obtaining a satisfactory mortgage". The court determined the phrase to be a condition. However, the condition was void because it was too vague to be enforceable. As the phrase was considered to be a condition precedent, the uncertainty destroyed not only this clause but the whole contract which was premised upon this clause. *Id.* at 779–780.

24. [1992] 1 HKLR at 3.

25. *Au Wing Cheung v Roseric Ltd* [1992] 1 HKC 149, CA involved a concluded preliminary agreement. Subsequent correspondence concerning the proposed formal sale and purchase agreement were headed "subject to contract". The Court of Appeal held that the letter had no legal effect upon the already binding preliminary agreement.

26. *Michael Richards Properties Ltd v Corporation of Wardens of St Saviour's Parish, Southwark* [1975] 3 All ER 416. In the case of *Hong Kong Housing Authority v Hung Pui* [1987] 3 HKC 495, the rent was already agreed and the lease was already binding before the "subject to contract" letter was sent.

27. The courts have approved this principle. See the cases of *Link Brain Ltd v Fujian Finance Co Ltd* [1990] 2 HKLR 353; *Yiu Yau-ping v Fong Yee-lan* [1992] 2 HKLR 167; *Wisecal Ltd v Conwell International Ltd* [2011] HKEC 967; and *Liverpool City Council v Irwin* [1977] AC 239. See also 16 HALSBURY'S at para. 230.195.

28. LexisNexis at 1632 translates *requisitions on title* as "業權要求".

29. For a discussion of the covenants for title, see 16 Halsbury's at paras. 230.361–230.369. For example, *id.* at para. 230.367 notes that:

> The implied covenant for quiet enjoyment is that the land may be quietly entered into and . . . be held and enjoyed by the purchaser . . . without any lawful interruption or disturbance. Such a covenant for quiet enjoyment limited to lawful disturbance by the covenantor or any other person for whose acts or omissions he is responsible is not broken by claims under title paramount to that of the covenantor, or by tortious acts other than those of the covenantor himself. Since the covenant is a future covenant, the damages seem to be measured by the loss to the covenantee when the disturbance takes place.

See also Student's Guide at 525–526 (duty to show title), 901–902 (breach) and 1130–1143 (assignment); HK Conveyancing, vol. 1(A), chapter V, at paras. 4–16. As the court stated in *Timmins v Moreland Street Property Co Ltd* [1958] 1 Ch 110, 132: "If no interest is mentioned [in the memorandum of agreement], then prima facie an unencumbered freehold interest will be implied."

30. *Chu Wing Ning v Ngan Hing Cheung*, unreported, (1992) HCA 9409/1991 para. 37.

See also the case of *Walford v Miles* [1992] 2 AC 128. The Miles owned a photograph processing business which they wished to sell along with the business premises. The Miles and Walford entered into a sale and purchase agreement. There was an alleged collateral "lock-out" agreement concluded 18 March between the parties that the Miles would end negotiations with any other potential buyers. Should the Miles receive a satisfactory proposal from any third party before the deadline, the Miles would not deal with that party or give further thought to any alternative.

The trial court found in favour of Walford's claims of repudiation of the contract and misrepresentation, concluding that the March 18th agreement was an enforceable collateral agreement to the main contract for the sale of the business and business property. On appeal, the court held that the March 18th agreement was an agreement to negotiate and thus unenforceable. A further appeal to the House of Lords confirmed that a contract to negotiate is unenforceable because it lacks certainty. Additionally, the March 18th lacked certainty because it did not specify the time the seller was prohibited from negotiating with other parties.

31. *Keung Shiu Tang v DH Shuttlecocks Ltd* [1994] 1 HKC 286, CA.

32. *Mak Lai Man v Lam Siu Yui Peter* [1993] 1 HKC 452.

33. Text of Rule 5C may be found at The Law of Society of Hong Kong, *The Hong Kong Solicitors' Guide to Professional Conduct*, vol. 2 Cap. 18 *Solicitors' Practice Rules* Rule 5C:

http://www.hklawsoc.org.hk/pub_e/professionalguide/volume2/default.
asp?cap=18#5C

34. *Conveyancing and Property Ordinance*, section 36 provides: "The covenants and conditions mentioned in the Second Schedule, or any of them, may be incorporated into any instrument by reference."

35. For a discussion of equitable estates, see, e.g., STUDENT'S GUIDE at 133–136.

36. *Rockeagle Ltd v Alsop Wilkinson* [1991] 3 WLR 573, 577–578.

Clause 13 of Part A of Schedule 2 provides, in regards to paying the remainder of the purchase price:
> (1) The vendor's solicitors are the vendor's agents for the purposes of the receipt of any money due under this agreement and any payment made under the agreement to the seller's solicitors shall be a full . . . discharge of the purchaser's obligation in respect of that payment.

Per this clause, the seller's solicitor receives the remainder of the purchase price as the seller's agent, rather than as a stakeholder. Again, this is intended to protect the buyer. If the purchase money is paid to a solicitor who steals the funds, the buyer must pay again if the solicitor were acting either as the buyer's agent or as a stakeholder. If the solicitor acts as the seller's agent, the funds considered as being received by the seller, and the buyer will not have to pay again. *Edward Wong Finance Co Ltd v Johnson, Stokes and Master* [1984] AC 296.

37. The topic of formal completion will be discussed in detail in section F below.

38. In *Prime Win Enterprises Ltd v Nova Management Consultants* [2004] 2 HKC 587 the parties agreed to a break lease. The landlord had inspected the empty premises; however, the tenant did not return the premises' keys to the landlord after the inspection. The tenant, instead, gave the keys to the management office which returned the keys to the landlord six months later. The court found the tenant liable for the rent for this six-month period as the landlord did not have control or vacant possession of the premises without the keys. In *Wealthy China Trading Ltd v Huie Man Kit* [1999] 3 HKC 832 the court found that a shop attached to an outside wall would affect the buyer's use of the exterior wall; therefore, the seller had failed to deliver vacant possession. However, a small amount of chattels left behind would come within the *de minimis* rule according to the court in *Grandwide Ltd v Bonaventure Textiles Ltd* [1990] 2 HKC 154.

See also 16 HALSBURY'S at para. 230.225, which states that:
> the property is sold with vacant possession. If no tenancies are disclosed and no statement is made as to possession, the implication is that the purchaser is to have vacant possession except in the case of the completion of a sub-sale in a confirmation transaction.

A confirmation transaction:
> occurs where the vendor sells to a purchaser under a Sale and Purchase Agreement (SPA), and prior to completion the purchaser

sells on to a sub-purchaser under a Sub-Sale and Purchase Agreement (SSPA). The SSPA is usually completed prior to the SPA, with the result that the purchaser is unable to give vacant possession until he receives it from the head vendor on completion of the SPA . . .

16 HALSBURY'S at para. 230.225 fn.2.

39. The *de minimis* rule only applies where time is not made of the essence: *World Ford Development Ltd v Ip Ming Wai* [1993] 1 HKC 98, CA. However, in *Chong Kai Tai v Lee Gee Kee* [1996] 1 HKC 105, CA; [1997] 1 HKC 359, PC, the court decided that time is of the essence is implied for completion in Hong Kong conveyancing transactions.

40. [1993] 1 HKC at 108.

41. *Yiu Ping Fong v Lam Lai Hing Lana* [1998] 4 HKC 476 held that the seller must explain the reason the original document is unavailable. See also the case of *Big Most Ltd v Chau Wa Hung* [2012] HKEC 1057 and the *Conveyancing and Property Ordinance*, sections 13 and 13A.

42. It is common to include a provision giving the buyer an express right to raise requisitions. This right will be implied by the courts unless the parties have expressly excluded this right. *Active Keen Industries v Fok Chi Keong* [1994] 2 HKC 67, CA. The term *requisitions* is defined below.

43. "Requisitions are demands or requests made by the purchaser in respect of those matters of concern arising from the title evidenced in the documents produced to the purchaser by the vendor." 16 HALSBURY'S at para. 230.209. See also STUDENT'S GUIDE at 682 and 692–718; HK CONVEYANCING, vol. 1(A), chapter VI, at paras. 319–334 and vol. 1(B), chapter XI, at paras. 3, 109–109.3 and vol. 2(D), chapter VI, at paras. 546–561.

> In the absence of any express stipulation as to title, a contract for the sale of land implies an agreement on the part of the vendor to show and give a good, that is, a marketable title to the property sold. He discharges this obligation obligation [sic] to show good title when he does forwards [sic] the title documents to the purchaser for the latter's inspection, and when he answers appropriate requisitions satisfactorily; and then when he shows that he, or some person or persons whose concurrence he can require, can assign to the purchaser the whole legal and beneficial interest in the land sold. In general, it is sufficient if the vendor shows that he has a good title by the time fixed for completion, but, if it appears before that time that he has not a title, and is not in a position to obtain one, the purchaser may repudiate the contract.

16 HALSBURY'S at para. 230.233. See STUDENT'S GUIDE at chapters 5 (Nature of the Title to be Given) and 6 (Proof of Title); HK CONVEYANCING, vol. 1(A), chapter V, at paras. 170–175; 16 HALSBURY'S at paras. 230.237–230.244.

44. See, e.g., the case of *Gold Check Investments Ltd v Star Investment Ltd*, unreported, (1992) HCMP 592/1992, which involved the requisition as to a missing Crown lease. Another example is the case of *Mark Dean Jones v*

Bohmann International Ltd [2012] HKEC 919 which involved a dispute whether a company director's signature complied with the company's Articles of Association. 16 HALSBURY'S at para. 230.209 states in part:

> The sale and purchase agreement usually provides that any requisition or objection arising on the title is to be made as soon as practicable after delivery [of] the title deeds, and not later than 14 days prior to the date of completion. . . . The purchaser is not precluded from making any requisition as to matters subsequently discovered which were not disclosed from the title deeds even if the time has expired. There is no time limit for the making of requisitions on title . . . The conditions may also specify a time within which the vendor must reply to the requisitions, and within which the purchaser must make observations on that reply.

Id. in fn.6 states in part:

> If a purchaser is not negligent in failing to spot a potential defect in the vendor's title, the requisition is not out of time . . . Even if a requisition goes to the root of title, if a purchaser, having used due diligence, is unaware of a potential defect in the vendor's title, the time limit imposed in the agreement does not run against him . . . Requisitions which go to the root of the title can be raised out of time. However, where a purchaser, having used due diligence, should have been aware of a potential title defect, he cannot, simply by virtue of the fact that the alleged defect goes to the root of the title, raise the requisition out of time . . .

The case of *Chinawell Management Ltd v Strong Huge Corp Ltd* [2012] 1 HKLRD 79 was decided in line with the above observations. See 16 HALSBURY'S at para. 230.243.

45. See also STUDENT'S GUIDE at 700–715 (citing *Hillier Development Ltd v Tread East Ltd* [1993] 1 HKC 285, CA); HK CONVEYANCING, vol. 2(D), chapter VI, at para. 550.

46. As explained in 16 HALSBURY'S at para. 230.211:

> If the purchaser insists on any requisition or objection as to title which the vendor is unable or on some reasonable ground unwilling to remove or comply with, then, notwithstanding any intermediate negotiation or litigation, or any attempt to remove or comply with the same, the vendor may by notice in writing annul the sale upon returning the deposit, and the purchaser will have to return the title deeds, or certified copies of them, and any other documents furnished to him.

A note of caution is provided in *id.* at para. 230.244:

> Some conditions of sale give the vendor the right to rescind the contract in the event of any requisition . . . being made which he is unable or unwilling to comply with, and it is . . . for the purchaser to take care that he does not, by making a requisition not really

essential, run the risk of losing the purchase. More usually the right of rescission is made to arise only when a requisition is persisted in, and the purchaser runs no such risk in making the requisition in the first instance. Requisitions should, however, never be frivolous or unnecessary. They should either call attention to a real or apprehended defect in the title, or ask for relevant information. The vendor cannot rely on the clause if he has no title, or if he acts in bad faith or recklessly.

47. 16 HALSBURY'S at para. 230.227 states:
> The vendor has no obligation to disclose any defect in the habitability or physical condition of the property, whether these defects are patent or, in some cases, latent, and he is not liable for physical defects nor is he obliged to abate the purchase price for any such defects.

Contrast this with the seller's obligation to disclose all latent defects in his title. If a seller: "wishes to prevent a purchaser from objecting to a defect he must do so in plain terms, stating clearly the exact nature of the defect to which the purchaser is not to make objection." *Id.* at para. 230.185.

48. *Conveyancing and Property Ordinance*, section 34A states in part:
> (1) This section applies to an agreement for the sale and purchase of undivided shares in land, together with a right to exclusive occupation of a unit or other interest–
>   (a) in an uncompleted development of the land; or
>   (b) in a completed development of the land where –
>   (i) the vendor is the developer of the whole development; and
>   (ii) no assignment of the unit or interest has been executed since the date on which the relevant occupation permit or certificate of compliance was issued in respect of the development.
> (2) This section also applies to an agreement for the sub-sale and sub-purchase of undivided shares in land, together with a right to exclusive occupation of a unit or other interest in an uncompleted or completed development referred to in subsection (1), but only where a solicitor or solicitor corporation, or 2 or more solicitors practising in partnership or association, is or are authorized, by or under the Legal Practitioners Ordinance (Cap 159), to act for both the sub-vendor and the sub-purchaser of those undivided shares.
> (3) Any provision of an agreement to which this section applies is void in so far as it would, but for this section, have the effect of requiring the purchaser or sub-purchaser of the undivided shares in the relevant land to pay the costs of the vendor or sub-vendor in or in relation to–

      (a) preparing, completing, stamping and registering the agreement; or

      (b) preparing, obtaining approval for and executing any instrument that gives effect to the agreement; or

      (c) preparing and executing any relevant preliminary agreement.

    (4) Subsection (3) has effect only where the vendor and purchaser, or the sub-vendor and sub-purchaser, under the agreement have separate legal representation.

    . . .

49. Some cases have held that the presence of illegal structures made the seller unable to give good title. See the cases of *Giant River Ltd v Asie Marketing Ltd* [1990] 1 HKLR 297; *Homyip Investment Ltd v Chu Kang Ming Trade Development Co Ltd* [1995] 2 HKC 458. In *Chi Kit Co Ltd v Lucky Health International Enterprise Ltd* [2000] 3 HKC 143, CFA, the property was encumbered by the obligation of the Owners' Incorporation to pay a portion of the damages in a negligence action.

50. The *BLIS Glossary* translates *licensee* as "認可証持有人".

51. *Crocodile Garments Ltd v Prudential Enterprise Ltd* [1989] 1 HKC 474 (assignee from covenantor not liable to repay deposit); *Hua Chiao Commercial Bank Ltd v Chiaphua Industries Ltd* [1987] 1 All ER 1110, PC (mortgagee not liable to repay deposit).

52. *Stamp Duty Ordinance*, section 29B(5) states in part:

    (5) The following matters are specified for the purposes of subsection (1) –

      (a) the name and address of the vendor and of the purchaser of the immovable property;

      (b) if the vendor or purchaser is an individual, his identification number;

      (c) if the vendor or purchaser is not an individual but is registered under the Business Registration Ordinance (Cap 310), the business registration number of the vendor or purchaser;

      (d) the description and location of the immovable property;

      (e) a statement as to whether the immovable property is residential property or non-residential property, within the meanings of section 29A(1);

      (f) the date on which the agreement for sale was made;

      (g) if the agreement for sale was preceded by an unwritten sale agreement, or an agreement for sale, made between the same parties and on the same terms, the date on which the first such agreement was made;

      (h) a statement as to whether or not a date has been agreed for a conveyance on sale pursuant to the agreement for sale and, if so, that date;

> (i) a statement as to whether or not there is an agreed consideration for the conveyance on sale that is to, or may, take place pursuant to the agreement for sale and, if so, the amount or value of the consideration;
>
> (j) the amount or value of any other consideration which each person executing the document knows has been paid or given, or has been agreed to be paid or given, to any person for or in connection with the agreement for sale or any conveyance on sale pursuant to that agreement (excluding legal expenses), together with the name, address, and the identification number or business registration number of each person receiving or to receive such consideration, and a description of the benefit to which the consideration relates;
>
> . . .

53. *Workers Trust and Merchant Bank Ltd v Dojap Investments Ltd* [1993] 2 WLR 702, PC. Hong Kong courts agreed with this decision in *Wan Moon Ling Wandy v Sino Gain Investment Ltd* [1997] 2 HKC 592; *China Pride Investments Ltd v Silverpole Ltd* [1994] 2 HKC 341; *Luen Wai Crane Engineering Co v Ajax Pong Construction Equipment Ltd*, unreported, (1994) HCA 5972/1992; *Dawson Enterprises Ltd v Talisteam Ltd* [1994] 2 HKC 327.

54. *Wan Moon Ling Wandy v Sino Gain Investment Ltd* [1997] 2 HKC 592, 599.

55. *Id.* at 600.

56. Only remedies available under contract law are discussed here. Other remedies available for a breach of the sale and purchase agreement may also be found in tort law, e.g., where misrepresentation or fraud is involved.

57. In *Wellfit Investments Ltd v Poly Commence Ltd* [1995] 3 HKC 56, the court decided that specific performance was appropriate as, inter alia, the property market had risen substantially.

58. An exception to this rule is found in Clause 11 in Part A of Schedule 2 to the *Conveyancing and Property Ordinance* which provides: "In the event of the vendor failing to complete the sale in accordance with the terms of the agreement it shall not be necessary for the purchaser to tender an assignment to the vendor for execution before taking proceedings to enforce specific performance of the agreement . . . "

59. See, e.g., *Charles Hunt, Ltd v Palmer* [1931] All ER Rep 815, where the court refused to grant specific performance to the seller who had represented the property as "valuable business premises" when, in fact, there were restrictive covenants that severely restricted the land's use and value. In *Re Puckett and Smith's Contract* [1902] 2 Ch 258, the court refused specific performance because the seller had described the land as suitable for building when there was an underground culvert preventing building on part of the land.

60. In *Chu Kit Yuk v Country Wide Industrial Ltd* [1995] 1 HKC 363, the original potential buyer sought specific performance but the court determined that the

property's subsequent purchaser, had committed considerable sums of money towards the purchase such that specific performance in favour of the original potential buyer would be unjust to the subsequent purchaser.

61. The *BLIS Glossary* translates *rescind the contract* as "撤銷合約"; *rescission* as "撤銷"; *repudiate the contract* as "悔約"; and, *repudiation of the contract* as "不履行 . . . . . . 合約".

62. [1981] ICR at 828.

63. See also the cases of *Chan Kam Hung v Light Ltd*, unreported, (1993) DCCI 16919/1992 where the buyer's submission of the engrossed assignment constituted waiver; *Chan Kin Leung v Lok Kar Cheong*, unreported, (1998) HCMP 3993/1997 where waiver was implied from the construction of the text of correspondence between the parties' solicitors.

64. The *BLIS Glossary* translates void ab initio as "從一開始無效".

65. For detailed discussion of this law, see, e.g., http://www.srpa.gov.hk/en/index.html

66. [1854] 9 Ex at 354.

67. HARVEY MCGREGOR, MCGREGOR ON DAMAGES para. 22–037 (18th ed. 2009): "the expenses of the abortive sale would have been incurred even had the buyer not defaulted; putting the seller into the position he would have been in had the contract been performed still entails his having incurred these expenses."

68. In *Cheng Wai Keung Daniel v Chui Ka Yuen Danny*, unreported, (1987) HCA 3766/1985 the buyer suffered substantial damages as the contract was on particularly favourable terms, such that the difference between the buyer's bargain price and market value was greater.

69. The court did not permit the recovery of conveyancing costs or stamp duty.
    [The claimant] cannot claim the benefit of the bargain, or, rather, the damages awarded to him for the loss of it, and also at the same time claim a refund of the money which he had to pay out by way of stamp duty to achieve the bargain in the first place.
    Kwok Chung Hon v Lo On Wa [1996] 4 HKC 191, 196.

70. See, e.g., the case of *Lee Hon Kai v Wellsburg Industrial Ltd*, unreported, (1995) HCA A1485/94 where the court held that the respondent must pay damages to compensate for the increased market value of the property, with the date of valuation based on the time claimant was notified that the sale would not be completed, when he has knowledge that the market is rising and fails to complete a sale.

71. In *Wing Wong Co Ltd v Chui Yuk Ming*, unreported, (1988) HCA 10099/1983, the buyer defaulted. The court found that the seller attempted to mitigate his loss by selling the property immediately but was unable to do so for three years. The court assessed damages on the difference between the contract price and the eventual price obtained on sale.

72. The court in *Wing Wong Co Ltd v Chui Yuk Ming* adopted this approach. In *Harmony Fit Co Ltd, Jade Fit Co Ltd v Faircal Ltd* [1998] HKCU 2037, the buyer defaulted on the contract and subsequently made a lower offer to be paid three months later. The seller rejected this offer; however, at the eventual resale, the property realised a lower price than the buyer had offered. The court held that the seller did not fail to mitigate its losses and had acted reasonably, not expecting a sudden downturn in the market. Contrast this decision with that of *Kwok Wai Kong v Luk Ping Hung* [1999] HKCU 1273 where the court ascertained damages at the time of the breach rather than at another date because the seller did not act reasonably, i.e., attempting to sell within a reasonable time. In the case of *Win Profit Corp Ltd v World Orient Investment Ltd* [2010] 2 HKLRD 1053, the defendant failed to purchase the property. After the breach, the plaintiff received offers for the property, at prices higher than the original sales price agreed with the defendant. However, the plaintiff did not act on these offers. The plaintiff sold the property seven months after the breach, when the sale price fell below the original sales price agreed with the defendant. The court decided that the plaintiff failed to minimize its loss by waiting seven months to sell the property. Consequently, the court decided that the plaintiff should recover nothing as it should have sold the property within several months of the breach, when the plaintiff could have made a profit greater than that of the original sale to the defendant.

73. This was the state of affairs in *Yuen Kong Ling Cana v Lai Kam Hon* [1993] 2 HKC 728.

74. See the case of *Bain v Fothergill* (1874) LR 7 HL 158 which set out this rule. Some judges have stated that this rule does not apply in Hong Kong. See, e.g., *Roseric Ltd v West River Development* [1993] 2 HKC 404; *Lee Siu Wai Florence v Priway Investments Ltd* [1998] 1 HKC 228. Yet, in *Ma Hon Ming v Lee Tsan Sum*, unreported, (2000) HCA 1620/1998 the court applied this rule. Later, another source stated:

> Previously it was thought that the rule in *Bain v Fothergill* . . . applied in Hong Kong. However it is now clear that the rule no longer applies, if it ever did. See *Grand Trade Development Ltd v Bonance International Ltd* [2001] 3 HKC 137, CA . . . "

16 HALSBURY'S at para. 230.312 fn.1.

75. In *Ma Hon Ming v Lee Tsan Sum* the court allowed recovery of the stamp duty but not the real estate agent's commission.

76. *Flureau v Thornhill* (1776) 2 Wm Bl 1078 is a case which decided that a buyer of real estate is not entitled to damages for loss of bargain when the title is defective and the seller cannot eliminate the defect.

77. *Wroth v Tyler* [1974] Ch 30 decided that specific performance was an unreasonable remedy when the seller's wife opposed the sale, but the claimant still could recover damages for increased real estate value as a substitute for specific performance.

78. *Malhotra v Choudhury* [1980] Ch 52 decided that a claimant is entitled to damages for the value of realty at the time of judgment when the respondent does not use his best efforts to carry out a contractual promise.

79. The Privy Council in *Workers Trust and Merchant Bank Ltd v Dojap Investments Ltd* held that forfeiture of a deposit is a penalty unless the forfeiture could be justified as a genuine pre-estimate of loss. This decision has been approved by Hong Kong courts in these cases which were cited above: *China Pride Investments Ltd v Silverpole Ltd*; *Luen Wai Crane Engineering Co v Ajax Pong Construction Equipment Ltd*; *Dawson Enterprises v Talisteam Ltd*.

80. A confirmation situation arises:

> When the purchaser has disposed of the land before the completion of the contract, it is usual to make the assignment direct to the second purchaser. The original purchaser usually executes the assignment as confirmor. The vendor may assign to the sub-purchaser directly if the purchaser causes the sub-purchaser to repudiate the Sub-Sale and Purchase Agreement, and the sub-purchaser wishes to obtain the land.

16 HALSBURY'S at para. 230.321. Confirmors and confirmations are discussed in section E.ii below.

81. [1997] 2 HKC at 599–600.

82. [2000] 2 HKC at 188.

83. *Id.* at 192.

84. *Kentex Investment Ltd v Hui Lap Ping Sam*, unreported, MP 3447/91. In *Wong Lai-fan v Lee Ha* [1992] 1 HKLR 125, 127, CA the contract clause provided:

> Should the Vendor after receiving the initial deposit paid hereunder fail to complete the sale in the manner herein contained the Vendor shall immediately compensate the Purchaser with a sum equivalent to the amount of the initial deposit as liquidated damages together with the refund of the initial deposit and the Purchaser shall not take any further action to claim for damages or to enforce specific performance.

The Court of Appeal determined that the intention of the clause was clear: the buyer could not enforce the agreement through an action for specific performance. Other courts reached similar conclusions in *Lee Tat Kwong v Choi Pui Kei Stephen* [1991] 2 HKC 109 and in *Cheerup Ltd v Wong Sau Fong* [1996] 4 HKC 92.

85. KRISHNAN ARJUNAN & ABDUL MAJID BIN NABI BAKSH, BUSINESS LAW IN HONG KONG *lix* (2nd ed. 2009) translates *contra proferentem* as "不利於提出合約的一方".

86. [1994] 3 HKC at 139. Affirmed by the Privy Council on other grounds at [1996] 4 HKC 130.

87. (1992) CACV 121/1992 at 8.

88. In *Wu Koon Tai v Wu Yau Loi* [1995] 2 HKC 732, CA (overruled by the Privy Council because of another point; see [1996] 3 WLR 778), the judge found to be void a conveyance written in Chinese and which failed to comply with section 4(1).

89. *Conveyancing and Property Ordinance*, section 4 states in full:
    (1) A legal estate in land may be created, extinguished or disposed of only by deed.
    (2) This section does not apply to –
        (a) an assent in writing by a personal representative;
        (b) a disclaimer made in accordance with section 59 of the Bankruptcy Ordinance (Cap 6) or section 268 of the Companies Ordinance (Cap 32);
        (c) a surrender by operation of law, including a surrender which may, by law, be effected without writing;
        (d) the grant, disposal or surrender of a lease taking effect in possession for a term not exceeding 3 years (whether or not the lessee is given power to extend the term) at the best rent which can be reasonably obtained without a premium;
        (e) other assurances not required by law to be made in writing;
        (f) a receipt not required by law to be under seal;
        (g) a vesting order or vesting declaration by a court or other competent authority;
        (h) a creation, extinguishment or disposal of a legal estate in land by operation of law.

90. The *BLIS Glossary* translates *equitable jurisdiction* as "衡平法司法管轄權".

91. E.g., if the assignee commits a breach or is not willing to perform its obligations. See the case of *Parker v Taswell* (1858) 2 De G & J 559. In the case of *Wu Koon Tai v Wu Yau Loi*, *supra* note 88, the parties did not sign the document.

92. *Walsh v Lonsdale* (1882) 21 Ch D 9. This is an application of the maxim that "equity regards as done that which ought to be done." Thus it is regarded in equity as if a decree of specific performance has already been granted.

93. See the case of *Town Bright Industries Ltd v Bermuda Trust (Hong Kong) Ltd*, unreported, (1999) CACV 137/1998, where the court found that:
    for the purposes of 53(1)(c) of the Law of Property Act, 1925 (on which section 5 of the local Ordinance is based) a [written] direction given to a trustee by a person entitled in equity directing it to hold the trust property in trust for another is a disposition of his equitable interest . . .
    Thus, property held by trustees may be assigned through a written document to the trustees.

94. BLACK'S LAW DICTIONARY at 588 defines *possessory estate* as "[a]n estate giving the holder the right to possess the property, with or without an ownership interest in the property."

95. LEXISNEXIS at 1512 translates *proprietary estoppel* as "所有人不容反悔".

96. As noted in 16 HALSBURY'S at para. 230.317:

> In general in the absence of agreement to the contrary, the purchaser prepares the draft assignment and submits it to the vendor for approval; however, where the property is contained in a large development it is usual for the vendor-developer's solicitor to prepare a standard form assignment.

97. [1995] 1 HKC at 206. The principles of the case are limited as its facts concerning the identification of the purchaser was the issue: the case was discussed and distinguished in *Liu Moon Ping v Wong Kwok Tung* [2006] 1 HKLRD 358.

98. For a definition of marketable title, see 16 HALSBURY'S at para. 230.233 fn.3. *Id.* at para. 230.262 explains:

> Upon the making of an enforceable contract for sale the purchaser becomes the owner of the land in equity, and can dispose of his beneficial (from the bare trust which comes into existence on the entry into the valid contract for the sale of land) or equitable interest (the interest arising traditionally under a valid contract for the sale of land) to a third person.
>
> It has been common for the purchaser to sub-sell the property prior to completion, and to provide that the sub-sale is to be completed immediately prior to the head sale. In most cases the assignment will be from the vendor to the final purchaser (the sub-purchaser) with the head purchaser (the sub-vendor) executing it as confirmor.

On the matter of confirmations see also STUDENT'S GUIDE at 1024–1029, 1138–1139; HK CONVEYANCING, vol. 1(B), chapter X, at paras. 64, 67–77.

99. Statement by Financial Secretary at press conference on "Economic Situation in Second Quarter of 2010 and Latest GDP and Price Forecasts for 2010" http://www.info.gov.hk/gia/general/201008/13/P201008130227.htm

100. HK CONVEYANCING, vol. 2(E), chapter X, at para. 504 explains that in the case of a nomination:

> Sometimes a purchaser does not intend to become the owner of the land, and, although not purchasing as agent for the intended owner, he will enter into the sale and purchase agreement with the intention that a third party will take the benefit of the assignment. This process is usually referred to as nomination and involves the purchaser nominating a third party as the ultimate party who is to be the assignee . . . In general the identity of the purchaser will not be a matter of concern to the vendor, and he will not be able to avoid the contract on the ground that the nominee was not a party to the contract . . . The right to nominate does not need to be included as a term of the contract . . . Nomination is sometimes used where the purchaser wishes to retain the beneficial interest in

the land for himself but makes use of the trust to distance himself from the legal ownership.

See 16 HALSBURY'S at para. 230.320; STUDENT'S GUIDE at 1024–1029, 1139; HK CONVEYANCING, vol. 1(B), chapter X, at paras. 64–77.

101. [1997] 3 HKC at 566–568.

102. *Conveyancing and Property Ordinance*, section 35 provides in part:

> (1A) The covenants implied under subsection (1)(a) shall be covenants to which section 41 applies.
>
> (1B) The benefit of the covenants implied under this section shall run with the land and shall be enforceable by the covenantee and his successors in title and persons deriving title under or through him or them.
>
> (1C) In paragraphs (a) to (d) of subsection (1), "assignment" (轉讓) does not include a legal charge.
>
> (1D) Unless the contrary intention is expressed, the liability of joint parties to any assignment or legal charge in respect of the covenants mentioned in subsection (1) shall be joint and several.
>
> (2) The covenants implied under this section may be excluded, varied or extended in the assignment or legal charge.

103. See, e.g., *Yeung Wah James v Alfa Sea Ltd* [1993] 1 HKC 440 (demolition of bedroom wall and replacement with glass window); *Owen v Gadd* [1956] 2 QB 99 (prevention of access); *Perera v Vandiyar* [1953] 1 WLR 672 (cutting off electricity).

104. This subject is discussed in 16 HALSBURY'S at para. 230.368, as follows:

> Under the covenant for further assurance the vendor is bound to do such further acts for the purpose of perfecting the purchaser's title as the purchaser may reasonably require and the vendor can properly do. The purchaser should tender a draft of the further assignment to which he considers that he is entitled, and should tender or offer to pay the vendor's costs. The vendor is entitled to a reasonable time to procure professional assistance. If the assignment is proper and he declines to execute it or to do any act which the purchaser can properly require, this constitutes a breach of the covenant. The purchaser cannot, by means of the covenant for further assurance, obtain a greater estate than that which was the subject of the original assignment, although if the vendor's title was defective the vendor may be required to assure an estate which he has got in since whether by devise or by purchase.

See, e.g., the case of *Goldsteady Investment Ltd v Fatima Estates Ltd*, unreported, (1995) MP 2943/95. The seller's assignment by way of power of attorney was defective because it had not been done according to the company's Memorandum and Articles of Association. A confirmatory assignment was ordered to make good the defect. See also STUDENT'S GUIDE at 1151; HK CONVEYANCING, vol. 2(E), chapter XII, at para. 65.

105. Several cases have examined this issue, e.g., *Lai Wing Ho v Chan Siu Fong* [1993] 1 HKLR 319 (seller attempted to sell exclusive right to roof without assigning his shares); *Modern Sino Ltd v Art Fair Co Ltd* [1999] 3 HKLRD 847 (the seller assigned shares to the buyer together with the right to exclusive possession of the house and subsequently assigned the right to exclusive possession of certain car parks with the intent and purpose that the car parks shall attach to the house; the court decided that when assigning the car parks, no shares were assigned; therefore, the buyer could only acquire a licence to the car parks); *Jumbo King Ltd v Faithful Properties Ltd* [1999] 4 HKC 707, CFA (the seller assigned shares to the buyer along with a right to the exclusive use of certain roofs and utility rooms; the court decided since the seller had the right to exclusive possession of the roofs and utility rooms, it could properly assign them to the buyer provided the seller assigned at the same time some shares in the building; the fact that no shares were allocated to the roofs and utility rooms was immaterial).

106. If the parties desire completion by way of mutual undertakings, an express provision should be included in the sale and purchase agreement as the courts will not imply this term into the agreement. *Chong Kai Tai v Lee Gee Kee*.

It should be noted that undertakings should be stated to be subject to the Law Society's Qualifications which stipulate where:

> If for any reason the party whose execution of a document (hereinafter called 'the relevant document') is required by the undertaking is unable or unwilling to execute the same, all moneys sent against the undertaking must immediately and in any event not later than the period prescribed in the undertaking be returned from whence they came and the undertaking given would thereupon automatically stand discharged without prejudice however to the rights of the parties to the transaction in question.

These qualifications would apply, e.g., upon the death or bankruptcy of the person giving the undertaking, or a court order restraining the party concerned from signing the document.

See THE LAW SOCIETY OF HONG KONG, *The Hong Kong Solicitors' Guide to Professional Conduct*, vol. 1, also available at:
http://www.hklawsoc.org.hk/pub_e/professionalguide/volume1/default.asp

107. In *Tse Chun Hung Herby v Chang Chung Paul* [1999] HKCU 375, the buyer's solicitors requested instructions from the seller's solicitors concerning the allocation of the outstanding purchase price, as the property was subject to a mortgage. The seller's solicitors did not respond and the sale fell through. The court decided that there was an implied term in the sale and purchase agreement that the balance of the purchase price would be paid by split cheques. The seller breached the agreement by failing to do so.

108. As noted at 16 HALSBURY'S at para. 230.349:

> A document requiring a stamp cannot be admitted in evidence in legal proceedings unless it is duly stamped or payment of the duty and certain further sums is made or an undertaking to pay is given. The proper stamping of title deeds is an important matter of title because, if the owner of the property is called upon to defend his right or to attack a wrongdoer with regard to the property, he must produce his title deeds in evidence and thus he cannot do so as long as the requirements for the admission of any deed have not been complied with.

See also STUDENT'S GUIDE at 1216–1218 and 1319–1323; HK CONVEYANCING, vol. 1(A), chapter VI, at para. 152.5 and vol. 2(F), chapter XIV, at paras. 2–4.4.

109. *Stamp Duty Ordinance*, section 2 defines *conveyance on sale* to mean: "every conveyance whereby any immovable property, upon the sale thereof, is transferred to or vested in a purchaser or any other person on his behalf or by his direction, and includes a foreclosure order".

110. See, e.g., Schedule 1 to the *Stamp Duty Ordinance* which sets out the fee schedule.

111. This does not apply to commercial and industrial property. The intention is to reduce speculation and slow rising property prices by having the parties pay the stamp duty on each sale and purchase agreement rather than on the assignment. Prior to the changes in the Ordinance, it was possible for a series of sale and purchase agreements to be entered into prior to completion, with each sale and purchase agreement being a transaction for a higher sales price of the property. There would thus be no stamp duty costs imposed upon these buyers turned sellers in the rising property market. See HK CONVEYANCING, vol. 1(B), chapter XIV, at para. 4; STUDENT'S GUIDE at 1216–1218, 1319–1323.

The current Hong Kong government, for the purpose of cooling down the real estate market in order to avoid a property "bubble", amended the stamp duty rates. Stamp duties on purchases of properties valued at HK$2 million or more were doubled to 8.5 percent. The government also raised the minimum down payment on properties worth more than HK$7 million; imposed a 20 percent stamp duty for re-sales of properties purchased within six months; and a ten percent duty for properties re-sold within one to three years of purchase. Another measure the government introduced was a 15 per cent buyer's stamp duty. See http://www.gov.hk/en/residents/taxes/stamp/stamp_duty_rates.htm

112. The *BLIS Glossary* translates the term "ad valorem" as "從價費".

113. Registration is:

> to protect priority of registration and to give notice of the registered interest to subsequent purchasers and mortgagees. A complementary result is that the register acts as a record of transactions so that these can be relied upon in establishing the details of the title to the land.

16 HALSBURY'S at para. 230.386.

114. *Id.* at paras. 230.382–230.383. See also STUDENT'S GUIDE at 1374–1375; HK CONVEYANCING, vol. 1(B), chapter XIV at para. 121 and vol. 2(F), chapter XIV, at para. 72.

115. 16 HALSBURY'S at para. 230.383. See also STUDENT'S GUIDE at 1374–1375, 1378–1383; HK CONVEYANCING, vol. 1(B), chapter XIV, at para. 123.

116. As defined in the *Land Registration Ordinance*, section 1A:

"lis pendens" (待決案件) means –
   (a) any action or proceeding pending in a court or tribunal that relates to land or any interest in or charge on land; and
   (b) a bankruptcy petition . . .

Lis pendens is "[a] pending lawsuit." BLACK'S LAW DICTIONARY at 950.

117. A court has stated that an option to purchase should be registered as it affects land or premises, even if the option to purchase is contained in a short term lease which itself need not be registered. *Markfaith Investment Ltd v Chiap Hua Flashlights Ltd* [1990] 2 WLR 1451.

118. *Land Registration Ordinance*, section 3(2) provides:

All such deeds, conveyances, and other instruments in writing, and judgments . . . which are not registered shall, as against any subsequent bona fide purchaser or mortgagee for valuable consideration of the same parcels of ground, tenements, or premises, be absolutely null and void to all intents and purposes:

Provided that nothing herein contained shall extend to bona fide leases at rack rent for any term not exceeding 3 years.

119. The *BLIS* Glossary. The *Land Registration Ordinance* at section 2A stipulates in part:

   (1) A document effecting a floating charge, whether or not it specifically identifies any land charged, is not, for the purposes of section 2, a deed, conveyance or other instrument in writing by which any parcel of ground, tenement or premises in Hong Kong may be affected.
   (2) A document effecting a floating charge created before, on or after 1 November 1984 –
      (a) becomes a fixed charge on the land intended to be affected; and
      (b) for the purposes of section 2, is a deed, conveyance or other instrument in writing by which any parcel of ground, tenement or premises in Hong Kong may be affected, upon crystallization of that charge . . . as evidenced by a certificate signed by or on behalf of the chargee.

120. Land Registration Regulations (Cap 128A), regulation 5 provides in part:
   (1) Registration of an instrument under the Ordinance shall be effected by delivering into the Land Registry such instrument

together with a memorial thereof in the form specified by the Land Registrar and by compliance with the Ordinance and these regulations.

. . .

(4) Subject to paragraph (5), the delivery of an instrument or memorial into the Land Registry by post shall be regarded as having been effected when the instrument or memorial is received by the Land Registrar.

(5) For the purposes of these regulations, the date of receipt of an instrument or memorial sent to the Land Registrar by post shall–

(a) where the instrument or memorial is received by the Land Registrar before 1.30 p.m. on any day on which the Land Registry is open to the public, be that day;

(b) where the instrument or memorial is received by the Land Registrar–

(i) after 1.30 p.m. on any day on which the Land Registry is open to the public; or

(ii) on any day on which the Land Registry is not open to the public, be deemed to be the next following day on which the Land Registry is open to the public.

For further information, see http://www.landreg.gov.hk.

121. *Land Registration Ordinance*, section 5 states:

All deeds, conveyances, and other instruments in writing, and judgments, which are . . . registered within one month after the time of execution thereof respectively, and all judgments which are registered within one month after the entering up or recording thereof, shall severally be in like manner entitled to priority, and shall take effect respectively by relation to the date thereof only in the same manner as if this Ordinance had not been passed.

122. As defined by BLACK'S LAW DICTIONARY at 1072 *nisi* is an order or such "having validity unless the adversely affected party appears and shows cause why it should be withdrawn." See *supra* Chapter Eight note 19.

123. These two examples were provided in Prof. Michael Wilkinson's lecture notes for the Overseas Lawyers Qualification Examination (June 2002).

124. Summarized from: http://www.landreg.gov.hk/consultation/en/background.html

125. http://www.landreg.gov.hk/en/title/faq_ltb.htm#G11. See also http://www.landreg.gov.hk/en/title/report2013.htm and http://www.legco.gov.hk/yr12–13/english/fc/fc/w_q/devb-pl-e.pdf at 630.

References

Books

Adams, John N., and Hector MacQueen, *Atiyah's Sale of Goods* (12th ed. 2010).

Arjunan, Krishnan, and Abdul Majid bin Nabi Baksh, *Business Law in Hong Kong* (2nd ed. 2009).

Black's Law Dictionary (9th ed. 2009) [hereinafter *Black's Law Dictionary*].

Bradbrook, Adrian J., Susan MacCallum, and Anthony Moore, *Australian Property Law: Cases and Materials* (3rd ed. 2007).

Bramwell, Hartley, *Conveyancing in Hong Kong* (1981).

Bridge, Michael, *Personal Property Law* (3rd ed. 2002).

Burn E. H., and J. Cartwright, eds., *Cheshire and Burn's Modern Law of Real Property* (18th ed. 2011).

Curzon L. B., and P. H. Richards, *The Longman Dictionary of Law* (8th ed. 2011) [hereinafter *Curzon*].

Dalton, P. J., *Land Law* (4th ed. 1996).

Dawson, I. J., and Robert A. Pearce, *Licences Relating to the Occupation or Use of Land* (1979) [hereinafter *Dawson and Pearce*].

Gaunt, J., and P. Morgan, *Gale on Easements* (19th ed. 2012).

Gleeson, Simon, *Personal Property Law* (1997).

Goo, S. H., and Alice Lee, *Land Law in Hong Kong* (3rd ed. 2010) [hereinafter *Goo and Lee*].

Gray, Kevin, and Susan Gray, *Elements of Land Law* (5th ed. 2009).

16 Halsbury's Laws of Hong Kong (2010) [hereinafter *16 Halsbury's*].

17 Halsbury's Laws of Hong Kong (2000) [hereinafter *17 Halsbury's*].

17(1) Halsbury's Laws of Hong Kong (2007) [hereinafter *17(1) Halsbury's*].

20 Halsbury's Laws of Hong Kong (2010) [hereinafter *20 Halsbury's*].

26(2) Halsbury's Laws of Hong Kong (2009).

Hong Kong Government, *Bilingual Laws Information System's English-Chinese Glossary of Legal Terms* [hereinafter *BLIS Glossary*].

LexisNexis, *Hong Kong English-Chinese Legal Dictionary* (2005) [hereinafter *LexisNexis*].

Lim, Hilary, and Kate Green, *Cases and Materials in Land Law* (2nd ed. 1995) [hereinafter *Lim and Green*].

Ma, Lawrence, *Equity and Trusts Law in Hong Kong* (2nd ed. 2009).

MacKenzie, Judith-Anne, and Mary Philips, *Textbook on Land Law* (14th ed. 2012) [hereinafter *MacKenzie and Philips*].

Mau, Stephen D., *Hong Kong Legal Principles: Important Topics for Students and Professionals* (2nd ed. 2013).

McGregor, Harvey, *McGregor on Damages* (18th ed. 2009).

McLoughlin, Daniel P., *Principles of Real Estate Law* (1992).

Megarry, Sir Robert, and William Wade, *The Law of Real Property* (8th ed. 2012) [hereinafter *Megarry and Wade*].

Mendes, Derek Da Costa, Richard Balfour, and Eileen Gillese, *Property Law: Cases, Text and Materials* (2nd ed. 1990) [hereinafter *Property Law: Cases, Text and Materials*].

Merry, Malcolm, and Paul Kent, *Building Management in Hong Kong* (2nd ed. 2008).

Merry Malcolm, *Hong Kong Tenancy Law: An Introduction to the Law of Landlord and Tenant* (4th ed. 2003) [hereinafter *Merry 2003*].

Merry, Malcolm, *Hong Kong Tenancy Law: An Introduction to the Law of Landlord and Tenant* (5th ed. 2010) [hereinafter *Merry*].

Nield, Sarah, *Hong Kong Land Law* (2nd ed. 1997) [hereinafter *Nield*].

Oakley, A. J., ed., *Megarry's Manual of the Law of Real Property* (8th ed. 2002) [hereinafter *Megarry's Manual*].

Shum, Clement, *General Principles of Hong Kong Law* (3rd ed. 1998) [hereinafter *Shum*].

Sihombing, Judith, *Goods: Sales and Securities* (3rd ed. 1997).

Sihombing, Judith, and Michael Wilkinson, *Hong Kong Conveyancing* (2009) [hereinafter *HK Conveyancing*].

Sihombing, Judith, and Michael Wilkinson, *A Student's Guide to Hong Kong Conveyancing* (6th ed. 2011) [hereinafter *Student's Guide*].

Law Reform Commission of Hong Kong, The, *Report on Law of Wills, Intestate Succession and Provision for Deceased Persons' Families and Dependents* (Topic 15) (1990).

Law Society of Hong Kong, The, *The Hong Kong Solicitors' Guide to Professional Conduct*, http://www.hklawsoc.org.hk/pub_e/professionalguide/volume1/default.asp

Thompson, M. P., *Co-ownership* (1988).

Thurston, John, and Deborah Annells, *A Practitioner's Guide to Trusts–Hong Kong Edition* (2007).

Welling, Bruce, *Property in Things in the Common Law System* (1996).

Worthington, Sarah, *Personal Property Law: Text, Cases and Materials* (2000).

Index